Muslim Women on the Move

Muslim Women on the Move

Moroccan Women and French Women of Moroccan Origin Speak Out

Doris H. Gray

LEXINGTON BOOKS

A division of
ROWMAN & LITTLEFIELD PUBLISHERS, INC.
Lanham • Boulder • New York • Toronto • Plymouth, UK

LEXINGTON BOOKS

A division of Rowman & Littlefield Publishers, Inc.
A wholly owned subsidary of The Rowman & Littlefield Publishing Group, Inc.
4501 Forbes Boulevard, Suite 200
Lanham, MD 20706

Estover Road
Plymouth PL6 7PY
United Kingdom

British Library Cataloguing in Publication Information Available

Library of Congress Cataloging-in-Publication Data

Gray, Doris H., 1955-
  Muslim women on the move : Moroccan women and French women of Moroccan origin
speak out / Doris H. Gray.
    p. cm.
  Includes bibliographical references and index.
  ISBN-13: 978-0-7391-1804-7 (cloth : alk. paper)
  ISBN-10: 0-7391-1804-8 (cloth : alk. paper)
  ISBN-13: 978-0-7391-1805-4 (pbk. : alk. paper)
  ISBN-10: 0-7391-1805-6 (pbk. : alk. paper)
   1. Muslim women—France. 2. Muslim women—France—Social conditions. 3.
Women—France. 4. Muslim women—Morocco. 5. Muslim women—Morocco—Social
conditions. 6. Morocco—Social conditions. 7. Women—Morocco. I. Title.
  HQ1170.G73 2007
  305.48'6970964--dc22

                                                                    2007033232

Printed in the United States of America

⊗™ The paper used in this publication meets the minimum requirements of American
National Standard for Information Sciences—Permanence of Paper for Printed Library
Materials, ANSI/NISO Z39.48–1992.

Contents

Acknowledgments

Without women in Morocco and in France opening their hearts and minds and often their homes, this book would not have been possible. Their courage and determination is a source of inspiration. They have shared with sincerity their ideas, hopes and agonies. Several people have helped shape this book. My foreign correspondent friend Sinikka Tarvainen has offered insights based on her extensive knowledge of African cultures and current events in Europe. Saadia Maski has given generously of her time in Paris and Rabat and challenged my early conclusions. Kelly Pemberton expertly commented on the first part of the book. Of my colleagues at Florida State University, Alec Hargreaves and William Cloonan have persistently supported me. The original inspiration for this book came from my oldest daughter Lancy who made friends in Morocco quickly and drew me into her circle of friends of young Moroccan women. The companionship of my daughters Tunuka and Khadijah, who traveled with me through Morocco and explored the impoverished suburbs of Paris, was invaluable. Their teenage curiosity and enthusiasm infused interviews with topics I would not have thought of. I could not have finished this book had not Steve Been, Kathy McGuire, Ellen Gwynn and Beverly Dayton taken charge of all mundane matters of our family. Most of all, this book could have not have been conceived without the steady and unwavering support of my husband Kenneth. Though he did not live to see its completion, his spirit continues to enfold me. To him I owe who I am today.

Introduction

This book offers a comparison of two Muslim populations that to date have not been compared in this way. The personal views of young, educated women in Morocco are compared with those of young, educated women of Moroccan immigrant origins in France. The study is based on extensive personal interviews with a range of women conducted over a period of three years in Morocco and France. The women who participated in this study have certain traits in common: they are educated, in most cases professionals, and the majority are under the age of thirty-five years. These groups of women are in a better position than illiterate or less educated women to comment on public policy such as legal reforms. They are more influential as agents of change.

The interviews were loosely structured around three main themes: Conceptions of the religion of Islam, legal changes affecting women in Morocco and Muslim women in France, and personal and professional goals and challenges. The text challenges the conventional dichotomy between the Western and the Muslim world. We shall hear the voices of a select group of individuals from each of these two different countries and see that despite their dissimilar national circumstances, they have more in common than is conventionally assumed. Individual perceptions are summarized and put into the larger context of Muslim women and their particular circumstances in two Western Mediterranean countries. Chapter 1 describes the methodology and summarizes some of the main problems involved in this research. Chapter 2 offers background information on Morocco and on France, particularly issues of migration. Chapter 3 discusses conceptions of Islam, chapter 4 pertains to the family law reform in Morocco and the ban on the Muslim headscarf in

French public schools and chapter 5 addresses personal and professional goals and challenges. Chapter 6 offers conclusions.

This book was inspired by personal tragedy. My oldest daughter Lancy died in a car accident in Morocco in the summer of 2000. At the time, my family had lived for only one year in North Africa. We were new arrivals in a foreign land, yet after our daughter's death, our family was surrounded by an outpouring of compassion, by prayer and support. People we barely knew reached out to us, came over to our apartment and quietly took care of everything that needed to be done. Grief has a way of breaking down religious, cultural and class barriers. Though I longed to be home with family and friends, I felt carried by the compassion of people we barely knew. They may have been strangers to me, but as in most developing world countries, no strangers to personal tragedies.

While in the process of writing this book, seven years later and back in the United States, my husband Kenneth suddenly died. Again I wondered why we go our separate ways in happy times, yet when we are in tears, we come together and hold on to each other in unexpected ways. Confronted with death, people tend to share their deepest beliefs and their sources of hope and faith. I have lived through this on two continents. These experiences also have washed away my inhibitions against talking with people about their beliefs, dreams and fears.

Cultural differences have fascinated me for a long time. For most of my adult life, I have lived in countries (South Africa, Kenya, Morocco) where I was an outsider, where I did not belong but had to make an effort to fit in and become accepted. In striving to become part of a society to which I had no natural affiliation, I learned to focus on the aspects people have in common. What set us apart—race, skin-color, ethnicity, culture, religion, traditions, language, cuisine, etc.—was apparent enough.

It came quite naturally that my academic inquiries followed along the same trajectory: to explore what people have in common and what sets them apart. Because I had last lived abroad in Morocco, this country seemed to be a natural starting point for my research. Global events involving conflict between the Western and the Muslim world coincided with my personal interests.

The following questions are at the heart of this study: Where do Muslim women move from and where do they imagine themselves moving to? Actually, "Muslim women" is such an overgeneralization that it is almost meaningless. Given that there are 1.3 billion Muslims in the world, spread out over the entire globe, Muslim women are a diverse, heterogeneous population. Twenty-one percent of the world's population belongs to the Islamic tradition. Only Christianity with 2.1 billion adherents (33 percent) is more widespread. Just as there is no uniformity of belief among Christians, neither does such homogeneity exist among Muslims. Though everyone born to a Muslim father is considered a Muslim, this does not necessarily mean that such an individual is a believer or a practicing Muslim. Despite my apprehension about the term "Muslim women," I acknowledge that we depend on categories for the purposes of analysis and, as will be explored later, other categories such as "Arab women" are equally flawed. "Maghrebi women" would have been the most accurate term, but in the Anglophone world this is not yet a commonly understood designation. The Maghreb is the region in North Africa that encompasses Tunisia, Algeria and Morocco and sometimes Mauritania.

A study of Muslim women would be incomplete without including a discussion of the religion of Islam. The goal of that part of my conversations was to gain insights into young women's own understanding of Islam. The focus is on individual conception of religion, regardless of dogma, institutional interpretation or official discourse. Women speak about their evolving understanding of Islam, what religion and spirituality means to them in their daily life and how they understand a life of faith.

Much scholarly research has been conducted on Islam in the West. Most studies attest to a trend toward secularization among the majority of Muslims in the Occident and radicalization of a small minority. Muslims residing in Europe or the United States tend to accept the separation of the public, secular sphere from the private, religious sphere. We want to examine whether this trend is particular to adherents of Islam living in a Western country such as France or if a comparable trend can be observed among Muslims residing in the heartland of a Muslim state such as Morocco.

Morocco and France have seen recent legal changes that directly affect women in these countries. In Morocco, a major reform of the Personal Status Code (in Western parlance called family law) has set the scene for considerable societal change in that country. The reform of the Personal Status Code (*moudawana*) changes the concept of the family from a unit presided over by a man to a unit with two equal partners before the law. This altered conception of family set in motion larger societal shifts. In the eyes of the law, men and women are now described as equal partners. In Morocco, the reform of the *moudawana* has officially been presented as a return to Qur'anic roots by abandoning cultural practices written into law upon Morocco's independence from France in 1956. As we shall see in chapter 4, certain critics of the reform said the changes were "un-Islamic." The majority of Moroccans welcomed the reform as a major step in the direction of granting women equal rights and thus bringing Morocco more into the mainstream of its neighbors on the northern shores of the Mediterranean.

In France the banning of selected religious insignia in public schools, including the Muslim headscarf, was the result of an ongoing debate concerning the secular nature of the French Republic. The greater visibility of Muslims in the public sphere has provoked increased official discourse on the Muslim minority in France. Whereas the Personal Status Code reform in Morocco is an indication of change, the ban on selected religious insignia can be interpreted as an indication of the French government's insistence on the status quo. According to Hargreaves (1995): "In the debate over Islam in France, no single incident has generated greater acrimony than the headscarf affair of 1989" (125). While the world was stunned by events surrounding the fall of the Berlin wall and the subsequent demise of communism in 1989, the French nation was fixated on the controversy over the expulsion of two girls wearing the Muslim headscarf to public school. Ever since then, the Muslim headscarf, *hijab*, has divided public opinion as France struggles to find a way to incorporate Islamic cultural and religious traditions into her European fabric.

The broad topic of personal and professional challenges and aspirations was chosen because it allowed women to raise issues of importance to them rather than imposing a set of narrow issues selected by the researcher. Little scholarly research has been conducted on this theme which gives women an opportunity to speak on their own terms. Women talk about the challenges they perceive as standing in the way of achieving their professional ambitions. They reveal their personal agonies that result from placing a high premium on higher education and a professional career. The stories of their personal hopes and visions, their disappointments and crushed dreams, speak most vividly to the risks these women are taking by discarding conventional roles and staking out new ground.

Muslim women in particular embody a phenomenon of our times, namely that of asserting multiple identities. Religion and culture, race, ethnicity, gender, nationality, sexual orientation, professional title or family status are some of the ingredients that make up an individual's identity. More and more people incorporate within themselves multiple cultural heritages or they find themselves in situations where they are required to move in and out of different cultural spheres. Routinely, it is the culturally distinguishing condition that is used for self-identification. For instance, in the West if one is a white male, one would not highlight this as the most important self-identifying feature. Yet if one is a black male, the fact that one is black would be the outstanding feature and the one that an individual is most likely to identify with. By the same token, being a Muslim in today's world has become a significant aspect of an individual's identity. This is certainly the case in places where Muslims are the exception. Even in Morocco, where the overwhelming majority of the population is Muslim, women emphasized that they were Muslims while at the same time being supportive of social change, rejecting a cultural emphasis on conformity and instead advocating individual choice.

In France, women frequently said they were culturally French and religiously Muslim.

In this book we will take a closer look at two particular Muslim populations, namely young, educated Moroccan women and women of Moroccan origin in France.

To date, 10 percent of the French population is of immigrant origin, the majority Muslims from North Africa. For France, a secular country with a marked Catholic heritage, this influx of peoples from different cultural and religious backgrounds poses a major challenge. However, this situation is not unique to France. In neighboring Germany, 8 percent of the population is of immigrant origins, mostly Muslims from Turkey. Likewise, Great Britain has a large Muslim minority, primarily of Asian origin (Pakistan, Bangladesh). In Belgium and the Netherlands, the largest minority populations stem, as in France, from North Africa. Yet in spite of the presence of millions of Muslims within Europe's borders, Islam is not treated as a part of the European religious and cultural fabric. For most people in the West today, Islam is perceived as the "other," intrinsically different from Western religious and cultural modes. Though Muslims—Moors mainly from North Africa—occupied the Iberian Peninsula from the eighth to the fifteenth centuries, the historic presence of Islam in Europe is often ignored.[1] Today, five centuries after the expulsion of Muslims, Islam is once more becoming a significant piece in the European mosaic.

Muslims who have successfully integrated into Western society are often believed to have loosened ties to their religious heritage. Such supposedly lax religious commitment of Muslims residing in a Western country is thought to differ from that of Muslims who live in predominantly Islamic societies. There, surrounded by Islamic cultures and traditions, a re-evaluation of customs and values is seen as less likely to occur. This perception contributes to the widespread understanding of a dichotomy between the Western and the Arab/Muslim world. This book sets out to question this divide.

Paying attention to individual attitudes allows us to discern larger trends. Women are an integral part of cultural and societal transformations, though they have often been ignored as agents of change. For the purpose of a valid comparison, educated, professional and urban Moroccan women and educated, professional women of Moroccan origin in France were the focus of this inquiry. The goal was to ascertain similarities and differences among them with regard to attitudes toward Islam, to legal changes affecting women in Morocco and in France, and to their personal and professional goals and challenges. This book examines ways in which social changes have been interpreted by particular groups of women and thereby straddles the boundaries of cultural studies and social sciences.

France and Morocco both border the Mediterranean basin. In the course of history, cultures from both spaces have ebbed and flowed and landed on each other's shores, moving further and further inland. Today, both countries are grappling with issues of cultural and social change. France is attempting to come to terms with the fact that Islamic religion and culture are becoming part of her national fabric, while Morocco is seeking to accommodate reforms that grant women more rights. Currently, 3 million Moroccan nationals, that is, 10 percent of the population, reside abroad. Eighty-six percent of these Moroccan expatriates live in countries of the European Union, the majority in France.[2] Thus, cultural and societal changes within Morocco and in France reverberate in both countries. An understanding of the changes occurring in these two countries will lead to a greater appreciation of the transformations underway in secular Western countries and parts of the Muslim world.

Geographically and culturally, Morocco is situated at a crossroads between Africa, the Arab world and Mediterranean Europe. Only nine miles separate Europe from North Africa at the Straits of Gibraltar. This close geographic proximity has led to deep historic, cultural and linguistic ties. However, due to France's colonial occupation of Morocco, French influence is more readily evident in Morocco than is Maghrebi influence in France. From 1912 until 1956, Morocco was a French protectorate. Geographically, Morocco is the closest developing world country to Europe. Due to the Spanish enclaves of Mellilia and Ceuta (also spelled Sebta), two Spanish cities on North African territory, this African country has in fact a common border with a European country. This oddity has often caused friction between Spain and Morocco. The international community becomes aware of this unique setting through reports of dramatic border crossings. Frequently, Africans risk their lives climbing over the fence, fortified with razor blades, to land on European territory in hopes of real or perceived better opportunities. In the past few years, the number of immigrants who try to reach the European mainland through Morocco via Mellilia and Ceuta has gone down and instead most Africans now risk the treacherous, long sea voyage from the West African coast to the Canary Islands.

The close proximity between the Maghreb and Europe, their historical relationship, and the fact that a significant number of families have members on both sides of the Western Mediterranean, allow for cross-fertilization of ideas, views and perceptions that influence and shape societies in both cultural spheres. Changes in Morocco occur as a result of pressures from within as much as from without.

Muslim women are particularly targeted and affected by legal changes in Morocco and in France. The ban on the Muslim headscarf in French public schools and the family law reform in Morocco specifically impact women.

Consequently, educated, professional and urban women in North Africa and Western Europe are rethinking their roles, private and public. In different ways, the government of France and that of Morocco have instituted a legal framework that guides specific aspects of the lives of Muslim women. Yet with or without legal changes, these women are exploring new ground. Changes on the individual level go hand in glove with larger cultural and societal transformations in both countries. Certainly, educated professional women are a minority in Morocco as are educated, professional Muslim women in France. In modern times, rights and freedoms of majority populations have often been improved by expanding rights and freedoms for minorities. In the United States, for example, the African American civil rights movement of the 1960s paved the way of more rights and better opportunities for white women.

Therefore, offering more rights and opportunities to Muslim women will in time enlarge opportunities for the majority populations of their respective countries. The women who contributed to this study in Morocco and France are minorities who are breaking with conventional roles assigned to them and are asserting their right to determine their personal and professional roles.

Nevertheless, the life experiences of women in Morocco and those of women of Moroccan origin in France differ significantly. They are not exposed to the same national contexts but are confronted with country-specific sets of circumstances. There are different social norms in matters such as relative gender equality in France versus, up until the recent reform of the family law, explicit gender inequality in Morocco. Furthermore, Morocco is a constitutional monarchy whereas France is a secular democracy.

An Islamic monarchy, Morocco knows no separation of the religious from the secular. This North African kingdom has a highly hierarchical, authoritarian structure. However, the traditional, patriarchal nature of this society is in a state of flux and the previously ascribed role of women is transforming. By most accounts, Morocco is one of the fastest changing countries in the Muslim world today.

France, a democratic country that guarantees basic liberties for its citizens, offers women of immigrant origins an opportunity to forge a new sense of personal and collective identity. The microcosm of France encapsulates the newly exacerbated, worldwide tensions between the Islamic and the Western world. Of critical importance are the real and perceived conflicts between Islam, Judeo-Christian values and those espoused by secular society. New legislation in France has restricted certain practices of Muslim women such as wearing the Muslim headscarf in public schools. As stated above, Muslims constitute the single largest immigrant minority in France and pose the greatest challenge in terms of identity, social cohesion and economic parity. Of critical importance is the extent to which the French government and French society at large can bring minorities into the mainstream. The possibility of their remaining an underprivileged underclass carries potentially serious risks ranging from petty crime to—in the extreme—terrorism.

This comparative study offers a fresh approach to understanding a certain segment of Muslim women. It has as its focus educated citizens but it does not draw primarily on experts, spokespersons, policy makers or religions. To round out personal views of ordinary women, the text also includes comments of certain influential women such as leaders of social service organizations, women's groups and Islamist movements. The actual names of women who are known in the public sphere are used. In all other cases pseudonyms are assigned.

This is not intended to be a comprehensive survey; instead it gives voice to women who otherwise remain silent in public discourse. Therefore, a word of caution is in order. This is not a representative study from which easy generalizations can be made. A larger context is provided by looking at relevant literature, scholarly texts as well as personal narratives and autobiographical novels.

Issues dealt with in this text revolve around a number of concepts and terms which can be interpreted in different ways. To avoid ambiguity, it is therefore important to make clear how these terms are used here.

A large portion of the book pertains to the "veil." There are a variety of religiously inspired garments for Muslim women, depending in style on geographical region or culture, variously called *tschador, burkha, shayla, al amira, khimar* or *hijab*, in the West most often simply called "veil." In the Qur'an the term *djillab* appears. In North Africa, the most common type of veil is the *hijab*, which is a headscarf that hides all hair but leaves the face and upper body uncovered, though a small minority of women also cover their faces with a *niqab*, or face veil. As the majority of Muslims in France are of North African origin, I use the term *hijab* or "Muslim headscarf."

As used here, "secular" refers to a condition in which church and state are separated, that is, there is little religious interference in government affairs and vice versa. The substantive concept from which that adjective derives is secularism which does not necessarily imply hostility toward religious beliefs. In France this concept is called *laïcité* and therefore this term is used. This concept is not applied in Morocco, an Islamic state where the King has the dual role of head of state and the nation's highest religious authority. Because of the historic connection between France and Morocco and the continued close relationship between those two countries, respondents in Morocco were familiar with the meaning of *laïcité*.

Several of the women described themselves as "Islamists." Islamism refers to movements, often characterized by moral conservatism, literalism, and an attempt to implement Islamic values in all aspects of life, that is, an Islamist worldview seeks to evaluate all aspects of private and public life based on the Qur'an and other sacred scriptures. However, there is not one single Islamist movement but several, which may differ and at times disagree with each other on matters of interpretation of sacred texts and practice. In Morocco, the largest Islamist movement is *Al Adl wa Ihsane* (Justice and Benevolence) which stands in the tradition of Sufism, the mystical branch of Islam that emphasizes personal experience and love for God over adherence to dogma. It is also a movement committed to non-violence. *Al Adl wa Ihsane* does not overtly participate in the political process of this country and does not field candidates in elections. Moroccan women who said they were Islamists or subscribed to Islamist positions referred to the positions taken by the *Al Adl wa Ihsane*. Because of its critical stance toward the monarchy, this movement is officially shunned and its leaders have been imprisoned or put under house arrest. There is in Morocco also a political Islamist group, the Party of Justice and Development (PJD) which has grown to become the second largest political party in the national parliament in 2007.

Morocco is also home to what could be termed "radical Islamists" as evidenced by the suicide bombings carried out by terrorists in five separate locations in Casablanca in 2003. The tragic events of May 16, 2003 in Casablanca marked a watershed for Morocco, comparable to the impact of the 9/11/2001 terrorist attacks on the World Trade Center in New York on public life in the United States. The international reach of Moroccan radical, violent Islamism can be seen in the predominance of Moroccans in the group that carried out the Madrid bombings of March 11, 2004 and the presence of Moroccans in international terrorist networks that have been uncovered in recent years. However, radical Islam is not the focus of this book.

In France, women who said they felt close to Islamism also emphasized their commitment to non-violence, which is different from radical groups that call themselves Islamists and support or engage in violence, including in extreme cases, terrorism. Some belonged to the French branch of the Justice and Benovolence Movement, which in France operates under the name *Participation et Spiritualité Musulmanes*. Most respondents however did not identify with a particular religious group. When the term "Islamist" is used in this book, it is based on this non-violent notion.

"Second-generation" refers to children of parents who emigrated from the Maghreb to France. This term is partly due to French citizenship laws, whereby a person born in France is not automatically entitled to French citizenship. Thus, women of Moroccan parentage for example, who were born in France and have never lived anywhere else, are not necessarily French nationals. In everyday language, "immigrants" in France most often suggests low-skilled workers with little formal education, even though juridically the term pertains to anyone from a foreign country taking up residence in France. I most often use the expression "women of Moroccan origin in France" rather than "Moroccan women in France" or "French women of Moroccan origin" because some of my respondents retained their Moroccan citizenship, some had dual citizenship, and some were French nationals only.

In the Western world, family law is part of civil law. In Morocco, as in most of the Muslim world, a separate, religiously based law, the Personal Status Code, governs matters such as marriage, divorce, custody and inheritance. In Morocco this Personal Status Code is called *moudawana*. Although parts of Moroccan civil and criminal law are also based on Islamic law, only the Personal Status Code is held to be based systematically on Islamic law. In civil law there are certain stipulations pertaining to real estate or property law that are based on Islamic law and in criminal law certain sections are based on Islamic law for example, breaking of the fast during the month of Ramadan, but other parts of civil or criminal law are derived from other sources, notably France. I use the terms Personal Status Code, family law and *moudawana* interchangeably.

The purpose of this book is not to explore the factual basis of attitudes but to understand individual perceptions. Often, individual perceptions differ from public discourse but are no less relevant with regard to social change. Because the war on terrorism is often perceived as a war of the West against the Muslim world, the way in which Muslim women make sense of their lives in a quickly changing world in which Islam has become a lightning rod is of critical importance.

NOTES

1. Some of the Moors—referred to also as "Arab-Berbers"—came from Syria. The last Moorish leader was expelled in 1492. During this same period, Jews were expelled from Spain as well.

2. According to *Jeune Afrique l'intelligent*, no. 2003, 27 février au 5 mars 2005, p. 49, 86 percent of Moroccan expatriates live in countries of the European Union, 9 percent in the Arab world and 5 percent in the United States and Canada.

1

Transgressing Boundaries

Changing attitudes and cultural changes are not easy to measure. Both are themes explored in this book. At the heart of this inquiry are the perceptions of individuals. What do individual women in Morocco and women of Moroccan origin in France believe and think about certain issues? The conflicts of our time are often presented in simplified terms and the more extreme views on either end of the spectrum are widely disseminated. Confrontations between radicals or fundamentalists on either side of the spectrum get most of the spotlight, leading to the misguided perception that a major clash of cultures, religions or civilizations is underway.[1] Public discourses tend to reflect the views of a certain elite on issues such as the legal reform of the family law in Morocco or the banning of selected religious insignia in French public schools. Meanwhile, the majority of women are struggling to make a living; and are decent citizens who do not subscribe to radical positions and stay out of the limelight and yet these ordinary people are affected by inflammatory public discourses. Opinions of large segments of the population are often drowned out in a spiral of silence.[2] Women who persistently but quietly pursue their personal and professional goals contribute just as much to societal transformations as those who can make their voices heard. It is on the individual level that grand issues can be understood in their complexity.

Societal changes are often tracked along specific geographic lines and thus we lose sight of the fact that similar phenomena can be observed in very different places. At present, there is little published scholarship with a comparative focus on women in Morocco and women of Moroccan origin in France. In part, this dearth has to do with the way the world has been divided.

1

THE KINGDOM OF THE WEST

Morocco is customarily studied within a Middle Eastern context. *Al-Mam-laka al-Maghribiya,* the official name of Morocco, translates as The Kingdom of the West. Moroccans commonly refer to their country as Al Maghrib, the West. This indicates that Morocco situates itself in relation to the Muslim East (Al Mashrik) rather than the vast continent of Africa to its south. (The name Morocco originates from the name of its former capital, Marrakech.) The countries of the Maghreb or the westernmost region of the Muslim world are considered part of the Arab world even though these countries, like Egypt, are in Africa. This designation is justified based on the fact that Islam is the dominant religion of all North African countries and therefore it is assumed that countries in which Islam is equally prevalent form a coherent unit. However, this can be countered by referring to Somalia, a country on the eastern coastline or the horn of Africa that has a larger percentage of Muslims than any of the nations in the Maghreb. Other African countries such as Mali, Senegal, Mauritania and Eritrea are predominantly Muslim as well. Another argument supporting the view that North Africa belongs to the Middle East or Arab world is based on ethnicity. All along the North African coastline, Arab peoples from the Middle East have settled since the end of the seventh century where they introduced not only their religion but also their culture and customs and therefore "the Arab world" is understood to be a coherent category. However, the original inhabitants of North Africa are various Berber (Amazigh) peoples who have no ethnic link—other than through intermarriages—with Arabs. Today Berber populations account for 40 percent of the population of the Maghreb. But because Arabs developed and settled primarily in the urban areas while Berbers remained a dispersed, largely rural population, Arabs have dominated public life.

Arab settlement has also occurred along the East African coastline where intermarriage with Africans has led to the development of Swahili culture. Yet Kenya or Tanzania—with the heavily Arab-influenced island of Zanzibar—are not considered part of the Arab world. One might wonder why only lighter-skinned North African peoples have earned the ethnic designation "Arab" whereas their predominantly darker-skinned fellow African Muslims remained "Africans?" Even though "race" has been discredited as a scientifically valid category, it is still used to separate North Africa from other African countries. There are black Moroccans and light-skinned, green-eyed Berbers. Every shade of skin color is also represented south of the Sahara—plus there are the white peoples of South Africa. Sudan, the largest country in Africa, is an exception because it is included in African and Middle Eastern Studies. Sudan's population is 70 percent Muslim, Arabic speaking and of

Arab descent and 30 percent are "black" Africans who are Christians or follow traditional African religions. And yet Africa continues to be divided into sub-Saharan Africa and North Africa—which in turn is linked to the Middle East—because African history is most often written from the perspective of the former colonizer—be they Arab or European—and categorization has historically been a useful tool in dividing and ruling colonized people.

Most African countries were at one point European colonies or protectorates. Algeria is the exception in the north of Africa because rather than being a colony of France it was actually an integral part of the French Republic. On the southernmost tip of the continent, the Republic of South Africa also has experienced a unique evolution because it had, like Algeria, significant European settlement and was not a colony in the same way most other African countries were.

Another reason given for situating North Africa in a Middle Eastern/Arab context is language. All the countries of North Africa use Arabic as one of their national languages. Other common languages are either French or English, depending on the former colonial power. Again, the Berber question arises. Nearly half of the population of North Africa speaks one of the Berber languages (Tamazight). Berber and Arabic share no linguistic connection. By contrast, Kiswahili, the lingua franca of several East African countries, is closely related to Arabic, *Swahel* being the Arab word for coast.

Without question, Morocco is an African country, inhabited by Africans, most of them Muslim. At the same time it is the only African country that is separated from Europe only by a hair's width and through the Spanish enclaves of Mellilia and Septa (also spelled Ceuta) actually shares a physical boarder with a Western European nation.

Morocco, a constitutional monarchy, is the only African country that is not currently a member of the African Union.[3] Instead, it is a member of the Arab League, the Arab Maghreb Union, the Organization of the Islamic Conference, and the Mediterranean Dialogue and is a major non-NATO ally. Thus, by its own assertion Morocco is not quite an African country—but neither is it a genuine Middle Eastern/Arab country. More recently, the designation "Mediterranean Region" has come into use. In sum: neat ways of dividing the world today is more problematic than ever.

What does this mean for our current discussion of contemporary Moroccan women and women of Moroccan origin in France? Moroccan immigrants in France are often called *arabe* (Arab) which is seen as a category apart from other immigrant population groups that emanate from other regions of the world. Employing the time-tested "divide and rule" strategy inhibits solidarity among various minority populations. Certainly, there are actual cultural and linguistic differences between migrants from North Africa and those who come from south of the Sahara, mainly former French colonies in West and Central Africa. There are also differences in terms of time scales in migration and settlement, different occupational structures, different positions in the French housing market etc. However, the validity of singling out the North African immigrant minority deserves to be drawn into question.

The flow of African immigrants into Europe has resulted in significant population shifts. Half a century after African nations won independence from their former European colonial masters, the histories of these two continents continue to be intertwined. The French population today is 10 percent Muslim, and other West European countries experience a similar rise in its Muslim populations. As Turkey is tenuously poised to become the first predominantly Islamic country to enter the European Union, integration of Muslim populations into the European mainstream is a pressing issue. Because the flow of immigration into Europe today is mostly from Muslim countries, one can no longer draw a hard and fast demarcation line between the "Muslim Orient" and the secular or Christian West. Women who have grown up in France, consider French their native language and who are at the same time Muslim, can serve as an important bridge between cultures and can contribute to overcoming stereotypes and preconceived notions about "Muslim women." By the same token, because Morocco historically has multiple identities—African, Arab, Middle Eastern, Berber—modern women in Morocco are also well placed to contribute to an altered understanding of Muslim women.

We shall now turn our attention to France where the majority of Moroccan immigrants have settled.

THE WESTERN HEXAGON

French school children still read textbooks that begin with the proverbial: "Our ancestors, the Gauls . . ." yet increasing numbers of French citizens do not have Gallic ancestors. Like any country, France adjusts slowly and with difficulty to its changing identity. We live in a progressively interconnected world where the flow of peoples from one geographic region to another alters the culture of their host county.

Unlike the United States, European countries view immigrants more suspiciously. France's population, like that of its European neighbors, used to be more or less homogenous. Discussions about assimilation of immigrants into the majority culture or integration—which allows for retention of distinct cultural or religious features—are therefore more visceral in Europe. The influx of foreign population groups shakes the foundations of deep cultural, historic, social, and national identities. A good immigrant, like a good child, is most appreciated when seen but not heard. In this book, we attempt to do the opposite, namely we want to give voice to women of immigrant origin.

An example of how France views new waves of immigrants from North Africa as intrinsically different is the fact that they are often referred to by their religion. "Muslim" is routinely used as a denominator for groups of people and in circumstances where religion plays no role. This became glaringly evident in national and international coverage of the tumultuous events in 2005.

In France, discussions about the Muslim minority reached an almost feverish pitch culminating in the debate on the headscarf ban in public schools in the spring of 2004. In the fall of 2005, the *banlieues* all over France erupted in flames as a result of an ill-fated police chase. Two teenagers had been electrocuted after climbing into an electrical sub-station in the eastern Paris suburb of Clichy-sous-Bois, in an attempt to hide from police. News of their deaths triggered riots in the area which is home to sizeable African communities.[4] These spontaneous riots made the larger French public aware of the pent-up frustrations and anger of mostly unemployed young men whose parents had immigrated to France, lured there by better professional opportunities than in their home countries in the developing world. Within days of the events in Clichy, cars were set ablaze in cities throughout France and young people rioted, smashed shop windows and even destroyed schools and nurseries. Still, most of this unrest occurred only in the outskirts and did not hit the city centers. The French government has long been aware of the simmering problems caused by failing measures aimed at integrating immigrants. A weighty report of nearly six hundred pages published in 2004 by the French *Cour des Comptes* (National Bureau of Statistics) examined the problem of immigration in France. The report concludes: "This crisis is not the product of immigration. It is the result of the way in which immigration was dealt with."[5]

Rioting "Muslim" youth in Paris showed the world the ugly side of France. Torched cars, vandalized stores, burnt down schools presented the world with images of the most violent unrest in France of the past forty years. The national crisis in the fall of 2005 brought to the fore an emblematic conflict of our times: that between a majority culture and minority ethnic groups. Variously referred to as the *intifada* of the suburbs, immigrant revolt, uprising of the underclass and *jihad* of Muslims against Europe, religion had actually little to do with the unrest. Though the majority of the rioters came from immigrant families, most of whom happen to be Muslim, the unrest ensued as a result of failed social and economic policies.

The fall riots were followed in the spring of 2006 by weeks-long protests and strikes—this time mostly by middle-class university students—against introduction of a new labor law. As these spring demonstrations carried on for weeks and occurred in the heart of Paris and other cities, then Prime Minister Dominique de Villepin announced the introduction of new labor law allowing employers to fire employees under the age of twenty-six within the first two years of employment. This CPE, Contract for First Employment (*Le Contrat première embauche*),[6] was intended to loosen strict labor protection laws in place in France with a view of creating new jobs. This should have made it easier for potential employers to hire people they would otherwise not employ, such as minorities. Students who protested this new law claimed it would turn them into the "Kleenex generation"—used and then discarded. In the United States such job guarantees are unheard of, but in France people are used to having jobs that last a lifetime—or conversely, remain unemployed. In the wake of these protests, my respondents felt more at ease to discuss their own, volatile job situations. These disturbances in France highlight social problems faced not only by this country but also neighboring ones that are host to large numbers of minorities of immigrant origins, such as Great Britain, Germany, Belgium, Italy and the Netherlands.

Religion was not at the core of the unrest, yet the largely unemployed young people who set cars, schools and businesses ablaze in the *banlieues*, the socially disadvantaged suburbs of Paris and other large cities, were frequently simply identified as Muslims. Local and international media reports often highlighted religious and cultural differences between the majority and the minority populations rather than directing attention to the social and economic causes.

Conspicuously absent in these riots were "Muslim" women, who were, however, like their largely unemployed peers, raised in the same destitute neighborhoods. This manifest female abstention from violent unrest points to a difference in approaching difficult situations. Throughout this book, we will meet women who explain how they deal with rejection, discrimination and social exclusion.

In his televised address[7] following the riots in France, former President Jacques Chirac spoke of a national identity crisis, a crisis of values and of inhumane urbanism. The question poses itself: Whose identity is in question and how can young rioters cause such a profound calamity? The rioters hit a raw nerve of mainstream France, the issue of integration of North African immigrants.

MEASURING OPINIONS

As mentioned above, women were conspicuously absent from the French riots, though they were equally affected by discriminatory housing and employment practices. In Morocco too, women deal with their adversities in a less brazen fashion. This is all the more reason to find out just how women deal with their particular situations and in what ways their approaches differ or are similar. This book zeroes in on individuals and their personal perceptions and then uses these individual testimonies as a basis for analyzing larger trends. This approach is called "grounded theory" because theories are developed inductively from a corpus of data. Such a case-oriented perspective assumes that variables interact in complex ways and defy strict statistical analysis.

Research methods in the social sciences are a dicey proposition. Some view social "science" with skepticism because social issues cannot be scientifically measured and therefore lack the validity of the natural sciences. This is especially the case in qualitative research on which this book is based. Qualitative research is a type of research that produces findings not arrived at by statistical procedures or other quantitative means. While some of the data may be quantified, such as demographic information, the greater part of the analysis is interpretative (Strauss and Corbin, 1998: 11). The choice of methodology was determined by the nature of the research. My goal was to gain a better understanding of attitudes of a specific group of people, their aspirations, thoughts, and feelings, by encouraging them to speak their minds on issues of importance to them. A questionnaire was used to acquire basic demographic information but the majority of the questions did not have a fixed catalogue of responses from which to choose. Instead, questions left room for open-ended answers.

Trying to understand people and issues from a culture other than one's own is always fraught with pitfalls and there is great potential for misunderstanding. However, absence of such effort is even more problematic. Even if one is unable to obtain a full understanding, crossing a cultural divide is a rewarding process because at the least, it allows for an appreciation of life's challenges as perceived by those who inhabit a different cultural space. Thus, engaging with women in Morocco and France was not a mechanical process of data collection in which questionnaires were filled out and answers checked off. Rather, it was a journey of discovery in which erstwhile strangers opened their doors and allowed a look inside. When Glaser and Strauss developed a "grounded theory" they intended it to be used for analysis which is grounded in themes supplied by concerned individuals or groups of individuals.

To the extent that significant differences in attitudes are found, the factors to which these can be attributed will be described. Where no significant differences can be ascertained, the reasons for similarities are explored. Because this study draws on a comparison of Muslim women in France with those in

Morocco, the extent of differences or similarities can serve as an indicator of how educated, professional women view themselves, where their loyalties lie, what they perceive as their main personal and professional challenges, and the extent to which they see themselves as vital parts of their respective societies. Modifications in attitudes are more fluid than legal changes, yet attitudes are of critical importance in social change.

WOMEN

The landmark Arab Human Development Report published by the United Nations Development Programme (UNDP) identifies the following main tasks in promoting human development: "Building, using and liberating the capabilities of the Arab people by advancing knowledge, freedom and women's empowerment." The Report, produced jointly with the Arab Fund for Economic and Social Development, offers an assessment and lays out a plan of action that emphasizes the role of women in national development. The Report states that because their rights to "self-determination have been grossly violated" in predominantly Muslim and Arab nations, women's contributions have been underutilized and undervalued (UNDP, 2003: III). The UN Report, compiled on the basis of data collected by hundreds of scholars, offers a comprehensive assessment of the situation of the peoples in various parts of the Muslim world. The report further asserts: "Knowledge is one of the key instruments of human development, be it in instituting good governance, guaranteeing health, producing the ingredients of material and moral welfare, or promoting economic growth" (ibid.: VI). Because knowledge is a key ingredient in the development of an individual as well as the nation, an advanced level of education was a factor in selecting women for this study. Higher levels of education enable individuals to evaluate their own culture and traditions more critically and can open the door to personal and professional advancement. These women are also more likely to have a say in the public sphere.

Most of this book is based on conversations with "ordinary" women, that is, women who do not occupy public positions, women who are not in the spotlight and who are not routinely looked up by policy makers or researchers. They are women whose opinions are rarely recorded, whose personal life stories have not made headlines. In Moroccan culture, as in many places in the world, women are encouraged to humbly lower their gaze and endure life in silence. Therefore, it is all the more important to break the spiral of silence and listen to what they have to say.

However, I also consulted experts including legal scholars and lawyers, political scientists, scholars of Islam, journalists and social workers. As Islamism is a rising force in Morocco, I sought out a spokesperson of the largest non-violent, Islamist Movement *Al Adl wa Ihsane* (Justice and Benevolence). Nadia Yassine is one of the most influential and, due to her critical stance toward the monarchy, controversial women in Morocco today. She also is the daughter of the founder and leader Sheikh Abdessalam Yassine. Her views represent those of large numbers of women not only members of the movement but also of those who are sympathetic to its positions on social issues.

In France, I sought out women who lead grassroots social service organizations. Sarah Oussékine directs a center for abused women, *Voix d'elles Rebelles* (Voice of the She Rebels), an organization that caters to troubled young women *(filles en difficultés)* in the *banlieues,* the socially disadvantaged neighborhoods comparable to the inner cities in the U.S. Though she does not nearly have the same status in France as Nadia Yassine has in Morocco, her opinions are important because she is involved on a daily basis with the struggles of women of North African immigrant origins. Her often controversial views have sparked public debate in France.

One might wonder about the usefulness of a study that focuses on a small minority rather than sampling from a larger population. The reason for focusing on educated, professional women lies in the comparative nature. To facilitate a valid comparison, the two groups needed to have significant criteria in common. Because the study has as its focus women in Morocco and women of Moroccan origin in France, certain commonalities can be taken for granted, for example the majority, if not all, are Muslim and have been—to varying degrees—inculcated with Moroccan culture and traditions. The reasons for choosing the additional criteria mentioned above are as follows:

Young: Young women are in the process of charting out their personal and professional lives and are an integral part of cultural shifts. Inasmuch as their lives differ from those of their mothers, young women are breaking new ground. The age of the women consulted for this research ranges between eighteen and thirty-five years.

Educated: As agents of change, educated women play a larger role in the public sphere of their countries than, for example, illiterate, rural women. According to World Bank statistics, Morocco has a literacy rate of 50.7 percent. Among women, the literacy rate is 38.3 percent: that is, more than 60 percent of Moroccan women are illiterate. The United Nations Educational, Scientific and Cultural Organization defines adult literacy as follows: "The adult literacy rate is the percentage of people aged fifteen and above who can, with understanding write a short, simple statement on their everyday life" (UNESCO Institute of Statistics, 2002). For France, no comparative data on literacy are available. It is, however, safe to assume that the literacy rate among women brought up in France, where the educational system is more developed, is considerably

higher than among women in Morocco. Given the disparities in overall educational levels between Morocco and France, interviewing educated women
in Morocco means focus on a small minority which is not representative of
the majority of women in that country. But as this investigation explores
viewpoints of women with similar educational attainments, thereby facilitat-
ing closer comparisons, this was a conscious choice and not an oversight.[8] All
the women interviewed for this study possessed at minimum a baccalaureate,
the majority in both samples held the equivalent of a Bachelor's degree, some
the equivalent of a Master's degree and some a Ph.D. The reasons why
women in the French sample generally have attained a less advanced degree
than those in the Moroccan sample lies in the fact that educated, professional
women in Morocco often come from a higher social class and therefore have
easier access to educational facilities. The issue and importance of social
class will be addressed throughout the book.

Professional: Professional women, that is, a growing number of women
with distinct qualifications for their jobs, are a relatively recent phenomenon
in Morocco. Likewise in France, second-generation professional women of
Moroccan origin are only now emerging. It was therefore of particular interest to ascertain the differences and similarities between two groups of people
who are among the first in their respective countries to enter the job market
in increasing numbers. Some of the women were between jobs and some were
unemployed at the time of my first meeting with them in 2004 but most had
found professional positions when I saw them again in 2005 and 2006.

Urban: For the purposes of a comparative study, urban residence was selected as a criterion. In metropolitan France, few second-generation women
live in a rural environment. Even the socially disadvantaged *banlieues* or *cités*
have basic services such as electricity, water and healthcare and children
growing up in these parts of town will attend school, which is not the case in
the rural areas and shantytowns on the outskirts of Moroccan cities such as
Casablanca. Therefore, the women I spoke with in Morocco came from an urban population, even though the families of some of the women originally
came from small towns across Morocco.[9]

Despite the commonalities with regard to the above criteria, there are significant differences as well. The single biggest difference between young, urban, educated and professional women in Morocco and a comparable group
of women of Moroccan origin in France was found to be social class. In Morocco, there are three identifiable social classes: the royal family and small
wealthy elite, a growing middle class and a large, often rural, lower class.

In Morocco, most young educated, professional women hail from middle-
or upper-middle-class backgrounds. The mothers of these young women are
literate, but most have not pursued a professional career, while their fathers

are often in the employ of the government or are highly skilled professionals such as medical doctors, pharmacists, academics or businessmen.

In France the majority of women of Moroccan origin come from working-class backgrounds and have grown up in the socially disadvantaged outskirts of industrial cities. Their mothers—and occasionally fathers—are often illiterate; if mothers were employed outside the home, they had menial jobs such as housekeepers. Most fathers work in low-skilled, low-wage jobs.

Because of these disparities concerning social class, particular effort was made to include young, educated, professional women in Morocco who come from modest backgrounds though these cases are still rare in a society that traditionally knows little upward social mobility. Women in that category are a particularly small minority but as the following chapters will show, they are also a particularly outspoken and active minority. In a similar way, in France, effort was made to include women of Moroccan origin whose parents come from middle-class backgrounds. These were women whose fathers had come to France to pursue university degrees and then found well-paying, high-skilled jobs and remained there. Others were businessmen who traded across the Mediterranean but maintained their residence in France or who worked for international companies.

To protect the confidentiality of my respondents, none of my interview partners will be referred to by their real name. Throughout, their names have been replaced with pseudonyms except in the case of well-known personalities who are used to being interviewed.

EDUCATION

Though this book gives voice to educated women, I rarely identify their exact level of education. This is due to the differences between educational systems in Morocco and in France. Though the two countries have similar educational systems, they are not identical. Even though a degree may have the same name, it is not always transferable from one French-speaking country to another. Several of the women had received their university education in the United States, Great Britain or at a Moroccan university that uses the American system of education. My respondents in both countries had completed at minimum the BAC (baccalauréate) Most had pursued a Bachelor's degree, the French equivalents *DEUG* (Diplôme d'Études Universitaires Générales) or *licence*. Some had obtained a Master's degree, *maîtrise* or *DEA* (diplôme d'études approfondies). An exact equivalency between French educational degrees with for example American university degrees is not easy to establish and depends on specifics of a given degree. Several women in Morocco and in

France had earned a doctorate or a Ph.D. When relevant, individual women's highest educational degree is mentioned in the following chapters. As this book focuses on educated women, the women mentioned here do have higher than average levels of education in both countries. This is particularly the case in Morocco, where no more than 36 percent of women are literate.[10]

TOPICS OF CONVERSATION

The topics for our conversations revolved around three main themes: conceptions of Islam, legal changes and personal and professional aspirations and challenges. Because religion is central to a believer's identity and because Islam in particular has become an important issue in current public discourse, women's individual perceptions and understandings of their religion were deemed an important theme. The extent to which attitudes of women in Morocco, a predominantly (Sunni) Islamic country, differ from or are similar to those of Muslim women in France, a secular state with a marked Roman Catholic heritage, serves as an indicator of a global phenomenon.

Both France and Morocco have recently seen important legal changes that directly impact women's lives; therefore this theme was deemed relevant. Certainly these changes are of a different magnitude in both countries. Again, the focus of the investigation was on how women in the two samples understood and perceived legal changes with regard to their own lives. Among other things, I wanted to find out how much women in France knew about the family law reform in Morocco and conversely how much women in Morocco had followed the debate on the banning of the Muslim headscarf in public schools in France.

The third theme concerned personal and professional challenges. For young women, decisions about marriage, family and/or a professional career are issues of immediate concern and therefore they can be expected to have much to say on this topic.

Weaving together family obligations and the demands of a professional life are of course challenges for women regardless of their cultural, religious or educational background. Marriage, however, presents a particular area of concern for Muslim women. Marriage is often understood as a fact of life and not primarily a matter of choice. Questions about early marriage, arranged marriage, the requirement to marry within the culture,[11] weigh particularly heavy on Muslim women.

The pursuit of professional ambitions is also of particular relevance for women in Morocco and women of Moroccan origin in France. In France, second-generation women whose North African parents came to Europe as low-skilled immigrants are the first of their kind to claim a place in the public sphere. Khosrokhavar described the emergence of a professional class among women of Maghrebi origins as follows: "The eruption of women in the public sphere is in new phenomenon in Islam" (1997: 115). He continues: "These young women emancipate rapidly yet their margin of available space is much more restricted [than that of men]" (121). In Morocco, a similar phenomenon occurs with increasing numbers of young, educated women seeking entrance into the workforce.

An increasing number of women in Morocco and France eschew early marriage to pursue higher education and a professional career; they are faced with the task of accommodating both personal and professional aspirations. In achieving a balance between the two, there are particular hurdles for women in the Muslim world because of a demarcation between the public and the private sphere. An understanding of this issue is important in order to appreciate the acuteness of the issue of personal and professional challenges for the two groups.

PUBLIC VERSUS PRIVATE

In Moroccan culture, as in most of the Muslim world, the public and the private are two distinct spheres. They are two separate worlds for which the rules of behavior are different. The public refers to the street, men's place, where everything is up for grabs, and where it is every man for himself. This is contrasted with the private that refers to the home, where all relationships are clearly defined and rules of behavior are unambiguous and actions are accounted for (Gray, 2005). Anyone who has traveled to North Africa will have experienced the somewhat rude behavior in the street which is in sharp contrast to the generous and kind hospitality in the home; widespread neglect of public spaces versus the immaculate cleanliness inside the house. There also is a marked absence of personal space and boundaries in public places which particularly for women can create uncomfortable situations (Hall, 1966: 159).

Families who moved from Morocco to France have a deep-seated sense of this distinction. Concern—even fear—among fathers, brothers and husbands of releasing their female relative into the unruly world outside is not merely a control issue as it is often presented, but it is also based on an understanding of the different rules governing social interaction in the private and the public spheres.

CONFIDENCE AND TRUST

Routinely, I discussed my conversations with experts in Morocco to search for hidden clues as well as a larger context. These scholars understood the nature of my inquiry and were at home in the culture of the women I spoke with.

They could shed insights on seemingly straightforward comments. Consequently, deeper meanings were unlocked. An example of this was my question: "Do you fast during Ramadan?" Almost all women in Morocco answered "yes." Yet in follow-up meetings the same women would say that they actually did not fast. Despite assurances of confidentiality, they were initially hesitant to admit that they did not fast during Ramadan. After we had met several times, they felt more comfortable to reveal themselves. In Morocco, the Ramadan fast is a national event in which all citizens are called to participate and eating in public is a criminal offense. According to the scholars I consulted, an admission of not fasting, even to an outsider and non-Muslim, was to be interpreted as a sign of trust and that I was held in confidence.

As our relationships deepened, women were more forthcoming in talking about various aspects of their lives. For example several women in France would simply state their profession without much further elaboration at our first conversation. During our second or third meeting, they would confide that they actually felt insecure in their present position, were overqualified but could not find another position or felt they could not move up within the company as they had expected. As the job situation in France for young people, particularly those of immigrant origins, became an issue of national concern following the riots in the fall of 2005 and came into even sharper focus with massive demonstrations by high school and university students, union representatives and teachers in the spring of 2006, my respondents also felt more confident in talking about their own situation.

In all human interaction, trust is an important matter. Especially when engaging with someone from a different culture for the first time, there is the risk that respondents will say what they believe is expected of them rather than reveal their actual views. Particularly in authoritarian societies such as Morocco, conformity is highly valued, therefore people may say what they believe the listener, especially an outsider, wants to hear. This was most apparent when discussing the Personal Status Code reform. Most respondents would initially repeat what the King had said when he first announced the reform, namely that it was firmly grounded in the Qur'an. Only in later conversations would they venture their own opinions about why the law had been changed.

FRIENDSHIP

One of the questions I wanted to explore was whether Muslim women had close personal friends who were not Muslims. While one might expect that this would be more common in France than in Morocco where the majority of the population is not Muslim, I found that given an opportunity to interact with people of different cultures, women in Morocco actually did seek them out and were interested in developing such relationships. It is however quite difficult to define "friendship" and so the extent of these cross-cultural relationships is hard to measure.

One particularly heartbreaking encounter in Morocco illustrates how hard it is to define friendship. I had met with a university student, Huda, who had not traveled much beyond her hometown and had lived all her life in the heartland of Morocco, several afternoons in a row. Huda came from a strict Islamist family and still lived at home from where her father monitored her relationships. And yet she told me she had friends who were not Muslim. I was curious as to where she would have met someone with a background different from her own. Eventually, I asked who her non-Muslim friends were to which she exclaimed: "Why, you!" In the course of our afternoons together, this shy woman said that nobody had ever shown such an interest in her opinions. At school and at home Huda felt constantly admonished as to what was right or wrong and her father in particular was prone to giving speeches rather than encouraging discussions. This I had experienced myself on some of my visits to her house. Huda said the encounter with my inquiry was her first opportunity to express her own views on religion, family, marriage, her dreams and hopes for her personal and professional life in such detail. And so she had concluded that despite our difference in age and background, we must be friends.

I had a similar encounter in France with an equally shy woman who came from a rather authoritarian home, albeit not a particularly religious one. After we had met a few times and she had begun to open up, she started e-mailing me digital friendship cards despite the fact that I was her mother's age. She continued to send such messages for years. Though they rarely included a personal message, in her own way, this woman wanted to continue a relationship that had allowed her to freely speak about issues she felt she mostly had to keep inside.

Other women felt quite differently; they were more detached and remained factual throughout our conversations. This was especially the case among women in France who identified themselves as "fundamentalist." I knew of a self-proclaimed fundamentalist woman with whom I had exchanged e-mail messages. Though we had arranged to meet several times, each time she stood me up. She had mentioned once that she attended classes at an Islamic Study Center on the outskirts of Paris every weekend. Rather than risking being left to wait in vain once more, I decided to find this center in hopes to see her there. It was not easy to locate this place as it was in an unmarked building in a back-alley in one of the *banlieues*. Because I had worked as a journalist for more than a decade in Africa where information is rarely freely available, I had developed skills that allowed me to track down people or "news sources" in obscure places. I found the Islamic study center, but it was for members only. Eventually, I was allowed to wait in the hallway where I started to chat with the women who walked in. I had hours to do so because Rhaba was nowhere to be seen. I rightly assumed that women who frequented this center knew each other by name. I was told that Rhaba was attending a special session and would come out as soon as the class was over. While sitting in the waiting area, I could observe through the slightly ajar door one of the study sessions in progress. A bearded man lectured on the role of women according to the Qur'an to a small, mostly female, veiled audience. The lecturer apparently was a native Arabic-speaker whereas the audience members knew little Arabic because he repeatedly invoked sayings in Arabic which he then translated into heavily accented French.

Eventually, Rhaba emerged and agreed to talk with me under the condition that the door of the room to which she guided me remained open. She also announced that she would end the conversation if I made her feel uncomfortable. She requested to read the notes I was going to take. Rhaba started out by telling me in her understanding of Islam there was no differentiation among people along national or ethnic lines. All true believers were brothers and sisters and national or ethnic background was not important. Though her parents were Moroccan, she considered herself first and foremost as part of the *umma*, the worldwide community of believers. Those who referred to their national or ethnic roots had, according to her, succumbed to a colonial mindset. She did not feel that her Moroccan origins had any bearing on her present identity and to illustrate this point she emphasized that her circle of friends included Muslims from various backgrounds.

This, in fact, is not unusual in France. Most immigrant families who come to France in search of menial labor have apartments in public housing complexes: large drab high-rise buildings which frequently are in various states of disrepair. Often, these neighborhoods take on a certain kind of village feel with outdoor markets and people sitting in groups outside. Neighbors know one another and often help each other out. The difficulty of adjusting to life in France diminishes enmities between their home countries. This was evident when I asked women if they could introduce me to some of their friends. Their circles of friends included people from other immigrant families, from Algeria, Tunisia, from Senegal and Mali. These friendships among people of Moroccan and Algerian backgrounds are in sharp contrast to the prevailing anti-Algerian attitude found in Morocco. Because of Algeria's support for the Polisario[12] movement that is fighting for independence of the Western Sahara, a territory claimed by Morocco, the two countries have had a long, acrimonious relationship which at times led to the closing of their common border. In France, these national hostilities had all but disappeared among the second generation. I also met several women in France, though none in Morocco, who came from mixed parentage, that is, one parent was Moroccan and the other from another African, or a Middle Eastern, country. Thus, Rhaba's statement actually reflected the reality of most second-generation immigrants in France.

Rhaba appeared defensive and torn between wanting to make her views heard and a deep mistrust for people who were not part of her community of believers. Another curious incident occurred on the subway shortly after I had left the Islamic Study Center. There, in a crowded Parisian metro, a young man stood beside me and introduced himself by asking if I spoke English. He too had attended a lecture at the Islamic center and noticed me sitting in the hallway. Originally from India, he had recently been assigned to the Paris branch of his bank. As he was new in town, he was looking for a community of fellow Muslims. Without much ado, he started unloading: "These French Muslims know so little about Islam, they really give Islam a bad name. All they know is what their African parents have taught them. They practice their rural uneducated culture, not Islam. And when they do want to know more, they come to these centers where they are taught Wahabism. I feel I have not really found any fellow Muslims here." We continued to chat for a while until we reached his exit station. The comments of this young man serve as a useful reminder of the diversity that exists within Muslim communities. The encounter with Rhaba also reflected the deep mistrust even of peaceful fundamentalist toward people who do not belong to their community.

BEHIND THE VEIL

In Morocco, there was no difference between women who wore a *hijab* and those who did not in terms of the ease with which they approached me. In France, women who wore the Muslim headscarf were considerably more cautious, for example in their choice of a meeting place. None of the covered women in France invited me to their homes and preferred to meet in places where women with headscarves were prevalent. In the present climate of the "war on terror" which can also be perceived as a conflict of the West against Islam, such precautions are understandable. At the same time it is a reminder of how international political conflicts impact personal lives and relationships. The precarious situation associated with the Muslim headscarf became apparent in an incident that occurred when I met with a group of young women at the university campus at the Université Paris X Nanterre on the outskirts of Paris. A university official approached me and demanded an explanation as to the nature of my meetings with "these women." While I was ready to get into a debate about such unwarranted intrusion, the women—apparently used to such forms of harassment—quickly said, "let's go to another place" and had disappeared before I could turn around.

RENDEZ-VOUS

An interesting aspect of how women saw themselves came to light when we arranged to meet. Over the phone, we exchanged particulars about our appearance so that we could recognize each other. This was mostly the case in France, because in Morocco, I could easily be identified as a foreigner. The way women in Morocco described themselves allowed me to spot them even in busy places such as in front of the main railway station in Rabat or at the edge of the medina of Fès, the walled-in part of town that has remained largely unchanged since the fourteenth century. Their self-descriptions matched their actual appearance.

By contrast in France, most women described themselves on the phone as looking "typically Moroccan." Routinely, the women would notice me before I saw them. What they viewed to be "typically Moroccan" could be lost on an outsider. Most were clad in fashionable Western attire, had brown, black or blonde hair, coiffed in a variety of styles, and did not stand out in a crowded street. Yet these women of Moroccan origin had a deep-seated sense of differentness which they believed could easily be noticed from a distance.

It was not uncommon that a group of women showed up for a *rendez-vous*. Invariably, they insisted that they were best friends, had no secrets from each other and we should just chat in a group. But as I was adamant about talking with one woman at a time, it happened that women revealed personal secrets their friends were unaware of.

There was one woman who admitted to having had sexual relationships despite keeping up the appearance of being a virgin in the eyes of her family and friends. Another spoke of an abortion—arranged by her mother—after she had become pregnant from a relationship with a non-Muslim boyfriend. Because of the shame and disgrace she felt afterwards, she agreed to a marriage arranged by her parents to a man she did not know prior to their engagement. Her friends knew nothing of the events that preceded this arranged marriage as she did not want them to know that hers was an arranged, meaning old-fashioned, marriage. She wanted her friends to believe that she had fallen in love. "Did you?" I asked her. She said she hoped that in time she would come to love her husband.

LANGUAGE

In France, all my conversations were in French, and in fact women often apologized for not knowing even verses from the Qur'an in the original Arabic. Occasionally, they would insert common expressions in Arabic such as

"*Inch'Allah*" (God willing), "*Mektub*" (it is written, meaning destiny). When I asked them if they spoke Arabic, some women in France responded by invoking the *fatiha,* the opening sentence of most *suras: "besmellah errahman errahim"* (In the name of Allah, most benevolent, ever merciful) or recite parts of the *shahada,* the profession of faith "*La ilaha il Allah*" (there is no God but God) and said this was the extent of their knowledge of classical Arabic. Women of the second generation in France described French as their primary language even though most spoke *Dereja* (Moroccan dialectical Arabic) or one of the Berber languages or a mixture of languages with their parents but used French with their siblings.

In Morocco, women chose to speak in French or English, or a mixture of French and Dereja or French, English and Dereja. Especially when discussing very private matters, some switched to the language furthest from their daily use, such as English. It is often easier to express sentiments that are considered taboo in one's own cultural context in a foreign language.

Language is often described as one of the hallmarks of identity. Thus the fact that women of Moroccan origin in France describe French as their mother tongue serves as an important indicator for their identification with France. In Morocco, language is certainly more complex because women of Berber origin speak one of the Amazigh languages with their families, use Dereja outside the home and often speak French at work. In most previously colonized countries, people are used to switching back and forth between languages.

Though Dereja is based on Arabic and uses the Arabic script in its written form, it is actually a mixture of Amazigh (Berber) languages, Arabic and French. Tamazight structures infuse the Moroccan Arabic to such an extent, that Dereja can often not be understood in Arab-speaking countries of the Middle East where a variety of Arabic dialects are spoken. This berberized Arabic is one of the distinguishing features of the Maghreb. Rosello contends that Maghrebis, "must first and foremost think *about* languages rather than *in* a certain language or even two or three" (Roselleo, 2005: 74). Code-switching on a daily basis is part of the complex identity of Moroccans and children of Moroccan immigrants in France.

Though the term "Berber" is commonly used, it is in fact a derogatory term. *Imazighen* (literally: the free people) is the name used by the original inhabitants of North Africa, whose presence in the Maghreb long preceded the advent of Arab invaders of the seventh century. The word Berber derives from "Barbarian," a designation originating with the Romans who followed the Greek custom of labeling native populations as "non-Greek speaking peoples." The three most common languages spoken in Morocco are Tamazight, Tachelhit and Tarifit.[13] Tamazight is the collective term for all Berber languages and has been a written language, on and off, for almost three thousand years; however, this tradition has been frequently disrupted by various invasions, colonial and post-colonial policies. The study of Tamazight was introduced into the Moroccan school system only in 2003 and the study of the Tifinagh alphabet has recently been re-introduced as an area of study in Morocco in the wake of official recognition of Amazigh cultures. Though in France immigrants from North Africa are often simply referred to as "Arabs" or "beurs," this belies the fact that the majority are not Arabs but Imazighen, or Berbers.

Though most women I met in France spoke a mixture of languages at home with their parents, they considered French their primary language. "I don't know if I will speak anything but French with my children," said Ilham. "It is a pity because my mother does not speak much French. But French really is my native tongue." She added, "outside of Morocco *Dereja* is useless and Tarifit even more so. When I was in Morocco as a child, I noticed that I could not speak as well as the other children. It is a shame to lose a language but what's the use here in France. I am better off learning English." I met few women in France who had some formal training in classical Arabic. Those who did had been sent to Qur'anic schools as children or they had taken it upon themselves to study Arabic as adults. The latter was primarily the case among veiled women. The lack of knowledge of classical Arabic also meant that they could not read the Qur'an in its original version. As the Qur'an is believed to be the directly revealed word of God to the Prophet Mohammed, any translation is considered an interpretation and therefore inferior to the Arab original. Some said their inability to read Arabic was one of the reasons why they had never read the Qur'an. Furthermore, their barely literate parents had never read the Qur'an either. This was especially the case in Tamazight-speaking families.

Despite questioning the continued usefulness of a Moroccan tongue, most women did enjoy being able to communicate in a language that could not be understood by the majority of French. Said Aïcha, a teacher near Paris, "It is fun to have sort of a secret language. When I am in the subway with my friends, and we don't want people around us to understand what we are saying, we can switch to *Dereja*." As language is closely tied to identity, the gradual loss of the languages of their parents also means a loosening of emotional ties to their country of origin.

WILL YOU TELL THE TRUTH?

Researchers who rely on personal interviews describe a frequently occurring experience, summarized by Joycelyne Cesari who quotes a young man in her

"Muslims and Republicans" (*Musulmanes et Republicains*): "We would very much like to contribute to your survey, but are you going to do the same as most others or will you tell the truth? Why do we always have to justify our-sevels?" (Cesari, 1999: 13). This outburst reflects the assumption that a West-ern researcher who asks questions about Islam must be concerned with ter-rorism and fundamentalism. In my encounters in France and Morocco, this sentiment was expressed frequently.

Most research about Muslims in the West, in this case France, is conducted from the vantage point of the Western world and examines its influence on changing attitudes among Muslims. My approach takes a Muslim country, Morocco, as a starting point and then looks to women of Moroccan origin in France. Therefore, the views of women in Morocco are often presented in greater detail because they allow for depth of understanding of the responses by those in France. It is also better suited for the purposes of this comparative analysis because it allows for a more nuanced understanding of how to inter-pret attitudinal changes of Muslim women.

Overall, despite being raised within a culture that treasures women's si-lence, I found that most women were eager to express their opinions and share their views.

NOTES

1. Samuel P. Huntington's seminal work "The Clash of Civilizations," Free Press, 2002, has contributed much to this simplified analysis, though Huntington himself of-fers a more complex view.

2. The Spiral of Silence is a concept developed by Elisabeth Noelle-Neumann in the 1960s, which postulates that large numbers of people do not express their opin-ions if they differ from public discourse.

3. This is due to the fact that the African Union supports independence of the West-ern Sahara, a territory claimed by Morocco.

4. For a timeline on the unrest, see: http://news.bbc.co.uk/2/hi/europe/4413964.stm.

5. http://www.Cour-des-comptes/publications/rapports/immigration/immigration.pdf.

6. See special edition of *Le Monde*: http://www.lemonde.fr/web/sequence/0, 2-734511,1-0,0.html

7. Televised national address, November 14, 2005.

8. First-generation Moroccan immigrants often have received only minimal schooling prior to moving to France; however, their daughters—the target population of this study—will have attended schools in France.

9. A hallmark of Moroccan society is its rural/urban dichotomy. About half of the population of thirty-two million lives in the rural areas and hinterlands, the other half in the urban centers. In the urban areas, there is great disparity between poor, socially

disadvantaged shantytowns, where dwellings may not have running water or electricity or adequate educational facilities and the middle- and upper-middle-class sections of big cities.

10. UNICEF statistics for 2000 for Morocco: Adult literacy rate for females: 36 percent, for males 62 percent.

11. Islam is a patrilineal religion, that is, a Muslim father is required for a child to be born a Muslim. Thus Muslim men are permitted to marry non-Muslim women whereas Muslim women are required to marry a Muslim man.

12. Polisario, from the Spanish abbreviation of Popular Front for the Liberation of Saguia el-Hamra and Río de Oro, is a movement working for the independence of Western Sahara since the 1970s.

13. In Algeria, Kabyle is the most widely spoken Berber language.

2

The Tar of My Country

At what point do children and grandchildren of Maghrebi immigrants stop being referred to as second or third generation and become simply French? Who determines their "Frenchness?" Minorities often find themselves with hyphenated designations or acronyms that link them to their ancestral places of origin, in the U.S. for example African American, Hispanic American or ABC (American-born-Chinese). Such terms are commonly assigned to minorities who have suffered state-sanctioned discrimination, regardless of whether they come from indigenous populations, are of immigrant background or, in the case of African Americans, were brought to the U.S. by force. While the United States has historically welcomed the role of immigrants in building the nation, European countries have viewed newcomers who speak a different language or have a different religion more suspiciously. In France where 77 percent of the population is Roman Catholic (despite the fact that 54 percent say they are atheist),[1] Muslims have a particularly hard stand. It has often been argued that France's Muslims are incapable of integrating because they owe allegiance to a religion which is fundamentally incompatible with the principles of the republic. However, religion is not the reason for the failure of integration. Instead, ill-conceived social and economic policies have led to perilous social exclusion. Referring to a minority population as "second generation" further alienates children of immigrants, because this term implies that these people are still newcomers or outsiders and therefore are not yet considered French. In addition, the complex and changing rules for acquiring French citizenship complicate matters. Whereas in the United States, *jus solis* (Latin for "right of soil") grants citizenship rights to every individual born on American territory, France, like several other European countries, employs the *jus sanguinis* (Latin for "right of blood") approach. This means that French parentage and ancestry are important considerations for acquiring citizenship and being born in France does not automatically entitle a person to French citizenship.

The majority of immigrants in France feel a strong allegiance to France; their children and grandchildren have benefited from the public school system and have been inculcated with French republican values. France generally has offered immigrants a better livelihood than their countries of origin and decent education for their children. The women I met considered themselves French and Muslim. They felt at ease with their multiple identities, yet the majority population continues to perceive a conflict between being Muslim and French. Muslims in France remain the "other." In the following, we will consider some of the larger issues impacting on the lives of women of Moroccan origin in France.

IMMIGRATION

Immigration is not a new or recent phenomenon in French history. To the contrary, immigration has a long tradition in France. In modern times, since about the middle of the nineteenth century, there has been a substantial flow of immigrants into the hexagon. In fact, France used to enjoy the reputation of being the European country most open to immigrants, including political refugees. Apart from wars and political turmoil, immigration generally is linked to the economic needs of a host country and tends to occur particularly during periods of rapid economic growth. In the time period between World Wars I and II, nearly three million, or six percent of the population, were of immigrant origins, mostly from neighboring countries, such as Italy, Spain, Belgium, or Portugal. In the years of economic expansion after World War II, when there was an acute labor shortage, immigration reached a particularly high level. More recently the immigrant stream came from North Africa, notably Algeria (an integral part of France until 1962) and the former protectorates of Morocco and Tunisia. Besides the Maghreb, people from French or former French territories in Central Africa, Asia, and the Americas provided an additional source of immigrants.

As the numbers of new immigrants—who were neither European nor Christian—grew, so did incidents of discrimination in housing and employment. Opposition to continued immigration from Africa in the late twentieth century increased and France's reputation as an immigrant-friendly country dropped. Initially, immigrants from Africa had been welcomed; they worked in undesirable, low-skilled occupations, lived in sub-standard housing out of sight of French neighborhoods. North African immigrants in particular were for the most part single males who had left their wives or families behind. As long as immigrants continued to work in jobs that Frenchmen were reluctant to accept, their presence did not pose a problem. Even the eventual re-unification of families went largely unnoticed. However, with the beginning of an economic downturn in 1974, French workers began to reclaim some of the jobs held by immigrants and the government started to restrict immigration. As the second generation moved through the French public school and university system and entered the job market, the presence of immigrants and their descendants within the hexagon became a fact of life—albeit a controversial one.

THE BEURS

Once they arrive in a host country, immigrants are often lumped together despite their very disparate origins. As far as mainstream France is concerned, a woman of Moroccan origin is a beur, or rather a beurette. The term "beur" was coined by inverting the syllables of the word *Arabe* which often carries a pejorative connotation in French. This expression originates in a word play called *verlan*[2] and is a form of French slang composed by inverting syllables. To take the sting out of being called "Arabs," the term *beur* was created by children of immigrants. This term is also used in Morocco where the second generation of Moroccan emigrants is now referred to as "the *Beurs* of the Mohammed VI generation."[3]

For our discussion of Moroccan women and women of Moroccan origin in France, it is essential to have a cursory understanding of differing North African national contexts. By far the largest flow of Maghrebi immigrants in France stems from Algeria. This country has a uniquely complicated history with France because it was never a French colony but was a region of France. Since their first arrival in Algeria in 1830, millions of French and other Europeans moved across the Mediterranean and settled there. A particularly bloody war for independence raged from 1954 until 1962 because the French did not want to let go of their territory on the other side of the Mediterranean. President Charles de Gaulle famously affirmed in 1958, "I have understood you . . ." reassuring French settlers in Algeria in the midst of the war that Algeria would forever continue to be part of France. It is one of the ironies of history that this exclamation was made by a man who arrived at the presidency (1958–1969) largely because he had led French resistance against German occupation during World War II. Eventually, France had to release Algeria into independence and a virtual exodus from Algeria to France took place. White settlers, the so-called *pieds-noirs* (literally "black feet"), were the first to be repatriated from Algeria to France. They were followed by the so-called *harkis*—native Algerians, that is, Arabs and Berbers—who had fought on the French side during this war. They fled to France because they were now considered traitors by the newly formed Algerian nation. In addition to these two groups came the flow of immigrants who left their impoverished country to find work in France. Consequently, there is a particularly complicated and complex dynamic concerning Algerian immigrants in France. Because Algerians arrived decades before Moroccans, there is by now not only a second but also a third generation in France, still collectively called *beurs*. As with African Americans, it is the historic problematic of mass movement of peoples across the waters that keeps these population groups distinct from the mainstream.

NO JOURNEY HOME

Moroccan immigration to France and Moroccan-French relations are by comparison less complicated. Morocco was a French protectorate from 1912–1956. For most of its post-independence history, Morocco and France have maintained amicable relations and people have been able to move back and forth with relative ease. This is particularly evident in the annual summer migration. Each July and August tens of thousands of cars packed to the gills, weighed down by gifts ranging from everyday household items to refrigerators, sofa sets, beds and other furniture strapped to the roof, clog southbound highways. At the wheel is the Moroccan head of the family while wife and children sit squeezed between packages. The journey is completed chiefly in two ways: either by road through France and Spain and then from Algeciras onto the short ferry ride across the Straits of Gibraltar to Tangiers; or by road to the southern French port of Sète and then onward via a twenty hour boat ride to Tangiers. This annual summer migration occurs with predicable regularity. The ports of Algeciras, Sète and Tangiers burst with activity and overworked customs guards on the Moroccan side reward themselves with bribes extracted from Moroccan expatriates. Most of the women I met in France could recount sometimes funny, sometimes horrifying tales of these annual expeditions to their parents' country of origin. In Morocco too, the arrival of the summer returnees has become an anticipated—or dreaded—annual event.

Despite the strong connection parents felt to the country of their birth and the effort they made to chauffeur their children across the continents, none of the women I met had ever seriously thought about the possibility of permanently moving to Morocco. A few had thought about relocating there temporarily if their job situation in France did not improve, but few had seriously engaged in a job search in Morocco. Like most people in the world, they preferred to remain in the country where they had spent all their lives. Occasionally I had a slip of the tongue and asked: "Have you ever thought about the possibility of permanently returning to Morocco?" which was immediately met with a correction such as: "I would not be returning, I am French," "I was born in France and lived all my life here, so if I go to Morocco I am not returning, I am visiting," or "Even though I still have a Moroccan passport, I have never lived in Morocco and therefore I wouldn't be returning."

Once I shared these comments with a woman in Morocco, who emphatically stated that I was mistaken in taking their word for fact: "They did not tell you the truth; of course they want to come back to Morocco. They are Moroccans. They just said that because you are a Westerner yourself and so they wanted you to believe that they too consider a Western country their home." This interpretation troubled me and so I asked a colleague in Rabat who had studied and lived abroad in various countries for several years. She offered this explanation: "Our women have to say that. They feel a sense of pride in being Moroccan and don't want to think that people who leave to settle elsewhere cut their ties with their home country." Another Moroccan scholar said: "Every summer, we see Morocco invaded by MREs (Moroccans residing abroad) and their families who are coming back for the summer. It seems there are more cars with French, Belgian, Dutch or German number plates in Morocco during the summer months than those with local number plates. This creates the impression that people working abroad still consider Morocco their home. It makes us feel good to see them coming home." Not everyone was pleased to see their relatives bring carloads of European goods. Said a young Rabati woman: "My brother comes back every year from France, his suitcases and boxes packed with stuff, most of which we can get here. But if something is from Europe and hand-delivered, people believe it is special, of superior quality. I told him to stop bringing us things. It is humiliating. We have what we need here. Last year, he came carrying just his backpack. I was so happy to see him like that but everyone in the family was terribly disappointed. It was actually quite a disaster because my parents felt it was a disgrace that my brother came home empty-handed. This longing for all things Western is schizophrenic because on the other side, people say they are so proud of living here. Proud of living in an Islamic country, yet wanting all the goods that come from the West, that's what I call schizophrenic!"

I did meet a few women in France who had actually come to work in Morocco for a short period of time, only to return to France because they did not feel at home in Morocco. A social worker in Paris had moved to Casablanca to work for a year in a center for abused women, directed by a relative. She said: "The problems I encountered at the center were not much different from what we deal with here, but I could not stand living there. I could not handle the Moroccan mentality. Even though I lived in a large, modern city, the way you are treated as a woman on an everyday basis was unacceptable to me. I left after only a few months. I think my cousin was very disappointed because we had worked well together." I asked what had bothered her the most. "First, I wanted to live by myself. But my relatives in Casablanca insisted I live with them. It was not just a matter of hospitality; they considered it indecent for me to live by myself. Plus, I don't know how many times I was asked when I would get married. I mean, there is no sense of privacy, every relative feels they can pry into your private life. When I am there I am considered Moroccan—100 percent. It does not matter that I actually lived my entire life in France and that I have different values. I could not stand it."

Uncertainty about their professional future in France was the main reason cited for a possible move to Morocco. More than 20 percent of France's eighteen- to twenty-five-year-olds are unemployed—a figure double the national average of 9.6 percent. Among the country's poorest communities, primarily those of immigrant backgrounds, youth unemployment stands at 40 percent. This large number of unemployed was one of the major causes for the riots that swept across France in the fall of 2005. Some women hoped that a French university degree might give them an advantage and make it easier to find a satisfying job in Morocco. However, this was based more on wishful thinking than on a consideration of the actual situation. In Morocco, according to the International Labor Organization, youth unemployment is estimated to be around 37 percent,[4] a figure not much different from that in France. If their careers in France did not take off the way they envisioned, some of my respondents hoped they had another option by looking for a position in Morocco. Professional opportunities—or the lack thereof—weighed heavily on the minds of most women I met. The emphasis on a job as the major reason for relocation became clear when I asked if they would move to North Africa if they were to marry a Moroccan man or if their future husband was to find a position there. These, almost all insisted, were not acceptable incentives for leaving France. For better or worse, they wanted to stay where they felt they belonged. The same was true of women in Morocco who felt equally stuck by the lack of professional opportunities.

All the women I met in France had family in Morocco whom they knew because of their summer visits. Upon becoming adults, these calls had become less frequent. On their own, none had gone to Morocco to visit their relatives. The excursions were part of their childhood and were never considered a journey home, because as I was told repeatedly, "my home is here in France."

There is another way of looking at this preference for staying in France in spite of the difficulties faced by the second generation. Their parents came from small, rural, mostly impoverished places. The rural/urban divide characterizes Moroccan society still today. On their visits to Morocco, they did not stay in the modern urban centers of Rabat or Casablanca but went back to the villages their parents had left decades ago. For women who had grown up in French cities, even the *banlieues*, rural life in a developing world country held little promise.

In fact, their parents had packed up and left these places because they could not make ends meet and did not see a future for themselves and their families in their homeland. One has to appreciate the drive and will-power of people who move from a rural African village to metropolitan France. Most did not speak French very well; they were equipped with little more than a determination to succeed in unfamiliar territory. Husbands left their wives and sometimes children behind for years until they had found steady employment and had saved enough money to move their families across the seas. Thus, from early childhood, these women understood the tremendous effort their parents had made by leaving everything familiar behind and carving out a living in a strange and foreign land. The tenacity of the second generation is, so to speak, in keeping with the family tradition.

EMIGRATION

For Moroccans emigration is a familiar concept. With 10 percent of its population of circa 30 million residing abroad, many families either have relatives abroad or know someone who does. Like their counterparts in France, most of my respondents said they would move overseas to find a better job. In the 1970s, the primary destination for Moroccan emigrants was France; in later decades Moroccans went to settle in Belgium, the Netherlands, Germany and Italy. Given the geographic proximity of North Africa and Europe and historic connections, Europe has traditionally seen the greatest influx of North Africans. I was interested to find out which country women considered their ideal destination. Canada was the country most frequently mentioned. This choice is revealing for a variety of reasons. First, it indicates that Moroccans are no longer singularly focused on France as its external reference point. Second, Canada shares many social, cultural and economic traits with the United States as its immediate neighbor. Third, despite similarities between the two North American countries, Canada has a significant francophone region. Considering the geographical distance between Morocco and Canada and the expense involved in trans-Atlantic travel, it is unlikely that women, who said they would like to move to Canada, would actually ever get there. However, the choice of Canada shows a remarkable skill in negotiating a balance between public Moroccan discourse, which in the wake of the invasion of Iraq and the recurring violence in the Middle East is decidedly anti-American, and personal preferences. With North America as the preferred destination, the old continent seemed to have lost much of its appeal.

None of the women mentioned an Arab or an African country for possible relocation. As fellow African countries face comparable economic hardships as Morocco, it is understandable that no one would consider moving within the continent. However, wealthy states in the Gulf region, the United Arab Emirates and Saudi Arabia are known to recruit professional labor from abroad and therefore it was surprising that women said they preferred countries of the Western world over other Arab or Muslim countries.[5] One woman said she had lived in Saudi Arabia for a year and another had received a job offer from Kuwait but had decided against moving there. In addition to real or perceived professional opportunities, Western Europe and North America also hold the promise of individual freedom. For a country where nearly half the population belongs to "the free people,"[6] this might not be an unusual priority. It also confirms Moroccan sociologist Fatima Mernissi's assertion that Moroccans are really "berberized Arabs" and allegiance with Arabs is not as strong as is often presumed.

Several women mentioned "the possibility of being myself" as a reason for choosing Canada. They said they felt overly bound to abide by traditions and customs in Morocco, even those they did not agree with. "I will tell you the story of my parents," Nadia, a civil servant in Rabat, told me.

> My father and mother are educated but it is stupid social customs that make life here difficult. Take the issue of owning a house. Socially speaking, it makes a big difference if ownership of the house is in the father or the mother's name. The head of the family, that is the father, is expected to own the house. For instance we say this is Mohammed's house, you don't ever hear this is Fatima's house or the house of Mohammed and Fatima. Yet, my father and mother built it together, they shared the expenses but my father is the owner. When I talked about this with my mother she said that my father expected her to trust him. I say, why does trust have to go one way only? And then she said this was also mandated by the religion. Everything is justified by religion here. So when my father died, my brothers inherited the house. They let my mother stay there, but guess who pays her daily expenses? I do. My brothers and I have had so many bitter arguments about this. Even though my mother sees all this, she tells me that when I get married I need to let my husband take the lead. She says I need to think about my image, the image of our family. Otherwise people will say why is he giving her authority over his property, why is she behaving this way?

Why does she want control? Does she not trust her husband? These things make me so mad. If you live here, you cannot escape these customs, that's what makes me think of leaving.

But after a pause, she added pensively, "even though I probably never will. There is a Moroccan proverb: The tar of my country is better than the honey of others."

HOME IS HERE

All women I met in France had visited Morocco but few thought they would ever want to live there. By contrast, regardless of whether they had traveled overseas, most Moroccan women said they could imagine themselves living somewhere else.

By and large educated, professional Moroccan women were more cosmopolitan than the women of Moroccan origin in France. Women in Morocco who had traveled abroad had been to a variety of countries, such as the United States, France, Spain, Norway, Malaysia, and various South American countries, Russia and Great Britain. In Morocco, but not in France, I met women who had been to Saudi Arabia to participate in the *haj*, the pilgrimage to the Muslim holy sites in Mecca and Medina. This wide range of international travel of the Moroccan sample shows that young, educated, professional women are not representative of the female population at large but are part of a small minority. This is again attributable to social class, that is, young, educated professional women in Morocco generally hail from middle- to upper-class families and therefore have opportunities for international travel. Another factor is that academic scholarships offering eligible candidates an opportunity to study abroad are more vigorously pursued by students in Morocco than by their counterparts in France.

Women of Moroccan origin in France generally had less international experience and their travel abroad had been mainly to Morocco. Some had gone on high school field trips to Great Britain or Germany and some had been to different countries as part of their jobs. None had been abroad as an exchange student.

It is more common for emigrants to return with their families to their country of origin than it is for Moroccans to go to abroad to visit their expatriate relatives. Emigrants had left as poor, unskilled workers but managed to amass enough of a fortune to finance an expedition back home—with the mandatory carload of gifts. Their—real or relative—success served as a constant reminder to those left behind, that it pays to take a risk and to uproot and that the grass is indeed greener on the other side. Certainly, some purchased more gifts than they could actually afford. Women told me that their parents went into debt just so they could buy gifts for their relatives in Morocco. Their children's insistence on remaining in France can be interpreted as part of that success story, namely that they had so effectively incorporated the values and lifestyle of their host country that they would rather battle discrimination and social exclusion than return to Morocco. Despite the fact that in Morocco, they were neither a religious nor an ethnic minority, my respondents clearly felt no longer part of their parent's home country.

CHANGE IS SLOW

For women who had lived abroad, mostly to pursue university studies, changes in their home country came too slowly. They said they had felt more at ease in a foreign society where they could express themselves freely and evaluate their customs and beliefs by comparing them to others. Unquestionably, studying abroad is a life-changing experience regardless of country of origin. Freed from parental control and norms imposed by one's own society, exchange students feel surrounded by an atmosphere of personal liberation and freedom. These students live in an almost norm-free zone because they are far from home, yet they are not bound into the cultural and social fabric of their host country. They experience a sense of freedom that could not be sustained if they were to become fully integrated into the host society. Empowered by this experience of personal freedom, Moroccan women were impatient with the pace of change upon their return home.

Occasionally, I heard a much more personal reason for wanting to move abroad: better marriage prospects. "Western men," one woman said bluntly, "don't have the same prejudice against marrying an older woman." By "older woman" she meant someone her own age. She was twenty-seven.

PROGRESSIVE CONSERVATIVES

When I asked women to describe themselves, it became apparent that conventional categories such as conservative, progressive, or feminist were infused with a variety of meanings. Women in both places said they considered it possible to be a practicing Muslim and progressive at the same time. Some described themselves as conservative and progressive simultaneously. Some with strong religious inclination said they saw a direct link between religious conviction and supporting social change. To be religious was not understood as being synonymous with conservative, that is, maintaining the status quo. Some used the term "Islamic feminist" to describe themselves, saying Western, secular models of feminism did not apply to them. This type of self-description illustrates the fact that women in different cultural contexts feel free to mix and match otherwise incompatible categories to construct approaches that meet their particular needs. Though Western feminism has moved through several stages over the past thirty years, it still is mostly associated with a secular inclination. Muslim feminists, Islamic feminists and even Islamist feminists[7] are becoming better-known self-descriptions that on one side reflect the heterogeneity among Muslim women and on the other that Western feminism is still often perceived as a neo-colonial project that presupposes the supremacy of Western values over those of other, less industrially developed, regions in the world. Though my respondents showed little interest in theoretical categorizations, their actual stances reflected the variety of approaches women employ to improve their lives and contribute to greater equality between the sexes. Some close to Islamist groups insisted that they were the "truly progressive" ones based on their understanding that modern societies, Western or Islamic, were morally bankrupt and therefore required radical change. Nadia Yassine, spokesperson of the Islamist movement Justice and Benevolence introduced the term "militant Neo-Sufi" to describe herself. Other respondents in France and Morocco were more cautious saying that power structures in their respective country betrayed their own mottos—in France that of the French Republic: *liberté, égalité fraternité* (liberty, equality, fraternity), and in Morocco the ideal of the *umma*, the community of believers as envisioned by the Prophet—and therefore they were unsure how best to describe themselves vis-à-vis these national ideals.

Certainly globalization contributes to the blurring of erstwhile hard and fast categories of self-description. Globalization offers easy access to French media in Morocco and Moroccan media in France; via the Internet people throughout the world can connect with the same virtual communities, transcending geographical boundaries. Women are exposed to similar trends in music, fashion, public discourses on the role of women, news and religion. The anonymity of cyberspace allows them to discuss private and intimate matters with co-religionists around the globe. Multi-lingual websites geared toward Muslim audiences, women in particular, are enjoying increasing popularity worldwide.[8] Though this book does not set out to study directly the impact of globalization, it is important to recognize that shifts in attitudes do not occur in a vacuum but are part of larger changes occurring in different parts of the world. Middle Eastern and North African countries currently experience the impact of the West with particular vehemence. Inasmuch as the perceptions of Muslims in France are influenced by exposure and immersion in secular, French society with a strong Catholic heritage, the presence of millions of Muslims[9] within the hexagon will in time leave its mark on mainstream French society.

Despite the very different social and cultural environments in France and Morocco, women in Morocco and women of Moroccan origin in France have important attitudinal traits in common. Certainly one never does justice to the uniqueness of each individual when generalizing; therefore these similarities are based on certain, limited factors. This said, we can observe that the differences between women living in a North African, Muslim country such as Morocco and those living in a European, secular, Western country such as France are often exaggerated. In the age of globalization, forces that touch the lives of women increasingly level the playing field and throw up comparable challenges regardless of country of residence. This also means that Muslim women tackle problems wherever they face them. They deal with the tar of their own country rather than seeking the honey offered elsewhere.

NOTES

1. Les Français et leurs croyances (The French and their Beliefs), 2003 csa-tmo survey. See: http://a1692.g.akamai.net/f/1692/2042/1h/medias.lemonde.fr/medias/pdf_obj/sondage030416.pdf.

2. The term *verlan* itself is the result of word play, originating in the word *l'envers,* meaning the other way around. Other common *verlan* words are *meuf* for femme (woman) or *keuf* for *flic* (policeman).

3. See Ahmed Ghayet: "Les Beurs Génération Mohammed VI." Mohammed VI is King of Morocco since 1999.

4. See: http://www.ilo.org/public/english/region/arpro/beirut/employment/youth employ/background.htm, last accessed August 2006.

5. Fatima Badry describes Moroccan women working in the UAE in a book chapter edited by Susan Ossman, *Places We Share: Migration, Subjecitivity, and Global Mobility.* Lanham, MD: Lexington Books, 2007.

6. The literal translation of Imazighen, Berbers, is "free people."

7. For treatment of feminisms in the Muslim world, see Leila Abu Lughod (ed.), *Remaking Women—Feminism and Modernity in the Middle East.* Princeton, NJ: Princeton University Press, 1998; and Margot Badran, "Understanding Islam, Islamism and Islamic Feminism," *Journal of Women's History,* vol. 13, no. 1, p. 47–52, 2001.

8. These websites are discussed in chapter 3.

9. The Muslim population in France is estimated at close to 10 percent of a total population of 61 million.

3

To God Belong the East and the West[1]

CONCEPTIONS OF ISLAM

The following chapter primarily addresses three issues: contemporary scholarly research on women in Islam, Islam in France and my respondents' conceptions of Islam. In my conversations with women in Morocco and France, the majority described themselves as "Muslim." I had asked if they saw themselves primarily as French, (or Moroccan), as women, as children of immigrants, as professionals or as something else altogether without suggesting a religious category. And yet women in both countries spontaneously gave similar responses: "I am a Muslim." In France, several added, "and I am French." Even women who said they were not particularly religious, or did not practice Islam in accordance with the five pillars,[2] believed that Islam was a major aspect of who they were. Individual identity can never be comprehensively or exactly enveloped in general categories. The precise meaning of being a Muslim no doubt varies from person to person—as it would among circa 1.2 billion Muslims throughout the world. No one would expect a uniform understanding among Christians, yet too often Islam is understood—or presented—as a religion that requires a homogeneous interpretation of its adherents. Nevertheless, it is remarkable that the majority of women I encountered north and south of the western Mediterranean chose the same broad category to describe themselves despite their different circumstances.

In France, women of Moroccan origin are a religious and ethnic minority, whereas Muslims in Morocco are not. In this chapter, we will explore the conceptions of Islam of two groups of women and how they are incorporating religious and cultural values based on Islam into their lives. First, we will provide a broader context by taking a brief look at what contemporary scholars of Islam have said about women.

WOMEN IN ISLAM

Women have always been the best friends of religion, but religion has generally not been a friend of women.[3]

This assessment of Indologist Mortiz Winternitz certainly applies to most major world religions and Islam is no exception. Women profess a religious identity even if this religion has not served them well from a historic or social point of view. In this day and age, discourse on the role of women according to Islam is not only of importance in Muslim societies. In *Believing Women*, Asma Barlas writes that Islamic thought and practice affects communities beyond the Muslim world. "Although the practice of Islam is of concern only to Muslims, Muslim practices are of concern to the community of nations in which we live" (Barlas, 2002: xii). Women of Moroccan origin in France come from families who have brought their culture, religion and traditions with them when they crossed the Mediterranean. Because Muslims now constitute the largest minority in France, questions of the role of women in Islam are indeed of concern beyond the Muslim world.

The Qur'an frequently refers to the role of women. Hence, a rich body of literature has accumulated throughout the centuries. In recent decades, a re-reading of sacred texts, that is, the Qur'an,[4] the *hadith* (sayings attributed to the prophet) and the *sunnah* (part of the *hadith,* pertaining to customs of the prophet), has resulted in Islamic feminist, post-colonial and other non-traditional readings of the Qur'an. As women have become central to the discourse on development and social change, religious and secular scholars have increasingly turned their attention to the role of women in Muslim societies and Muslim women in secular societies with a Christian heritage.

Ever since the inception of the religion of Islam in Saudi Arabia in the seventh century, the role of women in predominantly Islamic societies has been discussed. Religious scholars have interpreted the position of women as prescribed in the Qur'an and various *hadith* collections. Historians like Ira M. Lapidus, who have written extensively on the history of Islamic societies, have argued that with the spread of Islam throughout the Middle East and North Africa, the religion of Islam has adapted to and incorporated local traditions and customs: "An 'Islamic' state was also an expression of non-Islamic territorial and cultural identity" (Lapidus, 2002: 188). This view is supported by the majority of scholars who point to the fact that there is no central authority in Islam pronouncing religious dogma. To the contrary, Islamic scholars have always insisted on the importance of *fiqh*, jurisprudence based on Islam, which differs from one geographical region to another, and the privilege of *ijtihad* (judgment) or "rightful interpretation." Hence, there always has been room for interpretation. While scholars generally agree that Islam has improved the situation of women in pre-Islamic Arabic societies, regional and local customs remained a crucial factor in defining the role of women. "Islam was not necessarily the decisive element in the definition of gender in the region, but rather this religion encapsulated, reworked, and finally helped diffuse many older cultural practices of the region, including those defining of gender" (Nashat and Tucker, 1999: 2).

Applying a Western concept to the status of women, Leila Ahmed argues that women in the Muslim world are what the West calls a "minority." She explains this as follows: "In establishment Islamic thought, women, like minorities, are defined as different from and, in their legal rights, lesser than Muslim men. Unlike non-Muslim men, who might join the master-class by converting, women's differentness and inferiority within the system are immutable" (Ahmed, 1992: 7). In recent years, scholars of Islam have advocated a new, enlightened reading of the Qur'an which not only supports equality of women but also insists on the compatibility of Western and Islamic values (Arkoun, 1994 and 2002). In his seminal work *Rethinking Islam*, Mohammed Arkoun, an Algerian-born philosopher and scholar of Islam residing in France, takes issue with the way Islam is customarily studied in the West. "Islam is always considered apart from other religions and from European culture and thought. It is often excluded from departments of religion and taught instead as part of Oriental studies" (Arkoun, 1994: 8). This certainly has changed within the past decade but at the time of Arkoun's writing less than twenty years ago this was the case at least in France. Hence, despite the presence of millions of Muslims within its borders, Islam has not been treated as a part of the European religious and cultural fabric. Arkoun challenges an Orientalist approach that insists on an inherent difference between the West and the East. This vision is based on an ideological bias ostensibly suited to the concept of Orient as critiqued by Edward Said. Arkoun rejects this image of the "Orient," expressed as an entire system of thought and scholarship. Nevertheless, sweeping generalizations and misconceptions cloud understanding on both sides according to Arkoun (1994):

It is true that the sort of Islamic discourse common to fundamentalist movements, especially those engaged in the most decisive political battles, proposes the powerful image of a single, eternal Islam, the ideal model for historic action to liberate the world from western, imperialist, materialist model. . . . The field of perception is open to the confrontation of two imaginaries overheated by accumulated confusions about each other. (7)

Because this study offers a comparison between women in Morocco and women of Moroccan origin in France, Arkoun's analysis of Islam's historical influence on Western Europe is relevant. He emphasizes that Islam has for centuries been part of European history. Therefore Islam has had—albeit largely unacknowledged—an influence on European culture in general and the Mediterranean region in particular of which both Morocco and France are a part (ibid.):

> Another aggravating factor in the old quarrel between Islam and the West is that Islam, as a force in the historical rise of societies, took control of the Mediterranean area from the seventh to the twelfth centuries and again, with the direction of the Ottoman Turks, from the sixteenth to the eighteenth centuries. The cultures of the Mediterranean region share a single historical destiny that the scientific study of history, independent of the ideologies that divide the northern and southern or the eastern and western coasts of the Mediterranean, is far from confronting. The Mediterranean region I refer to is more cultural than geographic and strategic, it encompasses all those cultures that have been influenced historically by Iranian religions and the great cultures of the Near East, including the Mesopotamian, the Chaldean, the Syriac, the Aramaic, the Hebraic, and the Arabic—all before the intervention of Greece, Rome, Byzantium, and "Islam." (8)

Arkoun challenges the notion that the Christian West and the Islamic East are inherent opposites with few, if any, social and cultural commonalities. To him the cultures that developed along the Mediterranean coastline were shaped up until modern times by the same historical forces. This scholar also dispels the view that Islam is a static, backward looking religion.

Unlike most of Christianity, which, until the Protestant Reformation in the sixteenth century, was guided by the authority and dogma of the Catholic Church, Islam never had any comparable hierarchical structure. In his more recent *The Unthought in Contemporary Islamic Thought*, Arkoun emphasizes that there is in fact no single, common tradition in Islam: "Tradition is informed and conditioned by changing backgrounds, teaching, guiding and conditioning these backgrounds in return. This interaction is translated into self-entitlement of each Muslim community to incarnate and monopolize the authentic expression of the 'orthodox' tradition" (Arkoun, 2002: 251). Therefore, it is neither uncommon nor problematic to think of new ways of interpreting the Qur'an according to changing social, cultural and historic circumstances. This was also the view of most of my respondents in Morocco and France.

For decades, Moroccan sociologist Fatima Mernissi has been at the forefront of encouraging discourse about Islam and rethinking the role of women not only in her own country. She in fact credits discourse about religion as a major factor in the initial development of Islam. Mernissi explores the earliest phases of the religion as a period during which the new faith was perceived as "a religion of reasoning" (Mernissi, 1991: 35). She demands that this quality of reasoning should form the basis of modern understandings of the faith particularly with regard to the role of women (ibid.: 195).

Like other scholars exploring the theme of women in Islam, Mernissi traces the origins of assigning women an inferior role to some misogynist sayings in the *hadith*, such as the often cited: "Those who entrust their affairs to a woman will never know prosperity" (vol. 4, p. 226, Bukhari *hadith*).[5] She questions the veracity of these sayings because they contradict what the Qur'an says about women.

Mernissi studied the life of revered figures in Islamic history such as Abu Bakra, to whom the remark quoted above is ascribed. A companion to the prophet, Abu Huraya is "aligning women with dogs and asses and labeling her a disturbance . . . saying there is a fundamental contradiction between her essence and the divine" (ibid.: 69). Mernissi provocatively asserts that portions of the *hadith* are based more on hearsay or selective memory than on actual fact. She describes parts of Islamic history as "a tradition of misogyny" which is based on questionable pronouncements and unsubstantiated sayings attributed to the prophet rather than on the Qur'an. Mernissi argues that misogynistic *hadith* verses have become a persuasive moral force through institutional development. Because women remained uneducated for centuries after Islam was introduced, a certain image of women could be put in place that was quite different from the revelations received by the prophet, "the *imams* were able to take advantage of our [women's] ignorance of the sacred texts" (ibid.: 115). Mernissi insists that focus should be on the Qur'an because the sacred text emphasizes equality of believers, regardless of their gender.

Mernissi further probes the question why official Islamic historical discourse is purged of female heroes like A'isha, Sukayna and Umm Salama. "The answer without doubt is to be found in the time-mirror wherein the Muslim looks at himself to foresee his future. The image of 'his' woman will change when he feels the pressing need to root his future in a liberating memory. Perhaps the woman should help him do this through daily pressure for equality, thereby bringing him into a fabulous present" (ibid.: 195).

Amina Wadud also explores the role of women based on the scriptures in her book *Qur'an and Women* (1999). She too differentiates between the scriptures and the historical practice of Islam. "If the definite basis of what Islam means is determined by what Muslims do, then women and men are not equal" (Wadud,

1999: ix). Though the scripture clearly assigns a different role to women than to men, Wadud argues that these are based on functional considerations:

> Femininity and masculinity are not created characteristics imprinted into the very primordial nature of female and male persons, neither are they concepts the Qur'an discusses or alludes to. They are defined characteristics applied to female and male persons respectively on the basis of culturally determined factors of how each gender should function. (22)

According to this scholar, Qur'anic considerations of woman center on her relationship to the group, that is, as a member of a social system. When the Qur'an does refer to humans as individuals, it does not differentiate between male and female: that is, whatever the Qur'an says about the relationship between God and the individual is not conveyed in gender terms. "With reference to the individual, the Qur'an most often uses the term *nafs* (self/soul), a non gendered-term" (ibid.: 34).

Like Mernissi, Wadud points out that Qur'anic interpretation was up until recently a male prerogative and thus influenced by a specific cultural environment. "No interpretation is definite, limitation exists when specifically addressing the social situation in Arabia at the time of the revelation. No community will ever be exactly like another, therefore no community can be a duplicate of that original community. That most *tafasir* (exegetical works) are done by males indicates something about women and interpretation" (ibid.: 95). Interpretation occurs within a specific historic, geographic and cultural context and even divinely inspired texts fall prey to these earthly limitations. Therefore, the Qur'an has been interpreted to support a certain social system that benefited those doing the interpretation, in this case, men. "Sometimes the open-endedness of the Qur'an, which does not give explicit social functions or attribute explicit values to those functions, has been interpreted to mean that the Qur'an supports existing systems of evaluation—whether at the time of the prophet or in subsequent Muslim communities" (ibid.: 96).

The Qur'an, according to Wadud, is very much concerned with social justice in the sense that its message is intended to right the wrongs of this world. By this definition, it cannot be interpreted as supporting inequality. Wadud (1999) writes:

> With regard to social justice, it becomes necessary to challenge patriarchy—not for matriarchy, but for an efficient co-operative and egalitarian system which allows and encourages the maximum participation of each member of society. This system would truly respect each gender in its contributions, and all tasks that are contributed. This would allow for the growth and expansion of the individual and consequently society at large. (103)

The Qur'an, like the Bible, is not a "how to manual" that offers step-by-step guidance for daily affairs but is concerned with human being's eternal life and the meaning of earthly existence. The scriptures are concerned with humans' responsibility toward God and their responsibility toward each other. It is this absence of specific instructions, however, that allows for diverging interpretations, argues Wadud.

> The absence of explicit Qur'anic prescriptions for dividing labor allows and supports a myriad of variations. . . . Thus the Qur'anic guidance can be logically and equitably applied to the lives of humankind in whatever era, if the Qur'anic interpretation continues to be rendered by each generation in a manner which reflects its whole intent. (104)

Asma Barlas, a scholar of Pakistani origin, explains that change within Muslim societies can in the long run only be successful if it will be perceived by the population as being based on the Qur'an: "it is safe to say that no meaningful change can occur in these societies that does not derive its legitimacy from the Qur'an's teachings, a lesson secular Muslims everywhere are having to learn at their own detriment" (2002: 3). Barlas does not view herself as a feminist in the Western sense and insists that her reading of the Qur'an is based on conventional theological exegesis. She argues that no feminist reading of the Qur'an is required to come to the conclusion that the sacred text does not favor men over women. Instead, Barlas guides the reader through the Holy Book by highlighting the *suras* (chapters in the Qur'an) which emphasize equality between men and women:

> The most radical of the Qur'an's teachings, which establishes the ontic nature of sexual equality in Islam and which undermines the very notions of radical difference and hierarchy, has to do with the origin and nature of human creation . . . as both men and women originated in a single Self, have been endowed with the same natures, and make up two halves of a single pair. (133)

However, there is a *sura* in the Qur'an that states: "But I do not wish to absolve myself because the soul is prone to evil, unless my Lord have mercy" (12:53). As the term soul in the Arabic language is feminine, this sentence has often been used to support the notion of an inherently inferiority of women.

WOMEN AS RELIGIOUS LEADERS

The above mentioned Wadud is one of the foremost contemporary scholars of Islam in the United States. Her writings and actions are frequently referred to in Morocco, especially when discussing the role of women in religious affairs. In 2005, the African American scholar caused international controversy when she broke with century-old tradition and led the Friday prayers at a mosque in New York City. One year later, Morocco became the first Muslim country in modern times to appoint female prayer leaders, called *murshidat*[6] (guide). Samira Marzouk, one of the young *murchidats,* echoed the official royal position in an interview with the Public Broadcasting Service (PBS)[7]: "It is very normal for a Muslim country to reform its structure." With professional barriers thus broken down by royal decree, women in Morocco enjoy support from the highest authority to pursue their goals. As there is no separation of the secular and religious sphere in Morocco, these women, like imams, are state employees.

Lesser known is the fact that the Moroccan pioneer group of *murshidats* actually followed in the footsteps of an often forgotten tradition of female religious leaders in this country, so-called "circle-leaders" (*muqqamadat*) which according to Trimingham were common up until 1942 (Trimingham, 1971: 114). Especially in Amazigh communities, female religious leaders have a long tradition. Rausch (2006) writes:

> Throughout Africa, local Muslim scholars, in particular those affiliated with Sufi orders, endeavored to proliferate Islamic knowledge at the scholarly as well as popular level. In Morocco, like elsewhere in Africa, women were recognized as indispensable in the transmission of Islamic knowledge to other women. (173)

Rausch describes how women in the oral Amazigh tradition have been instrumental in shaping conceptions of Islam. These women relied on memorization and didactic poetry for offering religious instruction. Rausch emphasizes that these religious practices in Morocco are to be understood within an African and not an Arab/Middle Eastern context.

SUFISM

Scholars who do not specifically focus on gender issues also emphasize that the message of the Qur'an is one of equality of all humans vis-à-vis Allah. Annemarie Schimmel, a German scholar who taught at Harvard University, wrote extensively on Islamic mysticism, Sufism, and insists that the Qur'an addresses "man" as in "human being" and not with reference to gender. Schimmel spent considerable time in Morocco, where Sufism is particularly widespread. Because the Qur'an is concerned with lifting humans to a higher level of being, early Islam improved women's position in Arabia compared to pre-Islamic times. This, according to Schimmel, was based on the fact that "the 'man of God' was always mentioned as the idea of the true believer, but one should beware of taking 'man' here as gender related" (Schimmel, 1994: 197). Several of the women I met in France had read some of Schimmel's work[8] in an effort to gain a deeper understanding of their religion. Like other scholars cited above, Schimmel separates the text of the Qur'an from the practice of Islam: "It would be amazing if Islam were a religion that is against women as much as later developments give that impression" (198). She goes on to describe various female saints in Islamic history, which come from all parts of the Muslim world and are neither limited to one geographic region nor to a particular time period. In Morocco for example, honoring or paying respect to a saint is a widely accepted practice and some of those saints, like Lalla Mimuna, are women. This practice is frequently referred to as saint worship; however this term is questionable because in Islam, no intercession between God and the individual believer is necessary. Schimmel also sheds light on the little known fact of Islamic convents for women during the Middle Ages, especially in Egypt and Iraq. Women could seek refuge in these institutions after a divorce or find solace between marriages. These convents were led by a *shaykha*, a female sheikh, who also preached and led the women in prayer (199). Hence, there are historic precedents for having female religious leaders in Islam. Like their much earlier counterparts in the Middle Ages, female religious leaders in North Africa were often adherents of Sufism. Schimmel attributes the attraction of Sufism among women in Morocco to the fact that "mysticism was the only religious sphere where women could find a place" (ibid.: 18). Sufism is less concerned with adherence to dogma and instead emphasizes personal experience with the divine and the importance of love between God and man and between human beings. Given the historical preponderance of Sufism in Morocco, it is understandable why women in or of that region today feel less bound by orthodox doctrine and instead feel free to develop a religious understanding that suits their particular circumstances.

Schimmel also weighs in on the issue of the *hijab*, the Muslim headscarf. She argues that there is no theological justification for requiring women to wear the headscarf or the veil. She notes that covering a woman's head was initially a sign of class distinction, whereby noble women covered themselves in public whereas servants and lower-class women entered the public sphere with little more than the necessary clothing: "It was a distinction, not an onerous duty" (200). However, Schimmel (1994) observes:

> The insistence upon women's deficiencies (a term very much used also in the Christian Middle Ages) reveals the ascetic fear of women's power, and the ascetics in early Islam saw in women something horrible but—alas!—necessary. The *sunna's* insistence on married life left them between their wish to sever completely the bonds with this world (a world that appeared to them, as it did to

their Christian contemporaries, as a ghastly old hag, always ready to seduce and then to devour her unfortunate lovers) and a normal and normative family life. Marriage, to be sure, is no sacrament but a simple contract in which the bride is represented by her *wali,* "representative." (200)

This emphasis of the contractual nature of marriage is also at the heart of the concept of an Islamic Personal Status Code, an issue addressed in the following chapter.

Schimmel asserts nevertheless that a theological basis for assigning women a lower status than men can be derived from the Qu'ran: "One reason for the deteriorating image (and as a corollary, position) of women was the old ascetic equation between women and the *nafs,* the lower soul, *nafs* being a feminine term. As the *nafs* incites one to evil (sura 12:53), woman, too tries to divert man from his lofty goals—or so it was thought" (ibid.: 201). On this point Wadud (see above) disagrees with Schimmel because Wadud insists that *nafs* refers to "self" or "person" and does not carry a gendered meaning. The concept of *nafs* (self/soul), or *ruh* (soul), has occupied religious scholars throughout the centuries. In Islam, the soul denotes the inward dimension of the human being and possesses a variety of qualities but is not understood as a dual mind/body dichotomy. Rather, according to Murata (1992):

> The Qur'an makes no suggestion that the *nafs* of human beings and God are somehow intimately connected, as it does with the *ruh* and human beings and God. . . . Sufis usually looked at the spirit as intimately connected to God, while the soul or self represents the human being in an aspect of greater separation. (237)

German scholar Dorothee Sölle, a Christian theologian, explores the similarities of mystic traditions in various religions. She concludes that mysticism transcends dogma and therefore opens the way to a universalistic understanding of the human condition. Religion in the third millennium, she argues, "will either be mystical, or it will be dead."

Sölle recounts the story of one of the most well-known female Sufi saints, Rabi'a of Basra (circa 713–801). Rabi'a once walked the streets of her hometown in Iraq, holding a torch in one hand and a pail of water in the other. Asked why, she replied: "I want to put fire to paradise and pour water over hell so that these two veils disappear and it becomes plain who venerates God for love and not for fear of hell or hope for paradise" (Sölle, 2001: 35). In recent times, Rabi'a has become increasingly popular among young, educated Muslim women because of her image of fearlessness and her example of a woman whose faith transcended conventional dogma. Several of my respondents in Morocco and France referred to Rabi'a of Basra as a historical figure they admired.

This brief theoretical overview shows some points of discussion of experts who explore women in Islam. We shall now turn to current discussions of Islam in France.

ISLAM IN FRANCE

While Sufism is a venerated tradition in Morocco, several women in France said that there, Sufism sometimes was used in a derogatory sense and therefore they hesitated to use that term. One said that Sufism in the Western world is understood as "some new age feel-good mishmash of beliefs that lacks any kind of spiritual rigor." In France, access to Islamic religious discourse and literature is limited. Young Muslims, who want to explore their religious heritage beyond what has been transmitted to them by their parents, have to invest substantial effort. Not only is there no societal encouragement for religious pursuits, but also religious instruction in the homes of second-generation North Africans in France is often limited to the folkloristic and consists of little more than repeated recitation of prohibitions: no alcohol, no pork, no premarital sex (for girls, at any rate), no marriage to someone outside their community, etc. As the parents of most of these young Muslims were either illiterate or had little formal schooling, their own understanding of Islam was rather narrow. The young generation, educated in the French public schools, could in principle read the scriptures for themselves and seek out information on their own. However, because of their limited knowledge of the Arabic language, their access is further reduced to French texts. Despite these restrictions, a homegrown, French-educated Muslim population emerged within the hexagon which came about largely unnoticed by the majority culture.

Widespread ignorance and disinterest concerning Islam, changes in the conceptions of Islam among second-generation Muslims in France, have occurred largely unnoticed. In his early research on Muslims in France, Gilles Kepel observed that the French state failed to recognize Islam as a force of growing influence. It was not until the mid 1970s that France began to realize that Islam had become a fact of life (Kepel, 1984: 139). This recognition coincided with having to come to terms with the permanent presence of North African immigrants within its borders. As the title of Kepel's book suggests, *Les banlieues de l'Islam* (The ghettos of Islam), Islam up until then was perceived as a culture and religion of the *banlieues,* that is, it existed outside of the mainstream much as in the United States the Nation of Islam is often perceived as a fringe religion, whose adherents reside primarily in the poorer inner cities, the social if not geographical equivalent of the French *banlieues*. Kepel describes the phenomenon of "re-Islamization" which occurred chiefly as a result of social circumstances in the often-violent suburbs, which are marked by unemployment and deprivation. In his analysis of young Maghrebis who have "discovered" Islam, he finds "a mutation of values in the world of these young Maghrebis in France which came to the fore after the Beur movement had been stymied" (386).[9]

Unlike in Morocco, young French Muslims experience Islam not as an omnipresent reality but as the faith of a disenfranchised minority. It forms the basis of a culture that the second and third generation has to rediscover for itself. By attending religious gatherings of young Muslims all over France, Kepel (1984) observed that the questions asked demonstrate that these young people are thoroughly inculcated with French modes of thinking. The questions they posed to imams came from Western perspectives. Even though these young people were Muslims, they were surrounded by a culture that made no reference to Islam. Islam for them, writes Kepel, "is an orientation toward the future, it is a sort of utopia" (372).

Absent in Kepel's early writing on French Muslims is an acknowledgement of the different circumstances for men and women. However, in his most recent work *The War for Muslim Minds—Islam and the West* (2004), Kepel does approach the issue of young Muslim women: "As Islamist movements develop, the issue of gender equality becomes increasingly a field of contention in the battle for Europe" (282). Kepel explores the way in which modern technologies such as the Internet have allowed young people, women in particular, to seek answers to their religious questions from sources which previously were beyond their reach. Because of their inability to read Arabic, the majority of French Muslims of immigrant origins have no direct access to most of Islamic literature. However, a new discourse on Islam is emerging among Muslims in the West. One of the most prominent proponents of this new discourse on occidental Islam is Swiss-born philosopher Tariq Ramadan, grandson of Hassan al Banna, founder of the Muslim Brotherhood in Egypt, who is advocating dialogue among the various Muslim communities and proposes a new "occidental Islam" (2004). Ramadan's propositions are widely disseminated via Islamic websites and are discussed in chat rooms.

In fact, new information technologies cross linguistic boundaries as websites and chat rooms are often bi- or even trilingual. My respondents in France told me that they used chat rooms and Internet forums to discuss issues such as birth control and abortion, the veil and pre-marital sex. They said the anonymity guaranteed in cyberspace allowed them a freedom to express themselves in ways they did not feel comfortable in person-to-person discussions. Women in France said that Internet sites were one of their main sources of information about their religion.[10] The fact that they turn to these sites indicates that women often seek answers to life's questions within the context of their ancestral culture and religion. The increasing importance of cyber-space for young Muslims has also been addressed by Olivier Roy, who dedicates an entire chapter in his *Globalized Islam* (2004) to the virtual, online community of Muslims worldwide.

Moving in and out of the virtual and material world and between different cultural spheres is second nature for young Muslims in France. They are inculcated with Western values and for them Europe and what it represents is part of their everyday life experience. At the same time they are surrounded in their homes by Moroccan culture and the religion of Islam. Such cultural flexibility contrasts with the daily experience of the majority of Western Europeans, for whom Islam is a foreign concept. Because of their ability to traverse cultural divides, Bruno Etienne refers to the second generation as "the youth without borders" (Etienne, 1989: 260). This new generation of French Muslims creates a culture and religion based on diverse influences. Etienne argues that French Muslims—rather than representing an alien element in France—are in keeping with the finest of French traditions of reaching beyond borders for inspiration. Etienne proposes that these young people are no less "typically" French than so-called *Français de souche*: "the majority of French are not 'typical': therefore not being typical is the essence of the average French person. After all, we live in a country where the queens have always been foreigners" (264). This political scientist points to another common misperception, namely that "North African immigrant" is often understood as synonymous for "Muslim." Yet, the majority of today's Jews in France are also of North African decent (265). It is, for example, not uncommon to find butcheries in certain neighborhoods that advertise selling kosher and halal meat in the same store.

Yaël, a Jewish mother of three high-school age children, told me:

> Muslims and Jews in France have no problems with each other, we are both minorities here. The tension is with the Catholics. Even people who say they don't go to church or are atheist are inculcated with Catholic concepts which makes them so unwelcoming to outsiders. Look at the education system; it is totally elitist and geared toward pushing people down. Only a few can succeed. This is so hypocritical for a Western democratic country and especially one that has as its motto liberty, equality, fraternity.

When her children were younger, Yaël had sent them to Hebrew school, much like some Muslim parents send their children to Qur'anic schools on the weekend. "We need actively to preserve our culture and religion in France; this is not a country that encourages diversity. Sometimes I feel there is only one right way to be French, and being Jewish or Muslim of immigrant origin is not one of them."

Before it became a commonly used concept, Etienne advocated the notion of "multiple identities" which he called "*citoyenneté plurielle*" (plural citizenship). This certainly applies to French Muslims—and Jews—of immigrant descent. Most of my respondents felt quite at ease with their multiple identities. Yet the dominant culture adjusts with difficulty to a situation in which Muslims are an integral part of French society.

New ways of interpreting Islam among the children of North African immigrants are explored by French sociologist Leïla Babès. This Algerian-born scholar describes *Les nouvelles manières de croire* (New ways of believing) especially among women. She identifies the fact that young people consider religion a private matter as one of the most profound changes in conceptions of Islam (Babès, 1996: 7). France, and the Western world in general, place great value on individualism. Babès argues that this emphasis results in a personalization of faith with diminished adhesion to an institutionalized religion. A highly individualized interpretation of religion is particularly prevalent among women who seek to live their faith in the secular, less visible patriarchal society of France. Babès raises the fundamental question "Who defines what is religious?" and answers: "It is not up to a sociologist or some researcher to come up with a definition, . . . it is the believers themselves who determine the essence of what is considered religious" (15). This new religious understanding evolving in France does not mean the end of religion but rather a "transformation of beliefs" (177).

Islam in its new Western expressions is a nascent yet rapidly growing field of academic study. In her *L'Islam Positif* (Positive Islam), Babès observes that by conventional accounts, young, French Muslims are caught between a rock and a hard place, "they are either too religious or not enough" (Babès, 1997: 23). For the majority of young, French-educated, Muslims, the mosque is the place where their parents go, it is associated with the *bled*, the old country. The majority of the young generation rejects the institutional aspects of Islam. Having internalized Western individualism, they feel free to discover a personalized understanding of their religion.

Apart from the obvious influence of French society with its emphasis on *laïcité*, Babès attributes this "secularization of Islam" (94) in some measure to the presence of Christian or church-connected social service institutions in the *banlieues*. Young Muslims socialize in church-run community centers and benefit from secular outreach activities of Christian institutions. They experience church-run public service without the express purpose of proselytizing. In addition, young Muslim women use the official secular nature of France to pursue their own goals when these are against the wishes of their families and communities. They invoke French laws and the secular state to fight their own private battles. Another significant feature of French society is its pluralism, which according to this researcher, goes hand in glove with *laïcité*. As a result, "one of the most important consequences of this religious pluralism is the phenomenon of relativization of the religion to which one belongs" (102). I noticed this trend also in Morocco, especially among women who had either traveled abroad or had otherwise been exposed to extensive international interactions.

One of the most extensive surveys concerning religious practice among Muslims in France was conducted by sociologist Michèle Tribalat who published her findings in her book *From Immigration to Assimilation: A survey of Immigrant Populations in France* (1996).[11] Tribalat measured "religious practice" by using criteria such as attendance of a mosque, following dietary restrictions (abstaining from pork and alcohol) and fasting during Ramadan. Based on her data, she concluded that second-generation Algerians and Moroccans in France are less religious and closer to the values of *laïcité* dominant in French society than to the values of their parents. My approach differs from that of Tribalat in that I also inquired about practices not required by the religion of Islam such as reading the Qur'an and individual prayer. By whatever means, faith cannot easily be measured but I would contend that studying the scriptures is a stronger indicator than following rituals that have become part of a culture and tradition. Tribalat also finds that people of Moroccan origin in France show a comparatively higher religious inclination than those of Algerian or Tunisian backgrounds.

Whether the second generation is less religious (Tribalat) or religious in a different manner than their immigrant parents (Babès) is up for debate. Even the most obvious sign of adherence to Islam, the Muslim headscarf (*hijab*) does not reflect a uniform belief. This public display can be motivated by a form of radicalism or fundamentalism, a return to cultural and religious roots and may even be inspired by fashion but it does not equate with support for violence, certainly not terrorism, and therefore is not to be confused with the common use of the terms "radical" or "fundamentalist" (Nökel, 1999: 72).

LAÏCITÉ AND SECULARISM

Because of its emphasis on *laïcité*, France does not encourage the public recognition of Islam. *Laïcité* is a similar concept to that of secularism meaning the absence of religious interference in government affairs, and vice versa. There is no English word that captures the exact meaning of *laïcité* but it is related to the English word laity or laymen therefore "laicity" is the most accurate English rendering of the French term. There is however a difference between laicity, a political theory aimed at separating politics and religion with the goal of promoting religious freedom, and secularism in the sense of the declining importance of faith in individuals' daily lives. According to Arkoun, France is overemphasizing its secular nature at its own peril. "This combative secularism employed in the service of a specific political project—construction in France of a Republic that is 'one and indivisible'—neglects one of its own founding principles, that of philosophic openness to the study of all human channels for the production of meaning" (Arkoun, 2004: 96). Discouraging open discourse about religion and relegating it to the private sphere creates a situation in which extremism can flourish more easily:

> By "privatizing" religion, through its elimination from the teaching syllabus in state schools in the name of "national education," the French Republic's "compulsory, secular and free" principles for schooling equally all citizens has generated a lack of religious culture and abandoned religious affairs to the exclusive responsibility of the various "churches". . . Instead of this emancipating knowledge, the so-called secular schooling has enhanced among the citizens what sociologists describe as "the culture of disbelief," at a time when the question of the religious phenomenon, as I am trying to define it in this book, has become one of great political urgency, all the greater in that it was thought to have been dealt with for good by the progress of positivist scientific knowledge since the nineteenth century. (96)

In Morocco, the term secular or *laïcité* has historically not been used. Only recently, in the wake of the Berber Cultural Movement, have these concepts entered public discourse. The Berber Cultural Movement has used the notion of secular society to emphasize the value of Amazigh languages, which unlike Arabic, are not infused with comparable religious importance. This new discourse notwithstanding, Islam remains the state religion.

MOROCCO: ISLAM AS A STATE RELIGION

In Morocco, Islam is the one and only official religion. Freedom of religion as understood in the West is an absent concept. With a population that's 98.7 percent[12] Muslim, exposure to religions other than Islam is virtually non-existent. Most of the educated population is fluent in Arabic and therefore has access to a wide variety of literature on Islam. In a country where the King is at the same time head of state as well as Commander of the Faithful (ultimate religious authority in his country), the monarch determines the direction of new interpretations of Islam. This was evident when the King introduced the Personal Status Code—or family law—reform in 2004 and again when he took the bold step to appoint female prayer leaders in 2006. Though there is a lively public discourse on Islam within Morocco, certain themes are off-limits, such as questioning the legitimacy of the King. During the nearly four-decade long reign of the previous King Hassan II (1961–1999), political opponents were routinely jailed and tortured. The period following two failed coup attempts in the early 1970s are now referred as "the leaden years." As political and religious leadership are both in the hands of the King, people who questioned the religious authority of the King were equally punished. One of the most prominent of these critics is Skeikh Abdessalam Yassine, founder of the largest non-violent fundamentalist Sufi movements in Morocco, *Al Adl wa Ihsane* (Justice and Benevolence).[13] Yassine has variously been imprisoned, put into an insane asylum or put under house arrest. Though the overall political climate in Morocco has considerably softened under the leadership of Mohammed VI, Hassan's son, a tradition of open discourse takes time to establish. It was a sign of changing times that women in Morocco discussed their understanding of Islam with great frankness.

In ascertaining what the religion of Islam means to women who live in two different countries, one has to find issues that resonate in both places. For example, one question commonly used by Western researchers who attempt to understand the extent of Muslim's religious observance is attendance of a mosque. Yet, this practice is not simply a matter of faith but also of external infrastructure and therefore does not lend itself for a comparative study. In Morocco, there is a mosque in every neighborhood or within walking distance for most citizens. Many places of work have a designated room or place for daily prayers. This is not the case in France where it takes considerably more effort to get to a mosque or find an appropriate place for worship. Furthermore, public support for religious practices is virtually non-existent. French routine makes few, if any, provisions for Friday prayers.

In Morocco, practicing Islam is part of everyday normality whereas leading a life in accordance with this religion in France requires significantly more commitment. Fasting during the month of Ramadan is also often used as a determinant for religious observance. As it is one of the pillars of Islam, it is indeed an important part in the life of a Muslim. Yet, adhering to the month-long fast is obviously more complicated for Muslims in France than for those in Morocco. In Morocco fasting is a national event (eating in public during Ramadan is a criminal offense) and the schedule of public institutions is altered so as to accommodate a different daily routine during the holy month. There are no lunch breaks; instead work ends so as to allow everyone to gather for *ftour* (or *iftar*), the festive meal after sunset that breaks the daily fast. No such accommodations are offered to Muslims in France. The same applies to reading the Qur'an. In Morocco, almost all of my respondents were fluent in Arabic and had read sections of the Qur'an as part of their regular schooling, with the exception of those who attended private French schools. In France, few women had any formal exposure to the scripture during their adolescence.

WHAT MAKES A MUSLIM A MUSLIM

Rather than using such measures as attendance of a mosque or simply asking if they fasted during Ramadan, I asked women to describe what being a Muslim meant to them. In Islam, everyone born to a Muslim father is considered a lifelong Muslim, regardless of their actual practice or faith. Therefore, I wanted to know if they saw themselves as Muslims primarily by birth, by choice, or both. The majority of women in Morocco and France said they identified themselves as Muslims not merely because they were born to a Muslim father, but that it was their choice to affirm their faith and culture. In France certainly, it would have been relatively easy to discard their religion upon becoming adults. Women in France regarded *Aid al-Fitr* and *Aid al-Adha*[14] as their most festive days. This was the case even among those who described themselves as *laïques* or not practicing. Women in France also said they did not see a contradiction between being a Muslim and celebrating Christmas in some form. They recounted how their mothers had put up a Christmas tree in their apartment and how they exchanged small gifts on Christmas. Of course, one could argue that the Christmas tree is not truly a religious symbol but originates in pre-Christian European observance of winter solstice. But it is highly doubtful that barely literate Moroccan immigrant women would have explored the origins of the Christmas tree in great depth before placing a candle or an ornament on a pine.

In Morocco and France, some women stated they were Muslim by birth only, meaning they had ceased to practice the religion they were born into. Most said that this absence of any particular religious practice did not mean they were atheists but simply that they had adopted a more personalized understanding of spirituality. They did not rule out the possibility of developing an interest in Islam again at some point in their life. In Morocco, some women said being born a Muslim means being a Muslim for life and thus there was no need for further affirmation. But I also met a woman in Morocco who said that although she was born a Muslim, she was currently in the process of studying other religions in an effort to find a belief system that made most sense to her. This woman said in Morocco this was a difficult task as access to literature about religions other than Islam was limited and furthermore only the religions of the book (Judaism, Christianity and Islam) were considered religions; other faiths such as Buddhism or Hinduism were commonly considered philosophies. Another woman in Morocco offered this pragmatic assessment: "I am Muslim by birth and I am Muslim by culture, because of where I was born and where I live. But it was not my choice. There are many other ways to lead a righteous life."

Women in both countries stressed that in Islam, culture and religion are so closely intertwined that it was sometimes difficult for them to differentiate between culture and religion. They felt that some of the traditions and customs passed on to them were clearly not in accordance with their interpretation of the religion of Islam. It is often assumed that for Muslims in France the distinction between culture and religion is more evident as they live in a secular surrounding with a strong Christian heritage. My research however showed that educated Moroccans who live in an Islamic country are equally capable of making that distinction. Indeed, women frequently told me that their conception of Islam was at odds with the prevailing culture, particularly concerning the status of women.

Religious identity is influenced by a variety of factors, one of them being life experience. A person who has experienced significant personal loss or tragedy may come to a different understanding of religion than someone whose life has progressed without major disruptions. This also came to the fore in my discussions. Among the women who had turned to religion more fervently were those who had gone through some personal hardship. A librarian in Morocco explained: "After my daughter was diagnosed with a life-threatening illness, I began to pray. Though I have been a Muslim all my life, I never really cried out to God. Even after my daughter was cured, I felt I needed to become more religious. It just seemed important after what we had been through."

Nobel-prize winning Turkish novelist Orhan Pamuk, whose books are popular in Morocco, also makes a connection between social class and faith in his memoir *Istanbul* (2006). He writes:

> God was there for those in pain, to offer comfort to those who were so poor they could not educate their children, to care for the beggars in the street who were invoking forever Her[15] name, and to aid pure-hearted innocents in times of trouble. This is why, if my mother heard of a blizzard that closed the roads to remote villages or of an earthquake that had left the poor homeless, she would say, "May God help them!" It seemed not so much a petition as an expression of the fleeting guilt that well-to-do people like us felt at such times; it helped us get over the emptiness of knowing we were doing nothing about the situation. (176)

The issue of social class came up in my conversations in Morocco and France but less in the context of religion than concerning professional opportunities.

READING AND RECITING THE QUR'AN

As all my respondents were literate and well-educated, I asked whether they had read or were reading the Qur'an. As can be expected, comparatively more women in Morocco than in France said they had read parts or the entire Qur'an. However, I also did meet women in Morocco who said they had never read the scriptures. Some had attended a private French school in Rabat and their parents were part of the old Moroccan elite that preferred to speak French rather than Arabic even in the home. Another, daughter of a diplomat, had lived in Europe during her formative years. In France, the majority of women I met said they had never read the Qur'an. However, some women in Morocco and France said they did read the Qur'an during the month of Ramadan.

Women gave different reasons for reading the Qur'an. In Morocco, most said they had established a habit of reading the Qur'an when they were teenagers. Some said reading the Qur'an was a form of religious observance, and others said they had taken up serious study of the Qur'an more recently in the wake of the real or imagined worldwide conflict between the West and Muslim world. These women wanted to know and understand what the Qur'an said on certain issues, such as the headscarf, the role of women in general and on the issue of violence. This type of individual study confirms what Roy describes as follows: "The religious has been secularized . . . in the sense that the divine is an individual consideration and no longer belongs to a group of professionals who claim to represent and own its interpretation. The articulation of the religious and the social has thus been modified" (Roy, 2004: 100).

Women in France would often tell me that the only copy of the Qur'an in their parents' homes was an Arabic version that no one in the family could read properly. They also said that they did want to read the Qur'an at least once in their lifetime. Everyone without exception in Morocco and France said they had a copy of the Qur'an in their home and that they took it off the shelf from time to time to hold or look at. Some women in both countries even said that although they did not read the Qur'an, they always carried a miniature copy with them in their purse, which they proceeded to show me. When I asked how they could consider themselves Muslims if they had never read the scripture on which the religion is founded, some respondents in France seemed surprised. They felt there was little connection between reading the book and being a believer. Religious identity was understood as some internal disposition with a great variety of external expressions such as proclaiming the intention of wanting to read the Qur'an one day or carrying an (unread) copy of the Qur'an in the purse. One woman in Paris said: "The Qur'an is often difficult to understand. But I know it is the word of God and therefore I carry a copy in my purse." In Morocco, I heard similar statements: "I always carry the Qur'an with me. Sometimes, I read a few verses but it is important to have the word of God with me wherever I go."

Increased hostility toward Muslims in France led some women to study the Qur'an. Said Nadia in Paris:

> Growing up, I never read the Qur'an. I had no idea what it said about anything. Based on what I heard at home and at school, I thought Jesus is the man for Christians and Mohammed is for Muslims. So I grew up believing that we have nothing in common. I did not even know that the Qur'an speaks of Jesus or that Mary was a revered figure also for Muslims. I really did not know anything about Islam. I thought Christianity and Islam were two totally different religions and just accepted that. Now that I have read the Qur'an, I wonder why there is such acrimony between us [Muslims and Christians]. I don't know, but maybe the same is true of many Christians. They have no idea that we actually have more in common than they think, or else we would get along better.

But, she added:

> I have also studied Christianity a little bit and we Muslims certainly do not agree that Jesus is the son of God. God cannot have a son, He sends prophets. Also I don't accept that God is three, the Father, the Son and the Holy Ghost. We believe that God is only one. So there is a genuine difference but I am not sure that this could be the cause for such antagonism.

Reciting passages of the Qur'an by heart is one of the traditions practiced and appreciated by Muslims all over the world. In fact, all women I met in Morocco said they were able to do so. Even those who never read the Qur'an on their own, nor had done so as part of their French private schooling, were able to recite certain passages because of the omnipresence of Islam in Moroccan daily life. It was simply an element of growing up in a Muslim country. However, women were quick to add that being able to recite a verse was not synonymous with understanding its full meaning. Recitation of the Qur'an is a required component of the Moroccan school curriculum, yet questions about their meaning are discouraged. Thus, actual comprehension of the text is often limited. This is also due to the fact that the Arabic used in the Qur'an is of such a sophisticated quality that it requires more than common knowledge of the language to understand the connotation of certain words or expressions. The Arabic of the Qur'an differs significantly from *Dereja*,[16] the spoken Arabic of Morocco. In addition, critical thinking and individual inquisitiveness are not characteristics of the Moroccan educational system which stresses rote memorization and acquisition of established knowledge. Recitation of the Qur'an by adults can be compared with reciting the rosary in the Catholic Church. It is a religious practice observed in the spirit of worship and humility and not intended as an exercise in the exploration of meaning. Women in Morocco said they invoked the Qur'an because it offered them some serenity in their otherwise busy lives and because they could do so whenever they felt like it outside of any prescribed prayer ritual. They believed in the spiritual power of reciting sacred verses independent of a rational understanding of the recitation.

In Morocco, the mystical aspect of Islam as expressed in Sufism is widespread and *tariqas* or religious orders are common throughout the country. Belonging to *tariqa* however does not require renouncing the world as would be the case in some Christian monasteries, quite the contrary. A true Sufi is understood as someone who actively participates in public life and injects it with a spiritual dimension. Zoubida said she had been a serious student of Sufism for a number of years, though she did not belong to any particular organization: "For me it is a matter of living my faith. It is not a matter of dogma or following meaningless rituals. Hopefully, it is by example that I demonstrate my love for God."

Externally manifest acts, such as praying according to a prescribed formula or fasting, are a means to ascertain a degree of religious observance, but as my respondents repeatedly told me, this was not necessarily an indication of faith. Women in Morocco and France approached religion from a perspective of personal meaning and belief and did not consider adherence to prescribed rituals as a measure of their faith. One woman in France summed up what several others had expressed: "I often pray with my own words and in French. I know this is not what is commonly done by Muslims, but I have to offer what comes from my heart. Sometimes I include verses in Arabic from the Qur'an but I am not sure if I recite them properly."

RAMADAN AND PRAYER

No study about Islam is complete without considering Ramadan. Most Muslims take great pride in the fact that they are capable of enduring an entire month without ingesting any food or drink from sunrise to sunset, at the same time abstaining from sex and smoking. It is indeed remarkable to see heavy smokers bring their habit to an abrupt halt in observance of the holy month, yet lighting up again as soon as the required period of abstinence is over. When I asked a smoker why he (it is mostly men who smoke in Morocco) started smoking again after giving it up during Ramadan, he said: "I like smoking. By abstaining during Ramadan, I demonstrate that I am not addicted and that the mind is stronger than the body. This sort of self-discipline is the essence of Ramadan and is required of a good Muslim."

Fasting during Ramadan is not necessarily a straightforward practice. One might think that people either fast or do not. Because there is such great religious and cultural importance attached to the fast, it is an issue most young Muslims have thought about.

In Morocco the annual fast is a national affair in which all levels of society participate. Female television personalities wear no noticeable make-up during Ramadan, shedding their image of glamorous beauty and instead appearing modest and bland. I asked a prominent TV anchor if she found it difficult to go on the air without her usual heavy make-up, jewelry and fancy clothing. She said, no pun intended: "That is the beauty of being a Muslim. Once each year, we all are equal."

The different rhythm imposed during Ramadan and the sense of national and religious obligation makes it nearly impossible for Moroccans to admit that they are not fasting. Therefore it is quite remarkable that several women in Morocco said they adhered to the fast only "in public," meaning they kept up the appearance of abstaining from food and drink at their workplace but did not disclose to their colleagues that they were not actually fasting. Some explained that fasting was not merely refraining from food, drink, sex and smoking but its deeper meaning lay in strengthening the mind and cleansing it from bad thoughts and feelings. This internal aspect required great discipline and aided them in being true to the spirit of Islam. Ramadan, some asserted, had become more of a national tradition than a genuine religious practice. "The eating schedule simply changes during Ramadan," Hayat said. "We eat and feast all night and then fast during the day. Isn't it ironic that some people actually gain weight during the month of fasting?" Rachida, a teacher in Morocco said: "For me Ramadan is about becoming a better person. I try to fast from bad thoughts and that takes more energy than not eating."

In France, most women also claimed to fast during Ramadan. Some said they had fasted while they still lived with their parents, then stopped upon moving out but had taken up the practice again recently because they felt some personal desire to do so. Others said they fasted some years and not others and some said they fasted a few days but not the entire month. Though the fast is one of the five pillars of Islam and therefore not optional, the notion that fasting should be a personal choice, borne out of a desire to adhere to a religious command rather than being imposed by parents, family or society at large, is rather novel. Nearly all of my respondents insisted that fasting had to be a deliberate, personal decision. They saw no conflict between making individual choices on a matter that is a required tenet of the faith and still considering themselves "good" Muslims.

Praying in a prescribed manner is another pillar of Islam. Most of my respondents in Morocco and France said that this too was a matter of personal choice. While women in Morocco generally adhered more rigorously to this practice than women in France, there were a variety of viewpoints. Morocco is a country where one can see men rolling out little carpets on the side of the road and bowing for prayers in the direction of Mecca, where calls for prayer from the minarets are louder than most church bells in Europe and—with the help of modern technology—resonate through nearly every corner of every household; it is obvious that praying is an encouraged and accepted practice. In contemporary France, there is no comparable overt encouragement for prayer. Still, several women in France said they found a way to pray five times a day, most often unnoticed by their colleagues at work or school. Most said they did not pray in the prescribed manner but used their own words. "Prayer has to come from the heart, it is not a matter of following a ritual," was an explanation frequently offered. Women often described prayer as a personal expression. "In Islam there is too much focus on following the rules, I pray when I need to pray, but sometimes I use my own words," was how one woman in France put it. "Praying should not be an obligation, you should want to turn to God in prayer," said a woman in Morocco. Whenever women elaborated on their understanding of prayer, the views in Morocco and in France were strikingly similar. Assia in Saint Denis, on the outskirts of Paris, who described herself as devout, said: "There are what I call the 'five-pillar-Muslims,' meaning those who follow the prescribed rituals of Islam, but that is a rather low level of practice. A higher level is *imane,* faith, which requires more effort on the part of the individual because faith is an internal focus on a higher ideal. And the highest level is *ihsane,* doing-well, charity (in French) *bienfaisance* or what I think Buddhists call compassion."

Assia, who had a graduate degree in bio-chemistry, felt that Western researchers, as some Islamic scholars, were overly preoccupied with dogma and ritual and ignored the essence of a life of faith that should be evident in a person's behavior toward others. This, she insisted, could not easily be captured by conventional measures. She resented the commonly repeated observation that Muslims in the West are less religious than their counterparts in the Muslim world. "Imagine if we say we are not religious then we are accepted as having made the successful transformation into Western, secular society. People really like it when we Muslims say we are not religious. But if we openly admit to being religious and even go so far as wearing the headscarf, we are suspected of being close to terrorists." And with a smile, she added, "you see, it is not easy being a Muslim these days." Assia had prepared a beautiful couscous because she wanted to enjoy our discussions in a relaxed setting. She laughed while recounting how she had not been interested at all in religion as teenager. To this day she was the only one in her family of four sisters who wore the headscarf. "I just tried so hard being French in the way I thought was expected of me. And my mother said I should cut my hair so I would look more French and that I should look at what the other girls were doing to make it easier for me in school." But then, while a university student—with excellent grades, she emphasized—Assia came to realize that she needed to find out for herself who she was. Again, she said laughingly: "What am I if not French. I was born here, I never lived anywhere else. I recently started to study Arabic. I felt this emptiness inside and so I wanted to read the Qur'an in its original version. I did not even tell my family that I had become a serious student of religion—and I am a scientist too."

Assia's comments put the finger on a common perception namely that the majority of Muslims in the West are less religious as a result of living in a secular environment. She was adamant that a heightened sense of personal freedom led to more choices concerning religion. Taking charge of their lives, pursuing higher education and embarking on professional careers also led women to assume responsibility for decisions they made on matters of religion. Based on my research, a comparable trend can also be observed in Morocco.

INTERNATIONAL EXPOSURE

The most remarkable difference among women in Morocco was between those who had traveled abroad or were exposed to international contacts and those had not. In developing world countries travel or study abroad is generally a privilege of the affluent elite. Due to the comparative focus of this study, I made effort to find women who came from less affluent backgrounds but still who had an opportunity for extensive exposure to people from different cultures.

The late King Hassan II founded a university in Morocco that uses the American system of education and English as the language of instruction. His vision for this institution was the strengthening of a homegrown middle class and to stem the brain drain of academics and of gifted young people. Al Akhawayn University of Ifrane (AUI) was established in 1995 in the remote, picturesque Middle Atlas town of Ifrane, home of the late King's favorite palace resort. The faculty is a blend of international and local academics, and student exchange programs with American and European universities bring substantial numbers of international students to campus. In the dormitories, local students are intentionally paired with foreign students. Academic conferences and extra-curricular programs routinely revolve around themes of tolerance and inter-religious and intercultural dialogue.

As English is the language used on campus, even administrative staff must have a comparatively high degree of education because English is not commonly used in this Arab-francophone country. They also must be capable of adapting to an international environment and an American system of education. A reasonable number of staff positions are filled by people who possess the prerequisite qualifications rather than coming to their appointment by *coup de piston* (personal connections) as is often case in Morocco. The student body hails largely from middle- to upper-middle-class families, and 50 percent of students are female. AUI is the first private university in Morocco and tuition is—by Moroccan standards—extremely high. More recently, the university has been offering scholarships and introduced a system of work-study, common in the U.S. but previously unheard of in Morocco. This allows for recruitment of bright students from modest backgrounds. I purposely sought out students who benefited from these programs because their background is more in line with that of women I met in France.

Amal, a young woman from a small town near the Rif Mountains, had been the recipient of a scholarship and upon graduation had found a satisfying job in the computer field. She was in Ifrane for a visit with old friends when I met her. From a devout, religious family, she was the first in her family of four brothers and sisters to attend college. "Before I came to AUI, Islam was all I knew. I had never met a person who was not Muslim. When I came here, I met people from all over the world and I roomed with several American girls. My parents are very proud of me for being able to get this education but they were also a bit worried that I would loose my way." Amal said she planned on wearing a *hijab* after getting married. "Right now, it is just not practical for me to wear a headscarf. I played soccer while a student and I still like to run track. On campus, men and women freely interact with each other. With a headscarf, I feel I could not really do that. I know this is just my perception but that is how I feel."

She explained her evolving understanding of Islam. "Islam is one of the religions in the world. There are other religions too but this happens to be mine. For me Islam is my liberation, my freedom to express myself," she said. "It is the promise of peace and equality. Islam for me is a way of life, that means it is not just a faith but it informs everything I do and as a woman, Islam is the way to pursue women's rights because that is what the Qur'an states. We in Morocco need to get away from the cultural practices which have nothing to do with Islam but are presented as such. I constantly argue with my mother about that. I want to travel abroad and see what people in other countries do and if they are not Muslims, how are they are different?" Amal was enthusiastic about her student days at AUI. "I really liked my American roommates. I think, in the U.S., all kinds of people live side by side. I think you can really be yourself there." I asked Amal to elaborate on what she meant by "being yourself." She said she often felt restricted by Moroccan customs and social conventions and said that questioning her own religion was not encouraged. "By exploring Islam and looking critically at it, I feel I have become a better Muslim, but of course many in my family back home don't agree with that. They feel that I have changed, I have become too free, too critical of our customs." Amal emphasized her belief in tolerance. "I think we need to tolerate differences, it is actually not so difficult. I think because of their experience under the French, my parents and grandparents are skeptical of Christians and Westerners. But the key is education, we don't know enough about each other. Universities are the ideal environment where people of different backgrounds can interact." As happens often in Morocco, the Middle East conflict becomes a topic of conversation. Amal too, inserted the Palestinian question: "What about Jews? I am not sure they want to understand or tolerate us. Look at how Israelis treat Palestinians. That is a real problem. And America supports everything Israel does." Amal felt that through her studies she came to understand different aspects of Islam. "Education really is the key. The first word the Archangel[17] told the prophet was '*ikra*' (read or recite). He did not say that this message was intended for men only. The first order of Islam is the duty to educate but we have not followed this in our country. Otherwise we could not have such high illiteracy rates." When I met Amal the following year, she immediately told me that she had briefly visited the U.S. and had found it to be a deeply rewarding experience. Unlike the years before, she now wore a little gold pendant with the inscription "Allah" around her neck. She said this was an expression of her choice to be recognized as a Muslim.

Youssra, who had received a scholarship to pursue graduate studies in the United States and had lived two years in Iowa, wanted to share her understanding of Islam: "Islam is one of the religions in the world. When I lived in the U.S., I began to question the environment in which I grew up in here in Morocco. Life in the U.S. was so different from what I had been used to at home. While there, I studied other religions and now I am trying to find out which is the best religion for me. I never knew for instance that Buddhism was a real religion. Here, we only consider the religions of the Book proper religions; the others are considered philosophies because they are not based on direct revelation by God. But I found Buddhism very appealing. I have a hard time fitting back into Moroccan society; there are not many people with whom I can discuss my spiritual search. But now that I am back, I also want to study more about Islam, especially Sufism."

Like Amal, Youssra spoke of some conflict within her family, caused by her desire to re-assess her faith. However, she added, "I can understand them. I am venturing into territory unknown to them and they feel they can't protect me if I get lost. At the moment, honestly speaking, I don't really know where I am headed."

Jamila came to her interest in Islam by way of studying international finance. "Because I live in an Islamic society, I have not spent much time thinking about Islam. It has always been a part of my life that I have taken for granted. I mean, I have never asked myself why I am a Muslim. I have studied finance and sometimes we have to study some particularities of Islamic banking because for example, Islam does not allow charging interest. But at the university we studied different international systems of finance and the underlying philosophies that shaped those systems. That made me interested to study Islam more deeply with a view of understanding the social system based on this religion. And without realizing it at first, I became more and more fascinated with Islam and also realized that I actually have a deep belief in God."

Jamila grew increasingly animated as she tried to find the proper words to express her thoughts. "I know that faith can exist independently of a particular religious doctrine, but in my case, Islam made me realize that there is a larger purpose to our existence. I don't consider myself different from a Christian or a Jew, the spirit behind these religions is the same. It is just that for me, the door to a spiritual life was opened by Islam because that is the tradition I was born and raised in" and she added smiling, "and I deepened my belief by way of studying finance."

The views of Amal, Youssra and Jamila on the AUI campus were echoed by women in other parts of the country who had lived abroad. Said Ikram, a medical doctor in Rabat, who had earned her doctorate in France: "Islam is the religion of the people of Morocco. It is what holds our country together. It keeps people united. Of course, we are in a time of great social upheaval and we have an economic and social crisis in our country. Even though Islam is my personal religion, it is important to recognize that in Morocco it is also an important social force. It is the official religion, it is the basis of our educational system; Islam informs all aspects of life. It does not matter if one agrees or disagrees." Ikram paused for a minute before she continued. "In Morocco, Islam is based on instilling a sense of guilt. Here everyone proclaims to be a good Muslim, people don't say what they really think or believe. It is just a part of our social fabric. People tell me that my personal problems stem from the fact that I am not a good Muslim." She went on to clarify what she meant by personal problems: "At age 32, I am still not married, and yes, I have had a couple of boyfriends and occasionally I drink alcohol. Does that make me a bad person or a bad Muslim? I don't think so. I have been re-thinking my understanding of Islam, because I need to be able to live my life the way I think is best. It used to bother me when my colleagues made critical comments about my personal life. Anyway, it is not for others to judge if I am a good Muslim or not. There is too much of that going on here." I asked Ikram if she would feel less under public scrutiny if she lived in France. "In France, I may not have as good a professional position as I have here, I would be part of the North African immigrant minority and under a looking glass for different reasons. So, for me it is more a question of dealing with the devil I know here at home rather than trying to figure out how to be accepted in French society."

The above examples illustrate that women with significant exposure to people of a culture and religion other than their own perceived their religion as one faith among others. They also had a more critical view of the way Islam was practiced in their home country. I met one woman in Morocco who had converted to Christianity, secretly, because changing one's religion is illegal, and some in France who declared themselves atheist.

By contrast, women who had only minimally been exposed to people of different cultures or religions focused on the supremacy of Islam. Karima, a librarian in Morocco, said: "Islam is one of the three monotheistic religions. I don't know much about the differences between the three but the essence of all three is the promotion of peace. In Morocco, Islam is the basis for our culture, for our political and social life and it is the basis of our values. On a personal level, what I like about Islam is that there is no intermediary between man and God. Each believer can come to God directly. I don't like the concept of an intermediary when it comes to my relationship with God. We don't believe in a Son of God as Christians do. The Qur'an says Jesus was a prophet and we revere him as that. But Mohammed came after Jesus and was the last prophet. Therefore, Islam is [the] last revelation God gave. Islam means everything to me."

Loubna, a university student in Rabat, wearing the *hijab,* and by her own account close to an Islamist[18] position, said: "Islam is more than a religion, it is a complete way of life. It is not what is taught in the mosques here. The mosques just support the current system which is corrupt. What we have here in Morocco is not a true Islamic society or else we would not have such glaring injustices. I am very proud to be a Muslim, I believe in Islam. I believe a return to true Islam is the engine for change on all levels of society. We have to show the world that true Muslims are the bearers of peace and social justice." Another teacher said: "You must understand that Islam is the last revelation of God. Eventually Christians and Jews will come to understand that their religions prepared the world for the words revealed through Mohammed. This is only logical."

PEACE VERSUS TERRORISM

In Morocco, the theme of "peace" was frequently raised. Women voiced concern that Islam was perceived in the West as synonymous with terrorism. Indeed,

Morocco has had its own encounter with terrorism when forty-three people were killed in the deadliest attack in this country in Casablanca on May 16, 2003. The suicide bombings were carried out by fourteen self-proclaimed radical Islamists, members of the terrorist group Salafia Jihadia who came from the shanty towns of Sidi Moumen,[19] a poor suburb of Casablanca. Targets of the attacks were Spanish- and Italian-owned restaurants, a Jewish cemetery and community center, an international hotel and a site near the Belgian consulate. Shortly after the attacks, tens of thousands of people demonstrated in the streets of Casablanca in a "March against Terror."[20] In my conversations, I purposely steered clear of questions about terrorism as there is no natural link between terrorism and the religion of Islam. The bloody practices of the Spanish inquisition for instance are not held up as the norm as to how Christians deal with non-believers. These terrorist attacks had shocked a nation that felt itself immune to such atrocities. Everywhere people commented on this issue. Moroccans were also aware that a Moroccan had been implicated in the September 11, 2001 attack on the World Trade Center in New York and that Moroccans were involved in the bombings on a commuter train that killed 191 people in Madrid, Spain on March 11, 2004. In 2005 a Dutch citizen with Moroccan parents was sentenced to life in prison in the Netherlands for the murder in 2004 of filmmaker Theo van Gogh who had made a film critical of Islam. Given Moroccan presence in these murderous events, it is to be expected that Moroccans felt a need to address the issue of terrorism. Without exception, all women I spoke with, no matter where they stood on any other issue, said that Islam, the way they understood it, does not condone violence. "I can't even describe how terrible it is what the terrorists are doing to our religion," said Khalida, a school teacher in Azrou, home town of Zacharias Moussaoui's[21] mother. Several women expressed alarm that by linking Islam with terrorism, the West might use this connection to destroy Islam. "Islam means peace, love and goodness. It guides you through the dark hours which precede the daylight," said Amina, another school teacher. By dark hours, she referred to the darkness terrorism had thrown over the light of Islam.

In France by contrast, women rarely raised the theme of peace—or terrorism for that matter—when speaking about Islam. Some of the women who wore a headscarf made sure to emphasize that their fundamentalism was not to be equated with violence perpetuated in the name of Islam by terrorists. For the most part, women in France insisted that Islam, or religion in general, was an intensely personal matter. Karima, an Internet web designer in Paris, said: "Islam is something very personal for me. It guides me through this life and prepares me for the next. But I must not speak too much about this in a *laïc* (secular) state and I respect that. It is also a bit delicate to discuss religion in my family. I don't want to upset my parents with the questions I have about my religion."

For most women in France "parents" was a key issue when discussing Islam. They emphasized that their understanding of Islam was different than that of their parents. "Islam is the religion of my parents," said a high school teacher. "But my parents don't know the Qur'an very well. They did not have any choice with regards to religion. They were born and raised in an Islamic society. Even after they came to France, all their friends are Muslims and they live in a part of town where they are surrounded by other immigrants from North Africa. Even after all their years here in France, they have not learned much about other religions, other than the fact that Christmas is a big event here." This woman contrasted the experience of her parents with her own: "I grew up here, went to a French school. My colleagues at work are not Muslim. So, for me to be a true Muslim, not in name only, I would have to study the Qur'an and understand what it says. I hope to do that one day. Still, I am no less of a Muslim now."

Lila, a legal assistant, offered this perception of Islam: "For me, Islam offers simplicity in a very complicated life. It offers purity of spirit, tolerance and a sense of belonging. That's very important for me here in France." She spoke of the closeness she enjoyed with her friends who were of a similar background. Though they did not discuss religion explicitly, she said simply the fact that they were Muslims too made the relationship easier. With her co-religionist friends, she could discuss the difficulties she had with her parents which were similar to the conflicts they experienced. These conflicts were caused by such mundane issues as clothing—how tight can a t-shirt be and how short a skirt—but also more serious issues such as dating and marriage.

CHOICE

Women in France saw religious affiliation primarily as a matter of individual choice. But choice was almost always limited to exploring their own religion. Cases where women converted were exceedingly rare. In France I met one woman, Mariam, who was raised Catholic because her father was from Guadeloupe.[22] Her Moroccan mother had married this man after her first husband died shortly after Mariam's birth. This man had worked in a Catholic charity that had helped her get back on her feet after her husband's death. When she was in her early twenties, Mariam converted to Islam, her mother's religion, and now wore the Muslim headscarf.

Jihane, a graduate student in Paris who had recently decided to wear the *hijab*, said: "Islam means everything to me. It is my way of life, the basis for

my everyday behavior and for all the decisions I make. I am actively studying the Qur'an now and attend Qur'anic classes on the weekend. I did not
learn much about Islam from my parents but now I am beginning to understand what a great religion it is." Jihane said she was attracted to Islamism because of the coherent worldview it offered. "I rediscovered Islam when I was
at the university Saint-Denis.[23] There I met people who lived to please God.
I felt attracted to these people and I began asking myself whether Islam was
just another religion like Christianity or Judaism. I discovered that Islam was
a real treasure that one has to discover daily. It is a system for living one's
life. It is not just a religion."

Another university student offered a different view: "The more I studied
Islam, the more open I become towards others. There is no longer us and
them, there only is a we together and how to be kind to one another." I asked
this woman if she belonged to any particular group of if she attended some
kind of Qur'anic instruction. She said so far she had been studying the religious texts on her own, but mostly she consulted websites and logged into
chat rooms on the Internet. She also said that her parents had opposed her
wearing the headscarf. "They pushed me to go to university. Many of the
young people in our neighborhood don't have a proper profession or are unemployed. My parents wanted to make sure that I get out of that quagmire and
so they felt I should not be so demonstrative about my religion." In the course
of her university studies and her friendship with other young women who
were in a similar situation and who had already put on the headscarf, she became interested in exploring Islam. "It is really after I learned more about Islam that I became more serious about my studies. The Qur'an does not condone the way women are treated *chez nous.*"

Such newfound piety was not always supported by the mothers of these
young women. In a community center for aging North African immigrants
where elderly men gather to drink mint tea, play games, watch television or
just sit around and talk, I met 44-year-old Selma. Selma had been instrumental in creating the center because there are few facilities that cater to retired
immigrant workers, many of whom still live in the same old single-sex dormitories they had first moved into when they arrived in France decades ago.
These were men who had never managed to bring their wives and families to
France. Financed by the municipality of Paris, Selma spent her days organiz-
ing outings and lectures and often she simply listened to these lonely old men.
She described herself as liberal, secular and without much interest in religion.
Selma had a twenty-year-old daughter who recently developed a strong interest in Islam. "She started throwing the ham in the trash can and said she
wanted to reclaim her Moroccan heritage. I can live with that, but when she
announced she was going put on the *hijab*, I must say the veil is the limit,

that's where I draw the line." Selma had lived in France for more than twenty years and her daughter was born in Paris. "All my life I fought for women's rights and equality, especially in our immigrant Muslim community. I won't let my daughter regress. For me, the veil is too much a symbol of oppression. The battle for women's rights continues on both sides of the Mediterranean. I left Morocco hoping I would find more opportunity and freedom here so I cannot sit still and watch as my own daughter is trying to turn back the clock. To me it is not really religion she found, she wants to fit into this new group of friends and they indoctrinate her with all that dogma."

In Morocco and in France, some women found support for their personal ambitions through the study of Islam. For them, the realization that strict patriarchic structures were not a God-given system but that divine providence actually endowed them with rights and freedoms of their own offered them a deep sense of conviction that they were on the right path. Saadia, an aspiring academic who had just completed her Ph.D. in Rabat when we first met in the summer of 2004 and had started her career as a professor later that year, summarized her changing understanding of Islam: "When I was younger, I thought I had to make [a] choice between being modern and being a true Muslim. Now I understand I can be whatever I want and be a good Muslim at the same time. No one can tell me how to be a good Muslim. I do not have to make a radical choice instead I want to achieve balance within myself." Clad in fashionable Western clothes, Saadia declared herself as an "Islamic feminist."

I conducted a little experiment with myself after transcribing some responses without identifying the individual or in which country they were given. I put these notes aside and picked them up weeks later trying to match responses to countries. I wanted to see if it was immediately apparent if a response came from a woman in Morocco or from a woman in France. I failed to come up with the correct match. This affirms that assumptions based on geography are questionable.

Here are a few examples of some of those responses:

1. Islam informs my relationship with other people. I know I need to be patient, for example, and virtuous and need to educate my future children in the religion of Islam.

2. Every day I have an experience with Islam. I am very shy and solitary, so I don't talk much with others. But I do pray all the time and ask for guidance. Really, Islam is my source of strength especially in the work place where I have to deal with different people all the time.

3. I once had a wonderful boyfriend who was not Muslim. In fact, I don't even know if he believed in any religion at all. We really liked each other a lot. But then I got very disturbed thinking about our future together and that we may

raise children who are completely secular and without religious beliefs. And
so I broke off the relationship. Even though I am not at all a devout Muslim,
I feel I must not bring up my children without any faith.

4. I really don't want to speak so much about Islam as about faith. I pray during times of difficulty and in trying times and because I grew up in the religion of Islam, I pray the way I know how. If I was brought up in a different
   religion, I would probably pray differently.

5. Islam is part of my daily life. It is how I accept bad things that happen to me
   or to my family. Also when you start judging your deeds by yourself, I always feel there is an eye on me—some people say this is moral conscious-
   ness. But for me it is this reference that you are never alone at any moment.
   It also makes me accept my destiny, death, sickness and it gives me hope
   when all doors seem closed.

6. As an individual, God is a refuge for me. Faith is like therapy for me. God
   controls the universe. I know that from a spiritual perspective on life. And
   you know that from being a Muslim. And when I am happy, I can be grateful to God. Islam puts everything into a larger perspective for me.[24]

In sum, being Muslim was an important aspect of women's identity. Many
viewed their study of Islam as a liberalizing force and one that allowed them
to move forward with their personal and professional ambitions in the conviction that God was, so to speak, on their side. Even those who described
themselves as not practicing said Islam was part of who they were or at least
the trajectory from where they launched their lives. In Morocco where religious education is part of regular schooling, women were conversant with the
Qur'an. However, on becoming adults, several had taken it upon themselves
to explore Islam with a critical eye. In France, by contrast, none had received
comparable religious instruction and so they had to expend considerably
more effort in learning about Islam. Apart from what some have called a sen-
timental attachment of immigrant children to the religion of their parents,
most women actively sought to gain a better understanding of their religious
roots. Even those who had turned their back on the religion as practiced by
their parents said they had an interest in finding out what Islam was all about.
Their explorations led them to similar conclusions as their Moroccan counterparts. Recent perceived or real tensions between the West and the Islamic
world have contributed to this newly invigorated quest to understand this particular religion. It is therefore futile to speculate if similar resurgence of interest in Islam would have occurred had there not been such intense public
concern over some forms of life-threatening radical expressions of Islam.

Women in France and in Morocco differentiated between religion or their
personal faith and the cultural practices and traditions of their country or families. They emphasized that some practices, like the unequal treatment of

women, were part of the cultural fabric but were not in keeping with the spirit of the scriptures the way they understood it.

Women on both sides of the Mediterranean had developed a personal understanding of their religion. A major aspect of their conception was insistence on personal choice. In France young Muslim women often were caught in a conflict over religious matters with their parents whereas in Morocco women contrasted their views with those of prevailing social norms. An individualized approach to religion is a phenomenon commonly associated with the West. The views of my respondents indicate that the notion of personal faith can no longer be exclusively associated with the Occident. In Morocco, this trend was most succinctly articulated by women who had either lived abroad or had extensive interaction with people of a culture and/or religion different from their own. They saw religion primarily as a spiritual path and as one that allowed them to realize their potential as women.

The major differences concerning conceptions of Islam did not depend on geographical location. Instead, women who had Islamist leanings in Morocco held views similar to those with comparable interest in France. To varying degrees, they felt that Islam was not only a religion but an all-encompassing way of life, often perceived as superior to other religions. Their analysis of the society in which they lived was that it was corrupt and rife with discrimination and unequal distribution of wealth, in contradiction to the teachings of the Qur'an. Some advocated a strict implementation of Islamic law and a return to the "true faith" which could restore peace and eradicate glaring social differences.

However, it has to be stated repeatedly that wearing a *hijab* was not synonymous with a conservative or Islamist outlook on life. Both in Morocco and in France, there was a range of views among veiled women. Some veiled women held decidedly progressive views on certain social and even religious matters. Thus, the veil is not a useful indicator for assessing a woman's religious understanding or political leanings.

And conversely, women who held what conventionally was called "liberal" views concerning religion shared similarities regardless of where they lived. Globalization has become part and parcel of conceptions of Islam and the previously hard and fast demarcation line between the Arab/Muslim world and the secular Western world can be drawn into question, at least with regard to populations groups I studied, namely young, educated women.

NOTES

1. (Sura 2 The Cow, Ayat 115).
2. The five pillars of Islam: 1. *Shahada*: profession of faith ("There is no God but God and Mohammed is His prophet"); 2. *Salat*: daily prayers; 3. *Zakat*: giving of alms

or charity; 4. *Swam*: fast during the month of *Ramadan* in commemoration of the revelation of the Qur'an completed with the feast of *Id-al-Fitr*; 5. *Hajj*: pilgrimage of every physically and economically able Muslim to Mecca.

3. Quoted in Annemarie Schimmel's foreword to Sachiko Murata's book *The Tao of Islam*.

4. The Qur'an is understood as God's word as revealed to the prophet Mohammed. The *hadith* (lit: something new) are sayings attributed to the prophet. The *sunnah* are traditions and practices attributed to the prophet.

5. According to Schimmel, a *hadith*, a "saying tale," is part of the oral tradition; consequently a number of non-authentic tales may have infiltrated the text in the course of the first centuries (1992: 52).

6. In parts of the Arab world, the term *murshidat* applies to female nurses and health care workers.

7. PBS, Wide Angle: "Class of 2006," a program that aired July 25, 2006, http://www.pbs.org/wnet/wideangle/shows/morocco/video.html.

8. In France several women referred to Schimmel's book *Mon âme est une femme: la femme dans la pensée islamique* (My soul is a woman: women in Islamic thought). Paris: Jean-Paul Lattès, 1998.

9. The term "beur" was coined by inverting the syllables of the word "Arabe" which often carries a pejorative connotation in French. "Marche de Beurs" refers to a major political demonstration held in 1983 by younger members of the immigrant Maghrebi community. It's official title was "la marche pour l'égalité et contre le racisme."

10. In my interviews, the most frequently cited sites were www.oumma.com, www.sezame.info, www.islamfrance.free.fr and www.saphirnet.info.

11. Title of the original book: *De l'immigration à l'assimilation. Enquête sur les populations étrangère en France*.

12. According to the World Fact Book (2001) there are in Morocco: 98.7 percent Muslims, Christian 1.1 percent, Jewish 0.2 percent. In France: 83–88 percent Roman Catholic, 2 percent Protestant, 1 percent Jewish, 5–10 percent Muslim, 4 percent unaffiliated.

13. There are certainly other large Sufi movements in Morocco such as the Boutshishi tariqa of Skeikh Sidi Hamza but these are less politically active.

14. *Aid al-Fitr* is the day of celebration that marks the end of Ramadan. Children receive gifts or money from their relatives. *Aid al-Adha* or the Feast of Sacrifice takes place during the traditional time of pilgrimage to Mecca. It is celebrated by pilgrims in Mecca and by those who remain at home. *Aid al-Adha* commemorates Abraham's obedience to God by being willing to sacrifice his son. Each family is supposed to kill a sheep and prepares a feast using the meat.

15. Pamuk explains elsewhere in his book that he perceived God as female because of the nourishing and caring qualities ascribed to God.

16. Each Arab-speaking country has its own dialect. The Moroccan variety is probably most distant from Classical Arabic as it has incorporated Berber phrases and expressions as well as French words. The phrasing of the Qur'an can therefore not easily be understood by someone with limited comprehension of classical Arabic.

17. The Qur'an is believed to have been revealed to Mohammed by the Archangel Gabriel.

18. The Islamist point of view is explored in greater detail in chapter 4.

19. Sidi Moumen is inhabited by 170,000 people and is one of the shantytowns to which the newly appointed female prayer leaders were dispatched.

20. For more information on the bombings and the subsequent "march against terror" see the BBC world news website http://news.bbc.co.uk/1/hi/world/africa/2936918.stm (last accessed April 2005).

21. Zacharias Moussaoui is the only person who to date stood trial in the United States for the World Trade Center attacks on September 11, 2001.

22. Guadeloupe, in the eastern Caribbean Sea, is an overseas *département* (*département d'outre-mer, or DOM*) of France. Like the other DOMs, Guadeloupe is also one of the twenty-six *régions* of France (*as a région d'outre-mer*), and an integral part of the republic. As part of France, Guadeloupe is part of the European Union.

23. The university, otherwise known as Université Paris 8, is located in a suburb north of Paris with a large Muslim population.

24. Responses 1, 2, and 3 came from women in Morocco. Responses 4, 5, and 6 came from women in France.

4

Law of God, Law of Man

LEGAL CHANGES IN MOROCCO AND IN FRANCE

The close relation between religion and law is evident in Morocco's family law which vividly reveals cultural beliefs and understandings. The Personal Status Code, or family law, is based on the Qur'an and therefore is considered a divinely inspired law. In 2004, a major reform of the Moroccan Personal Status Code came into effect.

In the United States, debates about abortion and gay marriage illustrate a comparable close connection between law and religious beliefs. People's views on these issues are largely shaped by religious convictions and an understanding that laws need to reflect certain beliefs. In most Muslim countries, discourses on women's private and public roles, rights and responsibilities resembles in their intensity and polarization American exchanges about abortion and gay rights.

In France, laws reflect the values of the secular French Republic. The 2004 law banning ostentatious religious symbols—including the Muslim headscarf—in public schools is intended to maintain separation of the private, or religious, from the secular, public sphere. The new laws of Morocco and France which we discuss in this chapter specifically impact Muslim women.

Law, like religion, reflects categories of meaning. A change of law, therefore, marks a cultural shift and may reflect new religious understanding. Anthropologist and legal scholar Lawrence Rosen put it this way: "Though couched as statements of fact, legal discussions are, quite often, really creators of fact. Like religion, law is a kind of metasystem which creates order in a universe that is often experienced in a more disorderly way" (Rosen, 1989: 17). Over the course of a decade, Rosen[1] observed the courtroom proceedings of a local judge in a small town in the Atlas Mountains of Morocco. Based on this experience, his anthropological and legal training, he concludes:

> It appears more fruitful to view law as part of the larger culture, a system which, for all its distinctive institutional history and forms, partakes of concepts that extend across many domains of social life. In law, as in politics and marriage, one has the opportunity to see ordinary assumptions put to the test of scope and implication, and though the response may be peculiar to its own domain, analyzing the realm of the law as a cultural phenomenon is no more unusual than viewing aspects of a society through the behavior of its members in the public market-place, the family dwelling, or the house of worship. (5)

The family—nuclear and extended—constitutes the cornerstone of Muslim society and a legal code, based on religious law, is dedicated to issues pertaining to family matters: marriage, divorce (sanctioned in Islam), custody, inheritance. All countries of the Muslim world have a Personal Status Code,[2] in Morocco called *moudawana*,[3] which lays out the role of women within the family and in society in general. Any change in the Personal Status Code therefore has larger implications with regard to the status and role of women. While women in Morocco obviously are under the rule of Moroccan family law, the *moudawana* remains a point of reference to Moroccans residing abroad. Even after having spent decades in France and after adopting French citizenship, immigrant families maintain their traditions and customs. Family matters are often dealt with in accordance with the laws and traditions of their home countries rather than those of their host countries. For example, North African immigrant families may not call on the French court system when separating or have custody disputes, but handle those matters according to their traditions rather than French law. Often immigrant couples do not get a legal divorce but separate based on the practice of repudiation. In an effort to understand the changing legal status of contemporary Moroccan women and those of Moroccan origin in France, it is important to have some basic understanding of the Moroccan Personal Status Code and Islamic law in general.

SOURCES OF ISLAMIC LAW

The principles of Islamic law, *Sharia* (the way) are primarily based on four sources: the Qur'an, the *Sunnah* (traditions based on a custom of the Prophet, *Ijma* (consensus) and *Qiyas* (analogy). The Qur'an is believed to be the direct word of God, as revealed to and transmitted by the Prophet Mohammed. All sources of Islamic law must be in agreement with the Qur'an. However, in cases where the Qur'an does not address a certain subject, additional sources will be consulted. The *Sunnah*, or "the Qur'an in action" refers to the traditions based on known practices of the Prophet Mohammed, many of which have been recorded in the volumes of *Hadith* narratives. These texts include sayings of the Prophet and his deeds as recorded by his disciples. Mohammed is revered as a prophet and a human being; therefore there is a distinction between the word of God as revealed to the Prophet and Mohammed's own words. An additional source of law is found in the process of *Ijma* (consensus) which applies when scholars have not been able to find a specific legal ruling in the Qur'an or *Sunnah*. Consensus among select leaders of a community is an important concept because the Prophet is understood as having expressed that his community of believers would not agree on an error. Judges may furthermore use *Qiyas* (analogy) and legal precedent to implement new laws. These four sources were considered when reforming the Personal Status Code in Morocco in 2004.

As stated above, law is a reflection of culture and vice versa; inasmuch as law prescribes conduct, it becomes part of a people's culture. Hence, Islamic law, *sharia*, in general—of which Personal Status Code is one aspect—is described by Islamic scholar Tariq Ramadan as an expression of a way of life: "The *sharia* has nothing to do with the reductionist reading put forth by certain Muslims, Orientalists or journalists. . . . The *sharia* means how to be a Muslim and to behave as a Muslim, it is a path of faith, of staying faithful to the principles of a living faith, responsibility, justice, equality and respect for freedom" (Ramadan, 2002: 49). Ramadan's views reflect an Islamist perspective, namely that Islam is not merely a religious belief system, but a complete way of life that encompasses all aspects of personal and public life. Again, law and faith are closely—and openly—connected.

PERSONAL STATUS CODE AND THE ROLE OF WOMEN

Throughout the Muslim world, which today comprises roughly sixty states, Islamic law has been replaced with modern Western law in the areas of commercial, civil and much of criminal law. Despite these changes, family law has remained largely intact as a separate, religiously based form of law from precolonial through colonial and the present post-colonial period. This does not mean that the Personal Status Code has not been changed over the years; it simply means that family law remains religiously based law and changes have to be first and foremost justified by referring to the Qur'an. Because the Qur'an and the *Sunnah* contain numerous references concerning women and the family, changes in family law cannot be made without new interpretation of sacred texts and thus also connote an altered religious understanding. However, the demarcation line between pre-colonial, traditional and Western-inspired law is not always clear. The landmark Arab Human Development Report 2004 published by the United Nations Development Programme (UNDP) states:

> The colonial imprint can be marked. Indeed, it is often difficult to determine which legal processes are genuinely traditional and which can be seen as a hybrid by-product of colonial manipulation and control. An added complication in separating authentic from imposed practices is that colonial practice and its "civilizing mission" unilaterally claimed responsibility for introducing modern values, beliefs and institutions to the colonies. (58)

Legal pluralism is the hallmark of previously colonized countries. The same phenomenon occurs—though to a lesser extent—in countries such as Australia and Canada. Customary Law has not been disregarded or proscribed during the colonial or the post-colonial era. In African nations, the co-existence of different legal systems continues to lead to legal disputes and spurs public discourses.

One of the foremost scholars on Islam in the United States, John L. Esposito, argues that a change in Personal Status Code in Muslim societies is an "indicator of social change and reform, its methodology and problems" (Esposito, 1982: x). This Middle Eastern Studies scholar writes that Personal Status Code reform goes to the heart of establishing Islamic identity which includes re-examination of the question "What does it mean to be a Muslim woman?" (xi).

The Qur'an itself is not a legal text, but offers general moral guidelines and principles. In the centuries following Mohammed's death (632 C.E.), four major legal schools, *madhab*, developed which have become the basis for law in various countries. The Moroccan Personal Status Code is based on the Maliki code. Egypt for example uses the Hanafi code, Tunisia the Hanbali code, others the Shafii code. These schools differ on issues such as the proper age of marriage for a girl, whether or not a young woman has the right to reject a marriage arranged by her guardian *wali*, usually the father or grandfather, upon reaching adulthood.

Legal scholar Mohammed Ali Syed discusses how the revelation of the Qur'an elevated the status of women in pre-Islamic Arabia. The revelation of the Qur'an, understood as an expression of Divine Will for man, was the basis for a major reform of the status of women in Arabia. This reform pertained to three areas: marriage, divorce and inheritance. According to Islam, a woman is a legal partner in a marriage contract and not an object for sale as had been the case prior to the advent of the new religion in seventh century Arabia. Islam curtailed unlimited polygamy and men were restricted to marrying four wives with the stipulation that all wives are to be treated equally. Because it is in reality humanly impossible to treat different individuals in exactly the same way, this stipulation is interpreted by some as meaning that the Prophet was in fact discouraging the practice of polygamy. In the realm of divorce, a waiting period was instituted to allow for reconciliation. A pregnant woman could not be divorced by her husband until after the birth of the child. Inheritance customs changed through Qur'anic reform by de-emphasizing tribal allegiances and instead advocating solidarity with the community of believers (*umma*). As the family constituted the smallest unit of the newly formed, faith-based community, inheritance became an issue within the family and not, as had previously been the custom, a tribal matter.

Though it was often thought that Islamic law remained constant throughout the ages, "twentieth century scholarship has, in fact, demonstrated that the development of Islamic jurisprudence in general and *Sunnah* in particular was a much more dynamic and creative process than classical theory would suggest" (Esposito, 1982: 111). Syed argues that the questions of women's rights and obligations "appear to be the most controversial and most complex of all social problems" (Syed, 2004). Syed argues that the Qur'an and *hadith* place Muslim women on the same level as Muslim men. Syed provides an overview of these two sources and explores their respective roles in Islamic law, emphasizing the Qur'an's role as the supreme authority and questioning the authenticity of some of the alleged sayings attributed to the Prophet. Rather than analyzing the practice of Islamic family law, Syed focuses on the theoretical position of Muslim women as sanctioned by the Qur'an. Like scholars cited in the previous chapter, Syed too emphasizes the fact that most denigrating commentaries on women appear in *hadith* and not the Qur'an itself. He refers to sayings of the *hadith* which are used to support the inferiority of women: "I took a look at Paradise and noted that the majority of the people there were poor, I took a look at Hell, and noted that women were the majority" or: "I have not seen anyone more deficient in intelligence and religion than you women" (Bukhari 1:301).[4] Syed contrasts these sayings with specific examples of how the revelation of the Qur'an elevated the status of women from pre-Islamic Arabia. Hence he challenges assumptions of conservative framers of Islamic law who accorded a lesser status to women.

CHILD MARRIAGE AND CONCUBINES

Syed takes as a case in point the tribal custom of concubinage, whereby a man was entitled to have sexual relationships with any female slave or female prisoner of war. The Qur'an however demands that a man be married to the woman or women with whom he desires to have sexual relationships (Qur'an

24:32, 33). The same applies to child marriage. Proponents of child marriage often refer to the story of the marriage between the Prophet and Aïsha when she was only nine years old. Less known is the supposition that this marriage was not consummated until Aïsha reached the age of maturity. In addition, Syed points out that this marriage was contracted before the Prophet received revelations concerning marriage, though there are no explicit verses in the Qur'an proscribing child marriage. Hence, according to Syed, "pre-Islamic Arab customs that allowed child marriage played a major role in introducing child marriage to Islam" (Syed, 2004: 40). Unlike the Qur'an, various *hadith* collections do contain sayings pertaining to the permissibility of child marriage of both boys and girls. As minors have no right to enter into a binding contract, the concept of a guardian, *wali*, comes into play, vesting an adult male relative with the authority to marry their minor offspring without their consent. All schools of Islamic law have the provision of a *wali*, and consequently, child marriage became part of the *sharia*. However, Syed argues that adjustments to the *sharia* have been made throughout the ages and that modern times should be no exception.

The question of consent is also important concerning sexual relationships. A sexual relationship is acceptable if it is legally sanctioned and is not necessarily a matter of mutual consent. Acceptable sexual intercourse with an underage wife, for instance, does not require consent by the female partner. Sexual ethics in Islam is an important topic but as sex only rarely surfaced in my discussions with women in Morocco and in France, we shall not explore it further.

THE GUARDIAN (*WALI*)

Because of the centrality of the *wali* (guardian) in Islamic Personal Status Code, its abolition in the *moudawana* reform in Morocco is of critical importance. This concept is also one of the most controversial aspects of Islamic family law, which is why we will discuss it here in some detail. Generally, every female is under the lifelong tutelage of a *wali*. Until marriage the father or grandfather assumes this responsibility. This guardian can arrange marriage of his female child and, depending on the legal school a country has adopted, the young woman may or may not reject the marriage arrangement made by her *wali*. In accordance with the Personal Status Code implemented in Morocco after independence in 1956, women always lived under the protection of a man: a father, a husband, an uncle, a brother, etc. Until marriage, she was under the authority of her father, and then passed to that of her husband. Even without a father, a woman could not get married by herself. Consent of the *wali* is required for any marriage to be considered valid. In Morocco, a *wali* also needed to give his consent for such matters as obtaining a passport or opening a bank account or a business. Furthermore, the guardian is responsible for protecting his female charges from harm. This is particularly relevant in rural areas with large illiterate populations and few courts. As the concept of *wali* stems from the Qur'an, to abandon this type of guardianship represents a major religious re-interpretation.

The frequently dominant role of fathers or brothers in Muslim families in France, where this practice is often criticized by members of the majority ethnic population, has its roots in the concept of *wali*. What is perceived by the French majority simply as a backward cultural practice, is in fact rooted in Muslim law.

POLYGAMY

Polygamy is another important aspect of Islamic Personal Status Code and its abolition (with very limited exceptions) in Morocco's 2004 family law reform was nothing short of revolutionary. This is because the Qur'an explicitly allows a man to marry up to four wives under certain conditions. In practice, few men today actually live simultaneously with multiple wives, however what does happen with some frequency is that a husband leaves his first wife without divorcing her and moves in with another woman, declaring her his second wife. This leaves the first wife in a legal and financial limbo because absent a divorce, she can neither remarry nor claim alimony.

The Qur'an further stipulates that a man may marry a non-Muslim woman as long as she is Jewish or Christian, that is, a believer in one of the religions of the book. As Islam is inherited in a patrilineal fashion, a Muslim woman is not allowed to wed a non-Muslim unless the man converts. The issue of marriage with a non-Muslim was a recurring theme in my conversations with Muslim women in France and will be explored in the following chapter. The practice of *mut'a*[5] (temporary marriage) is mostly a Shiite custom and not prevalent in Morocco nor among Moroccan immigrants in France.

UPHOLDING TRADITION

Legal change is only one step in a process of social and cultural transformation. More profound are changes in attitude which take considerably more time to take root. According to Moroccan anthropologist Abdellah Hammoudi (1997), author of *Master and Disciple—The Cultural Foundations of Moroccan Authoritarianism*, maintaining traditions is an important aspect of

Moroccan society. In his analysis of the Moroccan social order, Hammoudi describes the Moroccan power structure as essentially resembling a traditional Sufi *tariqa* (brotherhood) model of a stern master with his obedient disciples. The king, according to Hammoudi, is viewed as an arbiter who transcends partisan struggles. To implement policies and to maintain stability and coherence, he relies on the unique Moroccan system of the *makhzen*. To put it simply, the *makhzen* encompasses notables and others beholding to the Moroccan throne and also includes a wide network of informants, casting an invisible net over the entire population. As there is no real power outside of the palace in Morocco, any substantive change emanates from the king. Likewise, loyalty to the king is akin to religious duty. Says Hammoudi: "This set of attitudes could not impose itself if it did not have as its source the historical roots of the ethos of humility, submission, service, and gift exchange" (Hammoudi, 1997: 43). The anthropologist describes the power structure as it exists in the Morocco of today as resembling the one put in place in the nineteenth century:

> To put it briefly, the arrangement was as follows: first the charismatic community, then the bureaucratic machine. Those with functions in the royal bureaucracy were put in a secondary position, while priority was given to those who ensured the perpetuation of the family of the Prophet and to the *ulema* (religious scholars), the custodians of his teachings and tradition. At the *mihrab* (niche in the mosque showing the direction of Mecca), the focal point of worship were the descendants of the Prophet, not the *ulema*.[6] The *chorfa*[7] derived their primacy from the fact that their presence was a tangible manifestation of the Prophet's "mystical body." (70)

The Moroccan King is not only the head of state but also holds the title of "Commander of the Faithful" (*Amir al Moumin*), which also makes him the highest religious authority in his country. This title dates back to the tenth century when the Amir Abdul Rahman III (912–961) assumed the caliphate in Cordoba, Spain, and declared himself *Amir al Moumin* (Abun-Nasr, 1987: 72). Any legal change announced by the monarch is therefore not merely of social or political importance but is viewed as a religious ruling.

The monarch's religious mandate has deep roots. The current ruler is heir to the Alaoui dynasty which has ruled Morocco, except for the forty-year interruption of the French protectorate, since the seventeenth century. Furthermore, the monarch holds the title of *sharif*, that is, he claims to be a direct descendant of the Prophet, a circumstance that endows him with special authority and *baraka*, that is, blessing and grace (ibid: 228). The power and importance of the Moroccan monarch, both as spiritual and as secular leader, cannot be overestimated.

Given this context, the King's announcement of the Moroccan Personal Status Code reform has to be viewed as a mandate to change an entire population's religious understanding. Social change has to be presented as being consistent with tenets of the religion. This unity between the religious and the secular is often misunderstood in the West, where a pragmatic approach to remedying social ills is favored.

LAW REFORM

To better understand this social shift based on a reform of the Personal Status Code, a brief explanation of the Moroccan legal system may be helpful. When Morocco achieved independence from France in 1956, the new nation adopted French civil law but retained a code of Islamic religious laws to govern matters within families. While the colonial legal system had influenced development of Morocco's civil and commercial law, traditional courts continued to apply Maliki jurisprudence to matters of family law. Following independence, a Code of Personal Status (*al-Moudawana*) was issued, based on dominant Maliki doctrine. Under Moroccan civil law, women were considered equal to men. However, under the *moudawana*, women needed permission from their *wali* (guardian) to get married. Men were free to marry multiple wives, issue unilateral divorces in accordance with the Islamic tradition of repudiation (*talaq*), and make decisions regarding their wives. Women could not normally request a divorce and had limited rights concerning property and inheritance.

Reforming the Personal Status Code was a long process. In the 1990s, the Union for Feminine Action (UAF), a women's rights group in Morocco, collected a million signatures for a petition urging a reform of the *moudawana*. The late King Hassan II referred the matter to a council of religious leaders, and in 1993, limited reforms were announced. After ascending to the throne after his father's death in 1999, King Mohammed VI appointed a commission which was charged with checking each article of the proposed reform against the Qur'an. If justification for change could be found in the sacred text, it was accepted. In 2004, the King announced the wide-ranging reform of Personal Status Code, *moudawana*. The King said the aim was to draw up a modern family law consistent with the spirit of "our tolerant religion" (Discours Royal, Site Officiel du Maroc).

It was Mohammed VI himself who first announced the reform of the Personal Status Code in the capital city of Rabat. The major aspects of the reform pertain to enhancing the rights and status of women. In essence, the reform changes the family from a unit presided over by a man to a unit with two equal partners before the law. Following is a brief summary, using common expressions instead of legal terms, of the main points of the Personal Status Code reform. The official text is available in Arabic and French but at the time of this printing, there is no official English translation of the legal text.[8]

Marriage age: The legal age of marriage for girls has been raised from fifteen to eighteen and now is the same as for men.

Polygamy: This practice permitted by Qur'an—has been outlawed except when a judge rules that there are significant reasons for a husband to take a second or third wife. Women are given a say in their husband's decision to marry a second wife: "Women have the right to impose a condition in the marriage contract preventing the husband from taking a second wife. If there were no conditions, the first wife should be summoned to secure her consent. The second wife should be informed that the husband was married to another woman and her consent should be obtained, and the first wife should be given the right to demand a divorce."

Repudiation: The Islamic practice of *talaq*, the right of a man to single-handedly repudiate his wife has been outlawed. This practice did not guarantee the livelihood for the repudiated woman and her children. The new law stipulates that divorce has to be granted by a court. "A new procedure for divorce has been established, requiring the court's prior authorization. Divorce cannot be registered until all money owed to the wife and the children has been paid in full by the husband." The law further states: "Divorce is the husband's prerogative but the wife may avail herself of this prerogative."

Divorce: The wife can ask for a divorce. Previously, a judge would not accept a request for divorce by a woman unless she could present a case of "suffering prejudice" and witnesses. A woman's request for a divorce will now be considered on its own merit without requiring witnesses.

Obedience: Previously, a woman's obedience to her husband was legally required. This provision was stricken from the Personal Status Code.

Inheritance: Whereas in the past, inheritance was patrilineal, the new law gives "the granddaughter and the grandson on the mother's side the right to inherit from their grandfather, as part of the legacy, just like the son's children." The same applies to inheriting from parents.

Guardianship: The wife no longer needs permission from a guardian (*wali*) in order to marry, which was required by the old law.

Civil Marriages: Marriages entered into outside of Morocco will be recognized by the new *moudawana,* provided two of the witnesses are Muslims.

Sharing of assets: Spouses may enter into a pre-nuptial agreement before marriage in order to ensure a fair sharing of acquired assets.

Child custody: In case of divorce, guardianship of children goes first to the mother, next to the father, next to the maternal grandmother or otherwise be decided by a court. Appropriate housing and child support must be guaranteed.

Children outside of marriage: The rights of children will be safeguarded in case the parents were not married. Before, children born out of wedlock did not have to be recognized by the father and hence the mother could not expect or claim child support.

Because of the male-centered nature of Moroccan society, the new law was explicitly described as not being a law that favors women. It was explained as reflecting the "true nature of a family law," namely the inclusion of all members of a family, father, mother and children. The reform was based on the concept of *ijtihad*, rightful interpretation of the Sacred Texts. In the words of King Muhammed VI:

> I cannot, in my capacity as Commander of the Faithful, authorize that which God has forbidden, nor can I forbid what the Lord has authorized. It is necessary that we are counseled by the intentions of the tolerant Islam which honors man and extols justice, equality and the harmonious co-existence, and to base ourselves on the homogeneity of the Malekite Code as well as on the concept of *ijtihad* which allows for Islam to be adapted to all places and all times, so as to formulate a modern Family Code which is in complete adherence with the spirit of our tolerant religion (Discours Royal, Site Officiel du Maroc).

The position of the King as both political and religious leader is particular to this country. Morocco has other traits that set it apart from other Muslim states. The reform of the Personal Status Code in Morocco has to be understood in the geographical, historical and cultural context of this North African kingdom and therefore, a few notes on the history follow below. It is however important to note that despite the particulars of the Moroccan nation, the 2004 legal reform reverberated throughout the Muslim world. The importance of this reform is reflected in the ongoing debates in many parts of the world where the role of Muslim women is discussed.

WEST OF EAST

Geographically, Morocco, as its Arabic name *Al Mamlakah al Maghribiyah* (The Kingdom of the West) indicates, is located on the farthest western end of the Muslim world. The Maghreb (literally: West) has seen itself historically in opposition to the Islamic *Mashrek* (literally: East). Ever since the first Arab incursions into the Maghreb under legendary Egyptian conqueror Uqba ben Nafi in the late seventh century, Morocco has developed its own Islamic identity. The country has a long history of keeping influences of Islamic empires to its east at bay. Unlike its neighbor Algeria, Morocco was never part of the Ottoman Empire.

Another distinguishing feature of Morocco is the sustained influence of its original Berber inhabitants. Various Berber (*Amazigh*) populations live in widely dispersed communities in the mountainous and desert regions throughout North Africa. At various times in history, Berbers have ruled Morocco. Unlike most population groups, Berbers have no common physical features. The black-skinned Tuareg nomads of the Sahara, often called the blue men of the desert, are Berbers just as the light-skinned, green-eyed, sedentary people of the Middle Atlas. It is variations of the *Tamazight* languages that provide the common bond between different Berber populations.

The unique Islamic society that has developed in this part of the Maghreb incorporates elements of the cultures of some of its earliest invaders. Some native Berber populations have variously embraced Judaism,[9] Christianity, and later Islam, all the while maintaining their own culture. I have seen Berber women in remote regions of Morocco making the sign of the Christian cross while at the same time invoking the name of Allah before starting to weave a blanket or carpet.

Successive Berber dynasties have ruled Morocco (and parts of southern Europe) during the golden age of Islam in the West from the Almoravids and Almohads in the twelfth and thirteenth centuries, to the Merinids and the Saadians from the thirteenth to the seventeenth centuries. At that time the reign of the Alaouis, the lineage from which the current monarch hails, began. The Alaouis originate from a family of Sufi holy men. Power has moved from urban centers along the Mediterranean coast into the hinterlands of the Atlas Mountains, with the center of power being located at some point in time in Marrakesh in the south under Ibn Tashfun in the twelfth century, in the Middle Atlas cities of Fès under Abu Hassan in the fourteenth century and in Meknès in the same region under Moulay Ismael in the seventeenth century, to Rabat in modern times.

While the mostly rural Berber communities have progressed according to their own rhythm, the urban centers have become increasingly arabized, sophisticated and prone to change. The particular Arab/Berber mix in Morocco is one of the distinguishing factors of this country. Today, the population is estimated to consist of about 60 percent Arab and 40 percent various Berber ethnicities who speak a variety of Berber languages.[10] However, there has been so much inter-marriage throughout the ages that Moroccans are sometimes referred to as "arabized Berbers."

RURAL-URBAN DIVIDE

Tension within Morocco today stems less from the Arab/Berber dichotomy, than from the economic and educational disparity between rural and urban areas. Life in the fast-paced, noisy, polluted economic capital of Casablanca is not much different from that in any industrialized city in the Western hemisphere. This is in sharp contrast to the quiet life in remote rural communities, where villagers—predominantly Berbers—still draw water from a communal well, their houses or goatskin tents are without electricity and the main means of transportation are donkeys.

Real and imagined differences between Arabs and Berbers were exploited during the four decades Morocco was a French protectorate. An important element in the development of Moroccan family law is the Berber *Dahir* (Royal Decree) of 1930 which the sultan of Morocco issued on behalf of the French colonial powers. Mounira Charrad, a U.S.-based sociologist, writes: "Exacerbating once again political and legal divisions between Berbers and Arabs, the decree reasserted the legitimacy of Berber customary law and tribal councils" (Charrad, 2001: 140). She describes the aim of the Berber decree as follows:

> The decree of 1930 was a continuation of the colonial policy of setting one part of Morocco against another. The French saw Berbers in the *bilad-al siba*[11] as potential allies. Catholic circles in Morocco believed that the distinctiveness of Berber customary law implied that Berber allegiance to Islam was shaky, even in the Islamisized areas. They entertained the notion that, with some encouragement, the Berbers could be weaned away from Islamic faith. (141)

However, French administrators had scant understanding of the complexity and heterogeneity of different Amazigh communities and simply grouped them together as "Berbers of the North" and "Berbers of the South." This lack of understanding made it virtually impossible to put an effective French administration in place.

In recent decades, the rural/urban dichotomy in Morocco comes into play again with the immigration of Moroccans to France. It was mostly Berbers from the poor, rural areas who crossed the Mediterranean to reach France in search of better living conditions. It is ironic that North Africans in France are often simply referred to as "Arabs" when in fact the largest contingents of North African immigrants hail from the rural Berber regions of the Rif mountains, the Middle or High Atlas regions in Morocco and Kabylia in Algeria. The majority of the women I spoke with in France traced their roots to a rural Berber region in Morocco.

After independence, the newly re-established monarchy used existing divisions to declare that family law differed from one ethnic group to another. From the viewpoint of nation-building, the absence of a uniform law that applied to all citizens alike fostered a sense of arbitrariness and uncertainty and rendered loyalty to palace the only constant. Charrad (2001) describes how the Moroccan monarchy after independence in 1956 used the family law to establish itself by drawing on regional tribal support as much as on the Arab/urban elite:

> The policy of family law after independence reflected the coalition between monarchy and tribe and the continued importance of kin-based solidarities in Morocco. Once victorious, the monarchy engaged in political actions and policies that protected—or avoided disturbing—the tribal order that provided it with its base for power. The policy on family law was part of this overall strategy. . . . The codification [of the Personal Status Code] institutionalized the model of the family as an extended patri-lineage based on agnatic ties, the kinship model that was the cornerstone of the tribal model. (147)

The first post-colonial monarchy took over the French divide–and–rule strategy. Existing rural/urban differences were exacerbated in an effort to exert control. The Personal Status Code was an important tool in this process.

A STEP IN THE RIGHT DIRECTION

Given the historic context, the reform of the Personal Status Code in Morocco represents a major societal shift and an altered religious understanding. It offers a degree of self-determination to women previously unheard of in this North African kingdom. It also has the potential of enhancing social cohesion by bringing the entire Moroccan population under one unified law. As this reform was implemented relatively recently, there has so far been little scholarly research on its long-term impact.

In Morocco, my goal was to find out how ordinary women perceived the legal reform. In France, my aim was to assess the degree of familiarity with the debate on the Personal Status Code reform and how these changes were viewed from the vantage point of women in France. In the following, we hear what individual women who are affected by these changes had to say.

Almost all women in Morocco and France welcomed the reform of the Personal Status Code. They felt it represented a "step in the right direction" or was part of an "evolution." However, most cautioned that a change of law was only a part of Morocco's move toward gender equality. Some women expressed concern that the new law was not entirely based on the Qur'an and could therefore impair Morocco's Islamic identity.

The main concern of women in both countries was how new laws in Morocco and in France affected their ability to assert control over their private and public lives. Though most did not care much about politics in their respective country, they followed with great interest legislation aimed at shaping the role of modern Muslim women in a changing world. This interest extended beyond the borders of their country of residence. Respondents in France followed the family law reform in Morocco just as their counterparts in Morocco kept informed about the ban on wearing "overt" religious insignia in French public schools. Due to the historic link between France and Morocco, mass media in Morocco cover events in France and French media frequently report on Morocco.

The reform in Morocco draws into question centuries-old customs concerning the roles of men and women. It mandates a new understanding of family and the role of women therein, with men and women now legally considered equal partners. With an increasing number of women entering the formal, documented workforce and playing a substantial role as wage earners in the family, a fundamental shift in the division of labor is already taking place. The Personal Status Code reform makes this transformation of women's role official by giving it a legal foundation.

While women in Morocco and France welcomed this momentous shift, they insisted that it was not only a matter of law, but a change of mentality and of culture was equally important. Modifying the law was an act of government that demonstrated a willingness of the ruling elite to set in motion a deeper societal change. A change of mentality among the population at large was seen as a slow process and one that required more of men than of women. This is because the reform has widely been viewed as curtailing men's rights and restricting their liberties, for example with regard to abolishing unilateral divorce (repudiation) and abolishing the clause that requires a woman's obedience to her husband. As one woman in Morocco put it: "The question for men is: what is in it for them? And quite frankly, from a man's point of view, not much."

King Mohammed VI presented the reform as in keeping "with our tolerant religion of Islam" and emphasized that it was based on *ijtihad*, rightful interpretation of the Qur'an. Critics of the reform, most notably certain Islamist groups, have argued that no one called to participate in a royal commission would dare to oppose guidelines provided by the monarch. Because such great emphasis was given to the Qur'anic basis for the reform, I wondered if women agreed with this assertion.

Opinions in Morocco were fairly equally divided among those who accepted the King's arguments and those who believed that religion actually had little to do with the reform. A fresh look at religious interpretation was seen as matter of social necessity. Said Farida, a young woman with a Master's degree in Business: "The question is not only if the new *moudawana* is based on the Qur'an, but we should ask ourselves if the old *moudawana* was based on the Qur'an. After all, the old *moudawana* had also been presented as the word of God. I don't believe that God changes, it must be our understanding that changes according to the times. This is normal for human beings." Farida felt it was not the religion of Islam that placed women in an inferior position to men in the first place. For her, discussion about the religious validity of the reform arose from a Moroccan cultural context, not from a genuine religious one. "But I understand that this is how the King has to present the reform, people would rebel if he said the law was altered purely for pragmatic reasons."

Laatifa, a woman wearing the *hijab* and on the fast track in a government department, echoed the opinion of the majority of respondents: "It is important that we stay true to our own cultural roots and the religion that forms the basis of our identity and of our family law." She said that Morocco should be more aware of the improvements to women's rights introduced by the Prophet during his lifetime instead of clinging to customs that had existed in North Africa before the arrival of Islam. Laatifa felt Morocco did not need to look to Europe or the United States to come to the conclusion that men and women were created equal. "People should read the Qur'an more carefully and not just take what suits them," she said. Laatifa emphasized that she wore the *hijab* out of religious conviction and to demonstrate her belief in the veracity of the revelation of the Prophet, gender equality included. Like most of her peers in Morocco, she did not view the *moudawana* reform through the lens of religion, but as a change born out of necessity. "We never really had a family law that was truly based on Islam." To her the reform marked a milestone in moving into a modern era.

Most women commended the King for having recognized that the Qur'an did not condone treating women as second-class citizens. He was frequently quoted as having said that living in harmony required equality. Yet most women were not sure just how quickly this reform would lead to a change in attitude, mentality and behavior. With few exceptions, young, educated professional women agreed that the Personal Status Code was at the heart of Moroccan society. Granting women substantially more rights also meant that Morocco's vision for the future had changed. "I feel now we have something to look forward to. If the *moudawana* can be reformed, other aspects of our society can be transformed too," said Lamiae in Casablanca.

At the same time, however, most of the women wondered just how quickly this reform would lead to a more deep-seated transformation of attitudes that underlie daily behavior. For some of the women, it was of paramount importance that legal change was framed within the context of Islam, because the identity of their country as an Islamic state was at stake. This position was voiced especially by women who felt close to Islamist organizations. They feared that Morocco would "lose its soul" if it implemented changes based on what they perceived as "Western models." They feared the real objective of the reform was to narrow the gap between Europe and this North African country.

JUSTICE AND BENEVOLENCE

The most vocal initial opposition to the reform of the *moudawana* was voiced by the largest Islamist[12] movement with a mass following in Morocco, the non-violent *Al Adl wa Ihsane* (Justice and Benevolence), founded by Sufi Sheikh Abdesslam Yassine.[13] This Islamist group first opposed the reform as not being based on the Qur'an; later it expressed concern that the reform did not go far enough in changing all aspects of law, civil and criminal, that discriminate against women. Because Islamist ideas echoed in some of my respondents' assessments of the family law reform, I sought out Nadia Yassine, spokesperson of the movement. When I asked her about the reform, she explained her basic premise, that religion is meant to uphold an ideal whereas politics deals with physical circumstances. Her movement intended to bring those two realms as closely together as possible.

Madame Yassine is in her late-forties, university-educated, highly articulate and married with four children and a growing number of grandchildren. She described herself as a "militant neo-Sufi"[14] as opposed to a feminist. She lives in a modest apartment in Salé, Rabat's twin city across the river. Because of Yassine's celebrity status and her controversial pronouncements, meeting with her aroused intense interest among my respondents. Some encouraged my visit because they believed Yassine could lay bare the complexities of the new law and explain its advantages and shortcomings. Others saw it as a waste of my time to talk to this—or any other—Islamist because they believed Islamists had nothing of substance to offer with regard to progress in Morocco. Islamists are presumed to advocate a return to the past rather than support a move forward. Some women insisted that I meet with them again after my *rendez-vous* with Nadia Yassine because they were keen to receive an account from an outsider as to what a leading member of "Justice and Benevolence" had to say. They thought Moroccan mass media often misrepresented the views of this particular Islamist movement in an effort to discredit it.

I had come to know Nadia Yassine during the time I lived in Morocco and had been a guest at her house in subsequent annual visits to North Africa. Because of her precarious status as a leading member of an organization that has a history of openly criticizing the King, a crime punishable by imprisonment, *Al Adl wa Ihsane* has officially been shunned.

Nadia Yassine's residence is located near the prison of Salé where her father had been incarcerated under the late King Hassan II. She usually advised me to wait next to the prison gate where she would send someone to meet and guide me to her home through the maze of unnamed streets. The effect of having to ask a taxi driver to take me to the prison was not lost on me. Generally, taxi drivers pretended not to understand my request, and more than once, I had to change vehicles because a driver felt uncomfortable taking a foreign woman to such a notorious site.

In her home, when no men are present, Madame Yassine lets down her hair and wears jewelry and make-up. This is in sharp contrast to her stark appearance in public where she covers her hair under a simple, dark veil, wears no jewelry and, other than the customary black henna around her eyes, no make-up.

During the decade that her father, Sheikh Yassine, spent in jail and under house arrest, Nadia Yassine rose to a leading role in his movement though she holds no official position other than "spokesperson." Eloquent, she is well-equipped to explain her fathers' message to the wider world. She resents Western-inspired reforms on the grounds that they impose a foreign agenda on the Moroccan people. However, she conceded that the change of the *moudawana* was based on a realistic assessment of a changing reality in Morocco yet had "precious little" to do with new insights into the Qur'an. Her critique of the reform was based on an assessment that it addresses the needs of an elite minority and not of the majority of Moroccans. As an example she cited a new legal provision that makes it easier for women to obtain a passport. "Is this an issue of national concern, given that more than 60 percent of our women are illiterate and live in the rural areas where they travel on foot or on donkeys from one village to the next?" she asked provocatively. "There is no new law that mandates building schools in the rural areas, there are no jobs for university graduates who do not have powerful connections. There is no proper health care in the rural areas and there are no realistic plans to rectify the glaring social inequalities. We are a poor country, a third world country as you say, yet our king is one of the richest men in the world. How can that be called an Islamic society?" With this rhetoric question Nadia Yassine was raising a recurring theme of her movement, namely questioning the legitimacy of the monarchy. For her, transformation of a highly stratified society and elimination of a rigid class system were the most pressing issues. In terms almost reminiscent of Marxist rhetoric, she decried the immense wealth of the King and that of a tiny, privileged elite which contrasts sharply with an average annual per capita income of 530 U.S. dollars for the majority of the population (United Nations Country Report, 2003).

Nadia Yassine also took issue with some more fundamental changes introduced in the new Personal Status Code, such as the raising of the marriage age and the abolition of polygamy. Again, referring to the majority of Moroccan women, she argued that raising the marriage age from fifteen to eighteen did not present advantages for the large number of rural, poor, under-educated women. For rural girls, early marriage offered protection and a safe way to grow into adulthood. She cited the problem of child labor that has widely been recognized as a major social ill, particularly the large numbers of *petites bonnes*, girls as young as seven years, who work as domestic servants and are prone to exploitation and sexual abuse at the hands of their employers. According to Yassine, early marriage, even as a second wife, offered a better prospect for a young girl in those circumstances. Furthermore, she feared that the abolition of polygamy would reduce chances of poor, rural girls to get married and, consequently, some girls might end up as *petites bonnes* or even as prostitutes.[15]

On the issue of the *wali*, guardian, Nadia Yassine explained the Islamist position as follows: Without a profound change of mentality, Moroccan women who are not under the protection of a *wali* would be susceptible to abuse. Men could easily prey on women if they did not have to fear retribution from a male guardian. The system of a *wali* was needed as long as the majority of Moroccan women remained illiterate, poor and without adequate access to the legal system. For this outspoken woman, the *moudawana* reform was not only pandering to a minority urban elite, but also "putting sand in the eyes of the West" by appearing to "modernize" the country in accordance with Western standards while ignoring the most pressing issues affecting the nation. She repeated that more urgent than a reform of the family law were improvements in education and employment opportunities. Her movement maintains that Islamic countries such as Morocco can reform from within and need not follow the lead of the Western world to address social ills. After all, she contended, the West was not responsible for the large-scale corruption that hindered genuine development in Morocco. Yassine felt her movement offered a better vision for the future of her country because it addressed the needs of the entire population and on an individual level took "the whole person, mind, soul and physical welfare into consideration."

During one visit, as we chatted in Nadia Yassine's living room, sipping strong mint tea and eating home-made Moroccan cookies, women "of the movement" came in, sat with us for a while and offered their own comments. All were veiled, articulate, educated, professional women who dedicated their spare time—and part of their income—to Islamist causes. Some were involved in campus outreach programs, where the activist stance of *Al Adl wa Ihsane* has attracted a large following among students. Of the women I interviewed on different university campuses throughout Morocco, quite a few were in some way connected or at least sympathetic to this Islamist movement. Even among women who did not wear the *hijab*, the movement enjoyed support because it put its finger on one of the main problems facing Morocco, namely widespread, high-level corruption.

Nadia Yassine also addressed the difficulties with the implementation of the new Personal Status Code caused by poorly trained judges, ill-equipped administrators and an illiterate population who was un- or misinformed about the reform. She had been to court herself to observe some of the proceedings required of petitioners to obtain a special dispensation to marry under the new legal age of eighteen. "The girls have to appear in front of a male judge and his assistants. They are asked in the presence of their fathers if they are still virgins and if they are willing to have their private parts checked by a medical examiner to confirm the veracity of their statements." These humiliating interrogations were tactics designed to discourage applications for early marriage, Yassine asserted. Other respondents had told me that families of young girls resorted to using the birth certificate of an older sister to get married. Instead of eliminating the root causes that necessitate early marriage, judges harassed petitioners in hopes that word would filter back to the rural areas that a trip to a court in the city had little chance of success. Training of female judges and grassroots campaigns were needed to explain the new laws instead of relying on the "typical Moroccan system of intimidation and fear," Yassine said.

During a visit the following year, our conversation turned from the *moudawana* reform to other topics of interest. Nadia Yassine had only recently been granted a passport and for the first time in her life had the opportunity to travel abroad. She recalled how surprised she was to find that most Americans she met were people of faith and that her Muslim headscarf had been of no obvious concern or interest to anyone. "I found a Bible in my hotel room and when I turned on the television, I saw all these channels with preachers." As I was accompanied by one of my teenage daughters, Nadia inquired about her preferences in music, movies, books and fashion. She asked my daughter if she dated boys and whether she had been exposed to drugs. She was intrigued to hear that a thoroughly Western outlook, including a preference for pop music and—by Islamist standards—immodest clothing,[16] did not correlate with loose morals or a lack of values. She admitted that her perception of the United States had changed as a result of her travels. As much as Islamists are misunderstood by the West, so is the West by Islamists.

Since obtaining a passport, Yassine has become a highly sought after guest speaker at international symposia and academic conferences. However because of her movement's opposition to the monarchy, some international organizations withdrew their invitations as a result of pressure from the Moroccan government. Throughout our conversations, she emphasized that her movement was committed to non-violence and had nothing in common with terrorists who claim to act in the name of Islam.

Nadia Yassine articulated the position of women I interviewed and who expressed reservations about the *moudawana* reform. At the same time, she had also echoed important issues raised by those who did support the legal changes, most importantly corruption, unequal application of the law and an entrenched rigid patriarchal system.

The majority of women agreed that the Personal Status Code and law generally depended on implementation by courts and judges. "If the mentality of the judges does not change, the new law is meaningless," said Mina, an aspiring manager in an international firm in Casablanca. "Anyone can buy a verdict here and, consequently, well-connected, wealthy men can obtain a ruling no matter what the new law says. Less fortunate men and women are at the mercy of old-fashioned judges, whose decisions they would not know how to appeal." Still, Mina maintained that the reformed family law was an important step forward for "the Moroccan woman."

THE MOROCCAN WOMAN

In my conversations in Morocco, it was striking how often "the Moroccan woman" was invoked. In the West, with its emphasis on individualism, differentiation and recent adversity to stereotyping, one would not speak of "the French woman," "the American woman," etc. But in this North African country, it is common to hear references to "the Moroccan woman." The reform, as I repeatedly heard, would allow "the Moroccan woman" to find her place in the modern world.

When probing deeper just who "the Moroccan woman" was, it became evident that my respondents were keenly aware of ethnic and especially class differences in their country and of the gulf that separates urban from rural women. There was some disagreement over who would benefit most from the new laws. Some argued that urban women were the primary beneficiaries because they had access to information and could claim their new rights, whereas rural, illiterate women remained at the mercy of those interpreting the changes for them. Others said that lower-class women stood to gain most because upper-class women already enjoyed many of provisions contained in the new law. Most agreed that the term "the Moroccan woman" did not capture the diversity of women in this country and that it presumed a sense of solidarity and shared experience which did in fact not exist. "The Moroccan woman" was invoked as a manner of speaking rather than capturing a non-existing commonality among Moroccan women.

During one of my excursions to the more remote areas of Morocco unreachable by road, I asked women who lived in a small settlement without running water and electricity what they thought about the Personal Status Code reform. They responded laughingly: "We are trying to survive. Our main interest is in the price of sheep, the price of wool and what everyday items cost in the *souk*."[17] Family law—old or new—was an issue for educated townsfolk. Up here in the mountains, where goats and sheep roam freely and the sky is so blue it looks almost artificial, marriages were arranged in accordance with age-old customs. There were no written contracts and divorce was mediated by an elder. Some of the smaller mountain communities I visited were noteworthy for their absence of men. When I inquired about husbands, fathers, brothers, I was told: "They are out herding sheep," or: "They are in town, working, looking for work or doing things." Men trekked home on weekends and the little communities seemed to function quite well in their absence. In keeping with the customary hospitality, I was invited to sit down on a homespun carpet in the simple abode and through an interpreter one woman told me the story of a recent divorce in this Atlas Mountain hamlet consisting of about twenty families. The husband, she said, was responsible for selling women's woven blankets and carpets in town and was found to be cheating with the revenue. "That's when we decided that some of us women needed to learn to read and write and do calculations. We now handle our finances ourselves and the elders separated the couple. Nobody went to town for this divorce. We handle these things up here by ourselves" the woman told me. She called out from the doorway of her hut and a young woman came running up the grass-covered hill. My hostess proudly introduced me to the new official bookkeeper of her hamlet who proudly showed me her pocket calculator and a notebook where she had recorded all transactions. My brief excursion into the Atlas Mountains brought home the continued urban/rural divide and the distance, not only geographically, that separates educated women in the cities from illiterate women in the countryside. "The Moroccan woman" indeed had many faces.

LAW, CULTURE AND RELIGION

In the cities, women saw the *moudawana* reform as a means of bringing Morocco more in line with its European neighbors to the north, while others pointed out that the model of reform of the Personal Status Code was to be found to the east, in Tunisia. "For us, the status of Tunisian women is the role model," said Zineb, a mid-level civil servant. "It has taken us more than forty years to catch up with our neighbor in the Maghreb," she added.

With regard to the legal status of women, Tunisia has long been ahead of most Arab or Muslim countries. Shortly after independence from France in 1958, Tunisia's Personal Status Code was single-handedly changed by its first president Habib Bourguiba, a French-educated lawyer. Polygamy was abolished and Bourguiba advocated discarding the veil for Tunisian women. He also promoted mandatory education for girls. My respondents in Morocco and in France frequently pointed to Tunisia as a model for the Personal Status Code. Most expressed that family laws should be compatible worldwide.

The fact that it took Morocco close to sixty years since independence to craft a new Personal Status Code is in line with anthropologist Hammoudi's assertion that the Moroccan elite is inherently averse to fast and dramatic change, especially changes that threaten its own, immensely privileged status (Hammoudi, 1997).

Compounding such adversity to change was the fact that distinctions between religion, local cultures and traditions are often unclear. Most women told me that though Morocco was an Islamic country, traditions had their roots in pre-Islamic Berber and Arab cultures. Women who had traveled abroad experienced the discrepancy between religion and culture first-hand especially when they encountered Muslims from other regions of the world. A case in point was a young science professor who upon completion of her doctoral degree had accepted a teaching position in Saudi Arabia. Though she described herself as a devout Muslim and wore a headscarf, she was shocked to see how the Prophet's country of birth "had perverted what He stood for." Breaking her contract, she left Saudi Arabia after only one year, chiefly because she considered the way women were treated in that country was in contradiction to what she believed to be an acceptable interpretation of the Qur'an. Her experience in Saudi Arabia led her to take a closer look at the customs and traditions in her own country. After returning to Morocco, the young professor became active in social causes in hopes of contributing to the development of an Islamic society the way she understood it.

Several respondents who did not have an opportunity to travel abroad said that their study of the Qur'an and the history of Islam had led them to an understanding that new interpretations according to changing social circumstances were acceptable. They argued that it was reasonable to present the reform as being based on *ijtihad*, rightful interpretation of the Qur'an. Said Sadia, who worked for an international aid organization in Rabat: "Slavery for example is a practice not prohibited in the Qur'an. The Qur'an contains several passages that admonish believers to treat slaves properly and justly, however without stating that the practice itself is an abomination. Still, slavery has long been outlawed in Morocco—as it should be." Abolishing slavery, according to Sadia, should not be interpreted as a sign of abandoning the tenets of Islam, but of the need for constant re-examination of the sacred text. Another example was child marriage (that is, under the age of fifteen), again a practice mentioned in the Qur'an but now outlawed in Morocco. Some argued that the *moudawana* reform should not be taken to mean that the country was adopting a more relaxed attitude toward religion nor as a move toward a more secular position.

Women in France for the most part did not pay close attention to the religious dimension of the Personal Status Code reform. Having grown up in a *laïc* (secular) state, they accepted that laws were reformed based on changing social circumstances. Most had followed with great interest news about the reform in Morocco. Whether or not the changes were based on the Qur'an made little difference in their overall assessment. Most expressed that this reform was long overdue and several used the exact same expression as their counterparts in Morocco, namely that this was "a step in the right direction." They understood that the reform all but abolished polygamy, made it possible for women to obtain a divorce and no longer required women to submit to their husbands. They said they were happy and relieved about the reform because they believed eventually the new laws would make life easier for women in Morocco. Like their counterparts in Morocco, women in France said a change in mentality and everyday behavior was even more important than legal reforms.

A more detailed assessment of the reform was offered by women who professed to be Islamists. They said the new law had to be examined "point by point." Jihane, a graduate student in Paris, said: "Polygamy is permitted by Islam, so I am against abolishing it. On the other side, divorce is also allowed by the Qur'an, so to make it easier for women to obtain a divorce is an acceptable change. It is also a good thing to raise the marriage age from fifteen to eighteen because the Qur'an does not give a specific age at which girls should get married." When I asked her if she could envision herself in a polygamous marriage, she hesitated and eventually would offer nothing more than "it depends." For this sociology student, the most important question was: "What is the vision behind this law? What vision does the King have for his country? Is this an occidental vision? One should ask these questions. In Islam, we are taught to be open, to ask questions, to be critical." Jihane was not alone with this view. I met other women, all of whom were wearing the headscarf, who also said they did not trust the King's motives and believed he would do anything to enhance his standing in the Western world. Nevertheless, for the most part, they welcomed the Personal Status Code reform: "This is just politics. If the outcome is good for the people, I am content. Islam is an easy religion. It does not want to make life difficult for people," said Jihane.

Several women in France recounted personal family stories to illustrate problems with the way family matters were handled in accordance with customary practices. Some recalled how the separation of their parents had left their mother in dire financial straits. Siham, a thirty-two-year-old teacher, was old enough to remember that her father had simply repudiated his wife. Her parents never obtained a legal divorce even after her father had moved in with another woman. Though this separation had occurred in France, Siham's illiterate mother was not familiar with French law and therefore accepted repudiation by her husband because she knew this practice was in accordance with Moroccan customs. Said Siham: "When you are left in such a desperate situation, you don't much care if laws are justified by the scripture. My mother always told me that I should not let something like this happen to me." Like Siham, other women recounted similar experiences in their families with practices justified by the old Personal Status Code. I found women in France to be more at ease recounting such painful family histories. This can be attributed in part to the fact that despite their difficulties in France, immigrant parents had to assure themselves that they had made the right decision by relocating to a European country. Most women told me that their (immigrant) mothers had always encouraged them "to study hard and make something of their lives in France."

In Morocco women were less forthcoming concerning family stories pertaining to the old Personal Status Code. However, when they did tell me of such incidents, they were remarkably similar to the ones I heard in France: a relative had been repudiated by her husband who proceeded to marry another woman without paying alimony or child support; an aunt or a cousin had wished to divorce her husband because of his repeated infidelity but could not obtain a divorce; a divorce left a woman impoverished because assets which had accrued during the marriage were not shared after the separation; and there were stories about women who had been coerced by their guardians or families to marry someone they did not want to share their lives with.

Overall, women in Morocco and in France were cautiously optimistic about the reform. "Things move so slowly here," said one young woman in Morocco, "it will take time before everyone in the country understands that things have changed." As an example of slow or half-hearted implementation, some referred to urban women's groups who had contributed to drawing up the reform and who had heralded it, but were now widely accused of not doing enough to propagate it in small towns and rural areas, confirming the Islamists' assertion that the reform catered to an urban elite. Most agreed that implementation of the reform had been rocky. "There has been some disappointment. The reform did not yet lead to wide-spread empowerment for women as some might have hoped," said a young computer engineer in Rabat. The government itself recognized difficulties with implementation and organized a conference in 2005 entitled: "One year after: What went wrong?"

Women younger than twenty-five years of age feared some very personal repercussions of the reform: the difficulty of finding a husband. "If a man is not allowed to discipline his wife, he may not want to marry at all," said Amal, a university student in Rabat. "Of course, I don't want to be beaten, but I'd rather have that than not getting married at all." Though I had not raised the issue of domestic violence at all, fear was a theme that recurred frequently. Some said one of the reasons for which they wanted their parents to take a leading role in finding a husband for them was that this would offer them a certain sense of protection in case difficulties arose in the marriage. "Difficulties," they specified, meant infidelity and physical violence. In conversations with more mature, married women it seemed that fear had given way to a sense of fatalism as their husband's infidelities were taken as a fact of life.

Because the new law stipulates that assets accrued during the marriage will have to be divided evenly upon divorce, some younger women worried that this would lead men to be apprehensive about getting married. "Morocco is in a state of uncertainty after the reform," said Aziza, another university student in Morocco, reiterating that a change in mentality would have to follow the legal changes. "Young men are afraid of getting married now. They don't know what to expect any more now that the law is no longer on their side." However, according to government statistics published in the summer of 2007, the number of marriages has gone up over the past three years while the number of divorces has decreased.

When I asked women in France what long-term changes they expected as a result of the Personal Status Code reform, the issue of fear resurfaced again. Fear was understood as an integral element of marriage and family life and one which carried over into other areas. Muslim women in France felt that the new law eventually would lead to a situation where women no longer needed to live in fear. An altered concept of family was expected to endow women with more confidence and also result in more freedom to pursue a professional career. However, most said they only had a cursory understanding of specifics of the new *moudawana* and that their assessment was based on a comparison with what they observed from having grown up in France. "I have lived in France all my life, so I know women have more rights here than in Morocco. The reform there should have taken place long ago, but I am doubtful it will bring about real, substantial change—at least not right away," said Lila, a teacher in Paris.

Repeatedly I was told that the life of Moroccan women was marked by fear: fear of their fathers, of their husbands, of what their neighbors might say, fear to express themselves openly. As with stories about experiences with the old *moudawana,* it is possible that because women in France could evaluate goings-on in Morocco from a distance, they cast a more critical eye on their parents' home country. When asked how they had come by this assessment of fear, they said they had witnessed this during their visits to Morocco. They recalled how they had been constantly admonished to dress or behave a certain way, told what and what not to say in public; they had felt their every move was scrutinized. "Women are just not free, they think that living in fear is some kind of religious duty—or maybe just a fact of life," said Fatma, a graduate student in Paris. "This new law will free them from this pervasive sense of fear and guilt. So often women in Morocco think that it is their fault when things don't work out, that it is *mektoub* (destiny) if bad things happen to them. In time the changes that will come as a result of the *moudawana* reform will allow women to shake off that sense of fatalism and step out and take charge of their lives."

The old family law obligated a husband to provide food, clothing and shelter for his wife, while she was expected to defer to him and obey. Women in France expressed relief that the new law raised the marriage age, abolished polygamy and adjusted divorce proceedings. Many said that their mothers had been married before the age of sixteen to their fathers through an arranged marriage. "I don't know if my mother was ever in love. She serves my father, she obeys him, she followed him to France, she had five children and she raised us. The new law will free women in Morocco to make their own decisions about marriage. This will allow them a whole new understanding of marriage, and that is an incredible change in Morocco," said Naima, a woman in her late twenties, who left home and had not been in contact with her family because her father had disapproved of her choosing a career over early marriage and her insistence on finding her own spouse.

Unlike their counterparts in Morocco, who said mainly men needed to change, women in France said that both sexes needed to modify their attitudes. "Women have lived with this system for so long, that is what they know, what they are used to. They may not know how to deal with their new rights and freedom and this can cause some confusion and conflict," said Malika, an airport security manager.

Others in France said that an organizational structure needed to be put into place to allow women to understand the new laws and their implications. "Women will need a lot of help, I think that is why so many new women's organizations sprout up all over Morocco," said Mouna, a lawyer in Paris. "This is a good time for women of Moroccan origin who have grown up abroad or studied in Europe to go to Morocco and help so that these reforms can take root in the society at large."

As in Morocco, French women too pointed to the example of Tunisia, where the family law had been changed in 1958. "Tunisian women have almost the same rights than women in France," said Fatima, a high school teacher in Paris. "And that is a Muslim country as well, so we should not make such a strong connection between Islam and what is going on in a given country," she added. They did however point out that Tunisia overall was not a free country and therefore rights of women and men were equally restricted concerning political and religious freedoms.

Because my respondent's working-class families had experienced some of the worst aspects of Moroccan society, they distinguished more clearly between religion and social reality than women in Morocco who often were members of the middle or upper class. Their immigrant parents had experienced inequality before the law, inequality of educational and professional opportunities, absence of social mobility and a pervasive sense of being ignored by the government. All these factors contributed to their exodus. It is therefore understandable that children of immigrants did not express a particular affinity or pride for an "Islamic state" as some of the professional women in Morocco had done. Though they cherished their Moroccan heritage, they considered Morocco a country held back by ancient customs and traditions. For them it was of little consequence whether the new family law was in keeping with the Qur'an. Nevertheless, they understood that the King had to present it that way to garner the support of the population. "The new King is young and progressive, he has a lot of good ideas and he wants to position Morocco to develop closer ties with the European Union. He is watching closely what is happening in Turkey and the changes Turkey is required to make to be even considered for entrance into the European Union. This reform shows that he is serious about modernizing his country and moving it closer to Europe," said Khadija, adding, "of course he has to keep Morocco's Islamic identity intact but that is just politics." Khadija works for a government-supported legal aid organization in the heart of Paris and displayed a keen interest in family law.

As women in France speculated on the changes that might come as a result of the family law reform, some differences in outlook between women in France and in Morocco became evident. Hiba, a young Moroccan diplomat charged with advising embassy and consulate personnel on how to apply the Personal Status Code reform in their dealings with Moroccan expatriates in Europe illustrates one reason for this difference: "These Moroccans [in France] are really funny. They live in a time warp. Their understanding of our society is based on the Morocco of thirty to forty years ago. Their mentality does not really exist anymore here, at least not among young, educated people in the cities." Hiba grew more and more animated as she compared herself and her peers with the second generation in France: "In many respects we are more modern than they are. For example, we believe women's rights come out of Islam, we believe we need more female judges, ambassadors, business executives. Young people of Moroccan origin in Europe don't have such high ambitions. They are so concerned with fitting into French society and feel they have to become more French before they can move up in that society. They think the Personal Status Code reform takes us out of the Stone Age, but they don't see all the other changes taking place in Morocco." In a provocative tone, she added: "How many female Muslim judges are there in France? How many high level Muslims—men or women—in government? Are there any French ambassadors who are Muslim? Surely, in the United States there are blacks in all levels of society but in France the Muslim minority still has a long way to go." For Hiba, the goals of Moroccan women are on a different scale than those of women of Moroccan origin in France. The headscarf ban in France illustrates the particular problematic of Muslims in France a theme to which we will now turn.

FRANCE UNVEILED

The reform of the family law in Morocco was seen as a reflection of social and cultural changes that most of my respondents regarded as progressive. In France legislation on select religious insignia, chiefly the Muslim headscarf in public schools, appeared more indicative of a trend toward conservative interpretations of the law. Women in France and Morocco found it considerably more difficult to assess the French ban on overt religious symbols which also was announced in 2004. The exact word in the law is "ostensiblement" for which overt is the closest rendering in English. There is no precise description in the law as to what is considered "overt." The wearing of Christian crosses, for example, is not disallowed and therefore the law can be interpreted to be directed at the wearing of the Muslim headscarf.

Women in Morocco and France were troubled by the perceived message implicit in this law because it was taken as an affront against Muslims in general and Muslim women in particular. Even those inclined to support the ban felt that the French government should have employed a less confrontational approach.

Since 1989,[18] the appearance of the *hijab* (Muslim headscarf) in French public schools has opened the most impassioned debate over the role of *laïcité* in French society since the separation of church and state was put into effect at the beginning of the twentieth century. Conflicts between Muslim adolescents and school authorities have extended beyond the schools to involve intellectuals, political actors, and religious authorities.

France, historically a predominantly Roman Catholic country, has wrestled to find a balance between secular and religious powers for centuries. The French Revolution in 1789 ended the Catholic Church's domination over the state. About a decade later, in 1801, Napoleon came to an agreement with the Catholic Church under a concordat which brought the church under state auspices and confined it to religious matters. A landmark law was passed in 1905 that instituted the separation of church and state and marked the beginning of *laïcité*, comparable but not the same as the separation of church and state in the U.S. This law was at its inception intended to keep the influence of the Catholic Church at bay. The past decades have put it to the test with the increasing visibility of Muslims within the hexagon, epitomized by the appearance of young Muslim women wearing headscarves. Once politicians and courts were called upon to legislate or rule on specific issues concerning the Muslim headscarf, the "headscarf debate" became a widespread public issue in France. The most publicized events revolve around the question of whether pupils in public schools may wear Muslim headscarves; other issues have also arisen, such as whether a company may fire an employee for covering her head at work. In 1989, when the world was stunned by the fall of the Berlin Wall and the subsequent end of communism, French media were preoccupied with the case of two girls from Creil who were suspended from school because they refused to abide by their school's rule and remove their headscarves. The French Conseil d'Etat, France's highest administrative court, ruled that religious signs are allowed in schools as long as they are not "ostentatoire" (ostentatious). As the Conseil d'Etat did not consider Islamic headscarves to be "ostentantoires," it was permissible for schoolgirls to wear them provided they did not contravene the law forbidding acts which "constitute an act of pressure, provocation, proselytism, or propaganda." Again in 2003 two teenage girls, this time from Aubervilliers, an industrial suburb of Paris, made headlines when they refused to take off their headscarves.

In 2004 the French government hoped to put an end to the headscarf debate and signed into law a ruling that would ban all overt religious symbols from public schools. This includes the Muslim headscarf, large crosses (the exact size is not specified), the turban worn by male members of the Sikh community and the yarmulke. The *Journal Officiel de la Republique Française*, dated March 15, 2004 (Loi no 2004-228)[19] and signed by then President Jacques Chirac, states:

> In the schools, including middle and high schools, the wearing of signs or clothes by which students manifestly and ostentatiously demonstrate adherence to a religious faith is forbidden. This rule requires putting in place a disciplinary procedure to be preceded by a dialogue with the student.

The interdiction on wearing a Muslim headscarf in public schools is seen by its proponents as an affirmation of France's commitment to separation of the religious from the secular sphere. This time the law is not directed at the Catholic Church but at France's second largest religion, Islam. Though Muslims have resided in France in large numbers for decades, they have lived on the periphery of mainstream French society. With second- and third-generation North Africans entering public schools, universities and public life in general,

Muslims are increasingly seen as a force to be reckoned with. According to Joycelyne Cesari, a French political scientist, the first wave of immigrants in the 1950s and 1960s introduced a "temporary Islam" into modern French society. In recent years however, France is confronted with a "stabilized religion to which adherents voluntarily subscribe and which has to be recognized" (Cesari, 1999).

Cesari observes a renewed Islamization whereby young French Muslims are looking for ways to assert their cultural and religious affinity which their parents' generation practiced in the shadows of mainstream culture. This trend can be observed among upwardly socially mobile young people. Cesari (1999) based her research on in-depth interviews with young French Muslims of immigrant origins. She describes the upwardly mobile as the ones who most openly embrace an Islamic identity: "Students, but also vendors and craftsmen are the categories in which Islamization of society is most noticeable and that is one of the surprises of this inquiry" (74). However, it is not clear how street vendors could be categorized as "upwardly mobile."

These young Muslims who have been forced to feel their differentness all their lives now re-assert the role assigned to them by the majority culture, and as a result, more and more young women wear the *hijab*. This self-assertion in turn is perceived as a provocation to the French state and its notions of *laïcité*, the strict separation of church and state.

Soheib Bencheikh, *mufti* (canon lawyer who can formulate a formal legal opinion) of the mosque in Marseille, points out that the concept of *laïcité* does not exist in the Arabic language. He insists that this is in fact a religious term which derives from the Catholic lexicon wherein "lay" people are non-ordained members of a Catholic congregation. Hence, ironically, the term *laïcité* itself has a distinct religious connotation which implicitly weakens the separation of the religious from the state (Bencheikh, 1998: 29). Even though Bencheikh questions the basic premise of *laïcité*, he nevertheless asserts that Islam in France enjoys a freedom not found anywhere in the Muslim world because, "political manipulation does not enter into religious reflections, the French law applies to all citizens equally" (ibid.: 273). Because of this emphasis on *laïcité*, France does not encourage public recognition of Islam. Arkoun argues that France is overemphasizing its secular nature at its own peril. "This combative secularism employed in the service of a specific political project—construction in France of a Republic that is 'one and indivisible'—neglects one of its own founding principles, that of philosophic openness to the study of all human channels for the production of meaning" (Arkoun, 2002: 96).

Some sociologists argue that the ban on the headscarf contradicts basic human rights which guarantee freedom of religion (Guénif-Souilamas, personal interview, May 2004). Others like journalist and author Fawzia Zouari are warning that the headscarf issue is threatening to tear France apart. Though Muslim feminists who do not cover their heads insist they have "no particular sympathy for the headscarf," they strongly advocate their co-religionists' right to express their faith (Zouari, 2004: 5). According Azouz Begag, sociologist and novelist who from 2005 to 2007 occupied a position equivalent to a Minister of Equal Opportunities in France,[20] the role of women is at the heart of the conflict between secular French society and its large Muslim minority. He ascribes the banning of the headscarf to a "fear of Islam," which will lead to a further isolation of Muslim youth. This will result in greater solidarity of second-generation members—believers and non-believers alike—of the Maghrebi immigrant community with the culture and religion of their ancestors (Begag, 2003: 100).

Khosrokhavar (1997) speaks of a distinct "feminine French Islam" of which the headscarf is a particular expression:

> The visible expression of French feminine Islam is the headscarf. In France, this signifies noticeable differences from mainstream French society. . . . In effect, the French headscarf has become increasingly popular among young girls who have attended French public schools since early childhood. They are in fact more deeply inculcated with French mentality and express themselves in highly sophisticated French, more so than one might imagine. (97)

In *L'une voilée, l'autre pas* (One Veiled, the Other Not) two French Muslim women of immigrant origins spar with each other over the issue of the veil. Dounia Bouzar, first female member of the French Council for Muslim Affairs (*Conseil français du Culte Musulman* CFCM), and Saïda Kada, self-described militant feminist of the women's organization "*Femmes françaises et musulman engagées*" (roughly translated: Active French Muslim Women), present their opposing viewpoints. Their jointly authored collection of essays includes testimonies of young French women who explain why they do or do not cover themselves in public. Bouzar opposes the *hijab* while Kada, covered herself, supports the headscarf of her co-religionists. As divided as they are on the headscarf, they agree on several points of importance, for instance that men should not rule on that issue. Bouzar and Kada (2003) write:

> French people who profess to be Muslim today look for a place in a universe where the rules are still made mostly by men for men. They no longer want to be identified by prescribed behaviors legitimized by a prefabricated Islam, modeled around male needs. (37)

Bouzar quotes the previously cited Bencheikh who makes the case that women are not compelled by the Qur'an to cover their heads. The purpose of the veil or the headscarf is to offer protection to women. In this day and age, Bencheikh (1998) argues, education is the single most important shield of protection for women:

> If the Qur'an recommends the veil, it is with the sole objective to preserve the dignity and the personality of women according to the means which were available at the time of the Revelation. If, today, the same means no longer serve the same goal, one should not insist on this but look for something else. Paradoxically, that which most safeguards the personality and the future of young women today is the public (secular) school which is at the same time free and mandatory. (144)

On the other side, Kada draws on the writings of Tariq Ramadan (2003) who insists on the continued relevance of the headscarf, the actual piece of fabric, for Muslim women. Ramadan feels that Muslim women need to be free to uphold their own traditions in the face of secular, Western influences: "The veil is a prescription based on freedom. Don't obey anything but your conscience!" In Ramadan's view, a woman's conscience should eventually direct her to wear the headscarf. In their essays, Bouzar and Kada (2003) place the *hijab* in a historical and cultural context. Kada stresses the notion of continuity:

> The veil came into existence *for* women and not *against* them. At the time of the Revelation, there was a need for this to assure their protection. One needed a sign so that they [the men of that time] respected women and stopped to assault them. (33)

For Kada, faith in the revelation of the Prophet is demonstrated outwardly by following the customs initiated by Mohammed. Bouzar, on the other side believes that the veil or the headscarf have to be understood within a specific historical context. As social circumstances change over time, the need for certain practices has to be re-examined. Bouzar suggests searching for the meaning behind practices like the wearing of a headscarf, and evaluating them in terms of their intended meaning, which according to Bouzar is to ensure the God-given equality between men and women.

Any dispute revolving around a religious question is complicated by the fact that faith is not a quantifiable entity. External symbols like the headscarf are nothing but an indicator and one to which its wearers attribute different meanings. As stated in the previous chapter, faith cannot easily be measured or evaluated. As my conversations revealed, the public discussion about the headscarf was understood by my respondents as missing the point of the problematic of Muslims in France, namely social exclusion, lack of opportunity and discrimination.

Though Bouzar and Kada do not quote the Qur'an in their book, it is worthwhile to take note of what the Holy Scripture says about covering a woman's head. Part of the reason for discord concerning the veil among Muslims themselves is because the 114 *Suras* of the Qur'an mentions the veil only twice.[21] Following is the most commonly cited *Sura*:

> O prophet, tell your wives and daughters,
> And the women of the faithful,
> To draw their wraps a little over them.
> They will thus be recognized and no harm will come to them.
> God is forgiving and kind. (Sura 33: 59)

This verse states that the veil serves two purposes: one, as a means of recognizing a Muslim woman and secondly, to protect women from harm. Tariq Ramadan's reading of "they will thus be recognized" can be understood as being synonymous with "bearing witness." According to Ramadan, this is an important reason for wearing a headscarf. For this philosopher, one of the principal characteristics of Muslim identity is in fact to "educate and bear witness" (Ramadan 2002: 30).

Ramadan's interpretation sheds some light on the underlying reasons why the headscarf is perceived as such a contentious issue in France. If this piece of fabric is used to distinguish an individual in terms of her religious affiliation, it may be interpreted as a tool for proselytizing. The veil is intended to impact others who shall recognize the wearer. This interpretation contributes to the tension surrounding the debate in France. Implicit in the scriptural exhortation is the idea that "their wrap" is concerned with the response of others: "They will thus be recognized and no harm will come to them."

However, it needs to be emphasized that there is a difference between bearing witness to one's faith by means of the headscarf and for asserting an otherness already imposed by society. Discussions about the headscarf reveal a nervousness concerning what Muslim women think, what Muslim men think and what the French community at large thinks. Another frequently cited reason for wearing a headscarf by women of Maghrebi origin in France is for self-protection. In the testimonies included in Bouzar and Kada's book, young women speak of the need to protect themselves from male violence prevalent in the *banlieues*.

Bouzar and Kada also agree on a uniquely French dimension on the debate over the headscarf:

> The headscarf is thus a French phenomenon. The young girls who wear it are French, they claim to be first and foremost French. The difference of this book lies in its analysis of the meaning of the veil in the French heartland. (16)

The particularly French aspect of the debate about the headscarf—revolving around the concept of *laïcité*—should not, according to Kada, be confused with a debate about Islam in general. She argues that the headscarf in the French context does not signify oppression of women as it is often understood in international debates about Muslim women's head covers. The dialogue between these two authors shows the existence of a vigorous internal debate on the headscarf among Muslims in France and that the headscarf debate is not merely a matter of the French state versus its Muslim citizens.

THE CROSS AND THE CRESCENT

Ambivalence best describes the assessment of respondents in France and Morocco concerning the ban on wearing overt religious insignia in French public schools. The majority of the women I spoke with were unsure if the new law served to advance the cause of national cohesion. The women in France said they understood and, more importantly, supported the concept of *laïcité*. In Morocco too, most claimed to be familiar with this principle of governance. Yet women in both countries were unclear about its application. They pointed to the fact that some of the most important public holidays in France were religiously based, such as Christmas, Easter, Pentecost, etc. In France women also referred to the lowering of the French flag throughout the country upon the death of Pope John Paul II in April of 2005. This, some women argued, was a clear indication of a state-sanctioned bias toward Catholicism. Being Catholic and being French was almost synonymous. "The cross is everywhere in France," said a young woman in Paris, "and that is OK because this is mostly a Christian country. All we want is to wear a scarf on our heads, we don't demand to have crescents displayed in public places."

The ban on overt religious insignia in public schools was perceived to be directed first and foremost against Muslims though officially the ban includes all demonstrative religious signs. The majority of women I spoke with felt that this new law increased tension between minority and majority cultures in France rather than reducing it. "Why," Nacera asked, "did such law become necessary just now? Students have been wearing crosses and Jewish skullcaps for centuries yet there has been no public debate about this. But now, the media can't get enough reporting about girls with headscarves."

Aïcha, an aspiring journalist in Paris commented: "When Moroccans move here, they know they are not coming to a Muslim country. They were not forced to come to this country. Actually, most left because they felt France was a better place for them than their homeland. They know they have to obey the laws of this country. And though the French government is within its rights to pass any law it deems necessary, it is a shame that with regard to us, they decided to go on a confrontation course." While Aïcha disagreed with the ban, she had not participated in demonstrations or other public expressions against it because she did not want to put her professional opportunities in jeopardy. Aïcha said she had thought about wearing the headscarf herself, but had decided against it because she felt this would make it even more difficult for her to enter the mainstream job market. "It is not a big issue for me, but I can understand that school girls and university students are willing to go all out to protest against this law."

The relative negative perception of the headscarf ban among women in France and Morocco stood in stark contrast to the view about the Moroccan family law reform. Even though women expressed uncertainty about the King's motives for introducing the Personal Status Code reform in Morocco, they felt confident that it would improve the situation of women and move society forward.

There certainly is a big difference between a law that grants more rights (the Personal Status Code) and one that restricts rights (the ban on wearing ostentatious religious insignia in public schools). Generally one would expect more support for a legal reform that promises more, rather than less, freedom. Yet all things considered, most women expressed remarkable goodwill toward their respective governments but women in France felt the French law "rewarded" their loyalty by further ostracizing them.

For the majority of young women, in France as in Morocco, wearing a *hijab* is a personal choice. For most women over the age of fifty, wearing a headscarf is as much a regional habit as it is an expression of their religious observance. We may need to remind ourselves that in many parts of Europe, women over a certain age wearing a headscarf was a common practice only two generations ago. This was the case as much in Nordic, protestant Finland as in southern, Catholic Spain and Italy and all the way over to the east in Russia. It is a comparatively recent phenomenon to associate the headscarf almost exclusively with Islam. I remember that my Lutheran grandmother never left the house without putting on a black scarf.

Today's generation of Muslim women in Morocco and in France feels much less bound by convention as became evident when comparing mothers and daughters. A mother's wearing of the Muslim headscarf had little bearing on the daughter's decision to put on the *hijab* and so there was no apparent correlation between the two. Young women who wore the headscarf often had mothers who did not and women who did not wear the veil had mothers who did. In fact, often women told me that their mothers were opposed to their decision to put on a headscarf, even if they wore it themselves.

Many of the women in France felt the "media hype" focused on an inconsequential issue while ignoring the main problems affecting Muslims of immigrant backgrounds, namely unemployment and discrimination. Also largely absent in the public discussion on the headscarf was a look at the reasons why girls wear it. French researchers have identified three main reasons: pressure from family or friends, conscious personal choice and/or to escape violence in the *banlieues*. This last reason has to do with an increase of violent attacks on unveiled girls in the outskirts. There have been reports of gang rapes and other atrocities, committed often by unemployed young men.

Le foulard, the veil, has indeed become a matter of public interest not only in France—and Western Europe—but also in predominantly Muslim countries. In Turkey, a predominantly Muslim state, the headscarf has been banned in all public places for decades. There, secularism has been the state ideology since Kemal Ataturk (1881–1938) founded the modern Turkish republic. Banning the headscarf in France in 2004 was seen by my respondents as an unnecessarily heavy-handed government approach to put an end to a public debate. Thus, it is not surprising that the majority of women felt that French government intervention of banning religious insignia did little to ease public tension.

Morocco does not have an official policy on the veil; it is neither forbidden, nor is it encouraged. The government discreetly favors women who are not covered. Nevertheless, in recent years, there has been a noticeable increase of young women wearing the *hijab* in Morocco and for that matter, in France. On the campus of any public university in Morocco, it is nowadays *de rigueur* to don a headscarf, especially one that matches the overall attire. Said a university professor in Rabat: "My students ask me why I am not veiled. I feel uncomfortable having to defend myself in front of them. Sometimes their reasons for wearing the veil appear shallow to me, but it has become so popular that some students feel they can ask a professor why she is not veiled. This would not have happened ten years ago. And then again, students are surprised to find out that often I know the Qur'an better than them." And she added: "It is a shame that there is so much emphasis on the *hijab*. That really should not be a major issue."

There are certainly many reasons why women put on the headscarf. In Morocco, the *hijab* has become a fashion item with colorful scarves matching the overall outfit. Occasionally, when I sat in one of the many outdoor cafés in Morocco, my companions made it a sport to point out passers-by in the streets whom they believed wore the *hijab* for religious reasons and those for whom it was a fashion statement. Obviously, one should not conclude that a more fashionable headscarf is synonymous with less religious sentiments. But it is important to reiterate that the Muslim headscarf is not in always an expression of religious devotion.

In France too, wearing the scarf was in some cases a fashion statement comparable to the way some young people in the West sport a T-shirt displaying an image of Che Guevara. The wearer of a Che-shirt signals a kind of rebellion against the establishment and asserts an identity without supporting a communist uprising. Most of the women I interviewed in France said they had put on the headscarf against their parents' wishes, even in cases where their own mother wore the *hijab*. Gilles Kepel describes the return to religious roots as the phenomenon of "re-Islamization" which occurred chiefly as a result of social circumstances in the often-violent suburbs, marked by unemployment and deprivation (Kepel, 1987). Being left out of the French mainstream, a renewed identification with the religion of Islam is seen as one way of asserting difference from the dominant culture. On a university campus in Saint Denis on the outskirts of Paris, women told me they wore the headscarf to assert their cultural identity.

I occasionally heard concerns that the banning of the Muslim headscarf would lead to further self-segregation of Muslim communities, such as the creation of Islamic schools. However, as Muslim communities in France are not affluent, funding for those schools would have to come from outside of France. As North African countries struggle to address illiteracy within their own boarders, it is unlikely they would invest in schools abroad. However the majority of mosques in France are financed by the governments of Algeria and Morocco.

No matter how complex the headscarf issue may be, most public schools had come to some sort of compromise with their Muslim students. In some instances, girls had been asked to wear a bandana instead of the scarf, in others they were asked to sit in the back of the classroom while in some schools girls took off her scarf on school premises but would put it back on as soon as they left campus. The majority of girls complied with the new law and took off the headscarf. Explained Naima whose younger sister recently graduated from high school: "Most of our families greatly value public education. They would not want to diminish their daughter's chances of getting a decent education. So it is often parents who admonish their children to comply with the law, even if they disagree with it."

Among young women who had just passed the *baccalauréate*, the French national high school exam, at the time of our meetings, the ruling evoked a strong reaction. Hayat who had completed high school near Etampes, a small town south of Paris, said she never wore the headscarf but she had classmates who did. She always felt awkward being pitted against her co-religionists by her French peers who felt closer to her because of her unveiled appearance. "But I am a Muslim just like the covered girls. Sometimes the veiled girls chided me for not wearing the *hijab*, telling me I was not a proper Muslim.

The other French girls thought I was more like them than the veiled girls. I wish there had not been this conflict and tension all the time. If none of us had been allowed to wear the headscarf, we would have looked alike and there would not have been all that bickering over who is a proper Muslim and who could be friends with whom. I think Muslims should be allowed to wear the headscarf if they feel it is their religious duty, but quite frankly I think we would have had a lot less conflict at school if no one wore the headscarf."

An interesting observation on the veil issue was offered by Loubna, a veiled professional in Rabat: "We have an Islamic state, so it should be taken for granted that citizens should be allowed to wear the *hijab*. But even here we have seen efforts to keep the headscarf out of the workplace. When I interviewed for a job at a bank,[22] I was asked if I would take off my *hijab* if I was given a position where I had to deal with customers. This is outrageous in an Islamic state but I could find no specific law that protected my right to wear the *hijab* at my place of work. So it is better to have rules on these matters. At least in France things are clear and everyone knows what the law is." What happened to Loubna was in fact not unusual. Since the terrorist attacks in Casablanca in May 2003, the government has discouraged women—without passing an explicit law—from wearing the veil, especially if they work in the police force, wish to attend military academies, or become air hostesses. For Loubna and others like her, the absence of clarity on the headscarf issue in Morocco created a sense of uncertainty.

VOICES OF THE SHE REBELS

On the north side of Paris is the département of Seine-Saint Denis which includes many "*quartiers sensibles*," areas containing dense concentrations of immigrant minorities where grey, identical towers of the HLM[23] public housing projects stand close to each other. Here a bi-weekly *souk* (outdoor market) brings this dreary-looking, artificial neighborhood to life. Women in colorful robes, often with babies strapped to their backs, bargain in their various native tongues. This is in sharp contrast to the impersonal shopping style in supermarkets in adjacent neighborhoods. The visitor finds it hard to believe that the Eiffel Tower or the Champs-Elysées are only a short subway ride away.

Hidden in one of those drab public housing towers is a center for "*filles en difficultés*" (girls in difficulties). The motto of this feminist association: "You are not born a citizen, you become one" sums up its educational focus, namely to enable women of immigrant background to become active French citizens. I spent several afternoons at the center, observing the goings on and talking to staff and visitors. Guests are offered mint tea in small, gold-rimmed glasses. Sarah Oussékine, who runs this outreach program, is a master of multi-tasking, talking on the phone while comforting a sobbing young woman sitting in front of her worn desk and telling an old woman in a *djellaba,* also in obvious distress, to sit down and be patient. She switched back and forth between French and Arabic, sprinkling in Berber expressions, and in between all this flurry of activity, she leaned over to talk to me.

By all accounts, Madame Oussékine is a liberal woman. Twice divorced, childless, living alone, fully supportive of French republican values, she once relocated to Morocco, the place her parents had left decades earlier, because she had been offered a promising professional opportunity. After only one year, she explained, she moved back to Paris, because even a modern city like Casablanca was "too backward in mentality" for her. But Sarah Oussékine adamantly disagreed with her liberal peers, intellectuals and feminists, who opposed the headscarf ban on the basis that this violated basic human rights. "I am sorry that I have to disagree with the people I would normally feel closest to. I know they are angry at me for supporting the ban on the headscarf. But I work here [in the projects], I see every day what goes on at the schools, how the girls are getting increasingly pressured to put on the *hijab*, and mind you, not by their fathers or mothers, it is now their brothers and their peers who insist that they cover their heads. We see girls here at the center all the time who say they have been threatened if they don't wear the *hijab.* The state has an obligation to protect these girls; nobody should be bullied into putting on what is essentially a religious garment. The *hijab* should be an expression of faith, but out here often it is not." Though not a practicing Muslim herself, she decided to read the Qur'an to see what it says on the issue of the headscarf and came away believing that the Qur'an did not require women to put on this particular piece of clothing. Oussékine reiterated that for some young women, the headscarf is a form of rebellion against a society that excludes them. Vigorously shaking her long, red-tinged, black curls, she argued that the French state handled the issue the wrong way: "I am not sure if the remedy is worse than the illness." She explained that most families who came to France from North Africa a few decades ago had no idea how the French public schools system worked. Coming from a country where there is no separation of the religious from the secular, immigrants did not understand how the concept of *laïcité* functions in everyday life. Also, they came from highly authoritarian places and were used to doing as they were told. But in France no one told them what to do with regard to their children's public school education. Sarah Oussékine felt, rather than coming down with a ham-fisted law, the government could have used its resources to have social workers visit immigrant families, or organize meetings for parents, and explain the French public school system to them. She went on: "Most parents are grateful that their daughters receive decent education in France and they could have been convinced without much difficulty that the headscarf is not appropriate in public schools here. It would not even have required much effort. These parents want the best for their children; this is one of the reasons why they came here in the first place. They certainly had no intention of going on a collision course with their host country. The last thing they would risk is to be forced to go back to Morocco or Algeria or wherever they came from. Instead, it had to come to all these conflicts and now it seems that the French state is on a confrontation course with its Muslim population."

For Sarah Oussékine and those who thought like her but were not equally as eloquent in expressing their position, unemployment is the real problem among the second generation. "Unemployed young men hang around in the neighborhoods and cause trouble. They need to gain some respect somewhere so they dominate or terrorize their sisters forcing them to wear the headscarf and behave in certain ways," the experienced social worker explained. "It is not the religion of Islam or the headscarf that are the main problems—it is unemployment and social exclusion. Girls in the *banlieues* are doubly discriminated against, as girls and as Muslims." Even though Oussékine's liberal outlook appeared in sharp contrast to the Islamist positions as explained by Nadia Yassine in Morocco, their analyses of the root causes of social tension were remarkably similar and their quest for social justice was fueled by a similar understanding of a state's responsibility to protect and provide equal opportunity for all its citizens.

Oussékine felt that once Muslims become an integral part of French society and members of this minority were seen as productive, loyal citizens, the veil would loose its provocative character. "One day, wearing a veil might be considered as ordinary as wearing a cross. But it is because we are perceived as a backward, troubled minority, volatile, prone to violence that overt expressions of our culture and religion are seen as a threat."

In Morocco women were also aware of the complexity underlying the French ban on the wearing of "overt" religious insignia. Most opposed the law on the grounds that the headscarf as a religious expression was a matter of personal choice and the state had no business interfering with a person's religious observance. They concluded that people needed to abide by the laws of the country in which they reside, whether they agree with those laws or not. At the same time, the French law and its repercussions were often not clearly understood. Many thought that France had banned the headscarf throughout. When hearing that the ban affected only girls in public schools, several women responded with surprise, asking: "Why would such young girls put on a headscarf?" Latifa, herself covered, explained that in her understanding of the Qur'an, covering one's head was a conscious decision made by an adult woman. "Once you put it on, you should not take it off again. It is not a decision made lightly by a teenage girl. Here, very few school girls wear the *hijab*." She continued: "Of course, here practically everyone is Muslim, so there may not be such a need to assert yourself early on. But I think the French state should not have caused its Muslim citizens to feel like victims. That is never a good course of action. There should have been more effort to teach these immigrants about their new environment so that their children could feel welcomed." But Latifa added that she could understand why Muslim families in France might exert more pressure on their daughters to put on a headscarf: "In France, you do not find religion in the streets, they do not teach religion in schools as they do here. Religious education is left to the families and maybe there they encourage their children more vigorously to put on the *hijab* as a means of being true to their religious identity. Here, we know everyone is a Muslim, we all study the Qur'an in school, there is no need for overt profession of your faith. Of course France has the right to ban the headscarf but they should remember that they initially welcomed all these immigrants to do the jobs the French did not want to do. The government should have considered the fact that immigrants from North Africa are Muslims and should have thought earlier about how they wanted to integrate them. To punish the second generation now is a sign that France never really thought about the religion and culture of these people when they first arrived." With contempt, she added: "Somehow, it was as if France imported machines in the form of humans. That they had feelings, a culture and come of an ancient civilization escaped them."

Women in Morocco were concerned that the French government and the majority population evidently found it difficult to live harmoniously with local Muslims. They saw the headscarf ban as a form of discrimination which would eventually lead to more severe problems. In the present climate of "war against terror" which often was perceived as a war of the West against Islam, this law confirmed that the West was not prepared to tolerate Islam as a viable religion. Women perceived a fundamental contradiction between France's posture of upholding human rights while banning the religious expression of a minority. "This confirms our suspicion that the West is an enemy of Islam and that ultimately they want to convert everyone to Christianity," said Khalida, a teacher in Rabat. "This ruling will lend more and more credibility to the Islamists, they are going to grow now in France and they will become more powerful, I have no doubt," she added. Samira, a French-trained psychologist in the capital city, said: "Muslims in France are already marginalized, this law is too brutal. Young people are given to revolt against the established system anyway, this will only fuel their anger and bring them together in a way that is detrimental.

This law is a trap." She pointed to Great Britain where there has been no comparable ban. Instead, Muslim police women for instance were offered a choice of uniform that conformed to their religious requirements and issued matching headscarves.

STANDARDIZING LAWS

Conversations about specific legal changes in Morocco and in France often turned to more abstract themes about the role of law in a modern society. In France some said they favored some degree of international standardization of family law particularly concerning legal marriage age, divorce proceedings and child custody. Moroccans on the other hand were intent on maintaining their Muslim identity on a state level. They feared that standardization or internationalization were euphemisms for imposing "French" laws. The Western world, they argued, would not be willing to incorporate any aspects of Muslim family law. Any attempt to standardize was understood as re-imposing French or European dominance and therefore would lead to an eradication of Muslim culture. The West, women in Morocco said, would not ever recognize contributions coming from a former colony and an Islamic one at that. Fouzia, a French-educated accountant for an international organization in Rabat, said: "We have two societies, two ways of being. We need to begin by acknowledging differences. The laws need to take cultural factors into consideration, but we should not think that Islamic law cannot adequately protect women and give them more rights. As we move forward and adjust our laws, there will be more compatibility—but it has to come from us, from within our culture."

By contrast, most women of Moroccan origin in France expressed that French laws had served them well and therefore Morocco stood to gain by adopting some of those laws. For the most part, they held pragmatic views and felt that their religious identity was generally not threatened by French laws. Khadija, a legal assistant in Paris whose firm works with immigrants and refugees, argued that uniformity of law was ultimately a necessity. She said there was an inherent problematic caused by difference in laws. "Especially concerning family matters, it would be much better to have a somewhat uniform law worldwide. This would help stem the tide of refugees. Our firm assists women who have fled their country because of some unbearable family situation and the failure of the laws in their home countries to adequately protect them."

In sum, educated, professional women in Morocco and women of Moroccan origin in France were reasonably well-informed about legal changes in both countries. They took an interest in developments that affect women on both sides of the Mediterranean. They approached interpretation and assessments of legal changes within contexts that made sense to them rather than subscribing to official discourses even though their views were certainly influenced by their environment. Women in France and Morocco were critical of the motives for legal changes in their own countries as well as of those across the shore. In Morocco, law and culture were seen as closely linked which confirms Rosen's assessment that like religion, law is a kind of metasystem which creates order in a universe that is often experienced in a more disorderly way. In France, women perceived a clear difference between the public and the private. Public French culture with its emphasis on *laïcité* was not understood as a threat to private Islamic identities but clashes may occur in the public sphere. The Personal Status Code reform in Morocco was welcomed by the majority of respondents in France and Morocco whereas the ban on wearing "overt" religious insignia in French public schools was viewed as a controversial, complex issue on which opinions varied. Beyond legal changes, women in both countries emphasized the need for a change of mentality and behavior.

NOTES

1. Rosen conducted this research in Sefrou, a town on the foothills of the Middle Atlas Mountains near Fès and in the same region as Azrou and Ifrane, where I conducted several interviews.

2. Administration of the PSC differs from country to country.

3. An unofficial English version of the *moudawana* can be viewed at: http://www.hrea.org/moudawana.html.

4. There are six collections of *hadiths*, the one gathered by Bukhari is considered the most comprehensive and authentic.

5. *Mut'a* refers to a practice that allows for a man and a woman to marry for a predetermined, mutually agreeable and possibly very short period, also referred to as "pleasure marriages." This allows the couple to go out together in public and to have licit sexual intercourse. According to historic Muslim practice, permissible sexual relations are not primarily a matter of consent; instead the issue is if intercourse is licit or illicit.

6. *Ulema*, singular *alim*, those who are trained in the religious sciences.

7. *Chorfa*, elevated place in the mosque for the imam.

8. An unofficial English translation is available at http://www.hrea.org/moudawana.html.

9. There exists a difference between the "toshavim," the pre-Islamic communities of the Atlas Mountains, and the "megorashim"—Jews fleeing Spain in the fifteenth century who settled mainly in the towns.

10. In Morocco the three main Berber languages are Tarifit in the Rif mountains of the North, Tamazight in the Middle Atlas and Tachelhit in southern Morocco.

11. Bilad (or bled) -al siba, lit.: place (city) of youth, here meaning "Lands of Dissidence" (until 1930s, Berber-dominated Rif, Atlas and Sahara).

12. Michael Willis, *Moroccan Islamism—Expansion or Decline*. Oxford: Oxford University Press, forthcoming.

13. Abdesslam Yassine has advocated the need to "Islamize modernity instead of modernizing Islam." He was imprisoned and later put under house arrest by the previous King Hassan II.

14. Sufism is the mystical branch of Islam that is popular in Morocco.

15. In Morocco, the term prostitute is also used to describe women who have sexual relations outside of marriage.

16. In this case immodest clothing refers to a sleeveless t-shirt and the absence of a headscarf.

17. *Souk* is an outdoor market where, in addition to fresh produce, all imaginable items—new or used—are offered. Fixed prices are rare; negotiation is part of the process of exchange.

18. For a comprehensive explanation of the "The headscarf affair" see Hargreaves, 1995: 125.

19. For the complete text of the law, see: http://admi.net/cgi-bin/admijo.pl?requete=Loi+no+2004-228.

20. Begag's official title was Ministre délégué à la Promotion de l'égalité des chances auprès du Premier ministre, Dominique de Villepin. Begag was the highest-ranking government official of North African immigrant origins. In the spring of 2007, Rachida Dati, a woman of Algerian-Moroccan parentage, was appointed to the considerably higher office of Minister of Justice under then newly elected President Nicholas Sarkozy.

21. The other verse in which the veil is mentioned is 24:31.

22. The "headscarf affair" at the BMCE Bank became public in 2004. In an effort to appear "modern," employees who dealt with customers were discouraged from wearing a *hijab*. Bank executives eventually offered an apology to their veiled staff.

23. HLM stands for habitation à loyer modéré, which means rent-controlled or public housing for low-income families.

5

A Journey of a Hundred Years

PERSONAL AND PROFESSIONAL GOALS AND CHALLENGES

The public face of France is changing. Young professionals of African immigrant background are entering the workforce in increasingly large numbers and contribute to a visible transformation of French society. Men and women of Moroccan origin form an integral part of this new French mosaic. Ahead of them are children and grandchildren of Algerian immigrants, who arrived decades earlier, in larger numbers and have already made their presence felt. One of the most beloved French heroes is Zinedine Zidane, team captain of the French national soccer team and three-time world player of the year. In 2005, Azouz Begag, well-known author, screenwriter and sociologist was named delegate minister for equal opportunities in the French government. Both men, fixtures in public life in France, are sons of Algerian immigrants and have used their considerable influence and popularity to draw attention to issues of discrimination and social exclusion faced by minority populations in France.

Across the Mediterranean, the public face of Morocco is changing with the emergence of a growing class of professional women. The minority[1] entering public life in this country is of a different gender and not, as in France, a religious or ethnic minority. What these women on the move in Morocco and France have in common is that they hail from lower-class families. In France second-generation women of immigrant backgrounds almost always come from a low social class and in Morocco professional women no longer stem exclusively from few elite families but now also come from lower-middle-class or even rural backgrounds. These particular groups of women transform the erstwhile monochrome tapestry in Morocco and France.

In these two countries, we witness Muslim women pressing forward into the public sphere for the first time. This is an exciting event. But as all first steps are uncertain and come with frequent falls and get-ups, this effort cannot be expected to be straightforward or to occur without occasional setbacks.

CHALLENGES, NOT PROBLEMS

The challenges faced by women who dare to chart new paths into previously unclaimed territories are numerous. In her research, sociologist Nacira Guénif-Souilamas, herself of Algerian immigrant background, identifies three major areas of concern for French women of immigrant origins: integration, subjectivity and individual identity. Integration pertains mostly to their public and professional lives, subjectivity to their desire and insistence on being in charge of their personal destiny, and identity to their understandings of themselves (Guénif-Souilamas, 2000: 345). Her findings are based on a series of interviews with young second- and third-generation women from immigrant families from the Maghreb, primarily Algeria. The three themes highlighted by this researcher also resonate, albeit in a different national context, with women in Morocco. In spite of the many obstacles they faced, the women I spoke with displayed for the most part a remarkable sense of determination and good will. As Farida, a social worker in France, put it: "I have nothing to go back to. Going forward, no matter how difficult, is the only way." Women's published narratives allow us a glimpse into the more commonly known and popularized themes of Muslim women and therefore, we shall take a brief look at some texts of this genre.

TAKING UP THE PEN IN FRANCE

The life of Maghrebi women has become the subject of a growing number of books in the past decade. In France, these texts are often in the form of first-person narratives and occasionally fiction. In Morocco, personal narratives are frequently presented in the form of fiction. Such personal narratives are a valuable tool for exploring social realities because they give voice to an often silent—or silenced—population group. The daily life experiences of Maghrebi women in France and of women in Morocco had previously rarely been recounted in public. When women take up the pen and tell their own stories, they break with conventional Moroccan mores. Proverbs abound which extol the virtue of a women whose tongue "does not go out of her mouth," or "Into a closed mouth, no flies can enter" and "Silence is wisdom and from it comes even greater wisdom."

In Morocco, texts produced in this new genre are categorized as "littérature féminine maghrébine," whereas comparable books in France are labeled "littérature beur."[2] Hargreaves (1997) has examined this literature in France and concluded that it consists mostly of first-person narratives of women (and men) who offer testimonies of their lives. They focus on "the key problematic which has preoccupied Beur writers: the articulation of a sense of personal identity, forged in the particular circumstances which are those of an ethnic minority in France" (1). These fictionalized personal narratives or testimonies usually have scant literary ambition, though it would be naïve to exclude them from literary studies. Even if they are a far cry from the quintessential female Muslim storyteller Sherazade whose tales are recounted in *One Thousand and One Arabian Nights*, contemporary female authors—like Sherazade—use the power of words to spare[3] or improve their lives.

French authors describe the difficulties of growing up in immigrant Maghrebi communities, their family conflicts, travails at school, discrimination and the problem of neither fitting in with the traditional structures of their extended families, nor French society in general. These texts describe how women are preoccupied by the question of personal emancipation vis-à-vis their community of origin. More recently, these works have been evaluated as "performative encounters," a term that implies the creation of new subject-positions rather than accepting pre-existing or predetermined identities. Rosello writes: "A performative encounter would be this exceptional moment when, in spite of an international or national conflict, in spite of the violence that reigns and imposes its rules, an unknown protocol replaces the script" (2005:2).

In writing their "own script," women authors of Moroccan origin come to terms with their multiplicity. In one of the early works of this genre, author Malika Mokkedem (1993) lends these words to her protagonist Sultana:

> I am rather like in-between, on a fracture line, inside the ruptures. In between modesty and disdain which reigns in my rebellion. In between the tension of refusing and breaking out which allows for freedom. In between alienation, fear even and escaping from reality by dreaming and imagining. I am in between two, searching for junctures between North and South, the landmarks and reference points in two cultures. (65)

As previously mentioned, multiple identities are common threads in the lives of immigrants in general and in the new generation of women of Maghrebi origin in France in particular. In *Ils disent que je suis une beurette*[4] (*They Say I Am a Beurette*, Nini, 1993), Soraya Nini describes the conflicts of an adolescent girl caught in such cross-cultural setting. She tells of the difficulties of second-generation North African women in leading a life that differs significantly from that of their mostly illiterate mothers who did not interact much with mainstream French society and never pursued a career outside the home. The second generation, by contrast, desires to be accepted and even blend in with mainstream French society.

One of the more successful books that has also been published in English is *Kiffe Kiffe Tomorrow* by Faïza Guène (2006). It tells the story of a teenage girl raised by Algerian immigrant parents. The young woman and her illiterate mother, abandoned by an alcoholic father, are stuck in a Paris housing project. Dependent on welfare and subjected to the obligatory succession of social workers, the two are determined to move forward, *kiffe kiffe*, slowly but surely. Guène wrote this book when she was nineteen years old. In *Née en France. Histoire d'une jeune beur* (Born in France. History of a young Beur, Benaïssa, 2000), the author recounts how she was sequestered by her parents in Algeria to curtail her ambition for personal freedom. Another writer, Djura, tells the story of a woman of Maghrebi immigrant origin who marries a French man (Djura, 1990). Rather dramatically, the book describes the attempted murder of the author/protagonist by members of her family upon learning that she was pregnant by a French man. Islamic dogma forbids Muslim women to marry a non-Muslim unless he converts and thereby ensures that children of such a union are born as Muslims.

Marriage, arranged, forced or to a non-Muslim, is a recurring theme in the narratives of second-generation North African authors. Leila—no last name given—writes in *Mariée de force* (Married by force, Leila, 2004) of the travails of a young woman, forced by her parents to marry a man she did not know prior to the marriage and did not love.

Some of these testimonials are a call to action, such as the memoir *Vivre libre* (Living Free) by Loubna Méliane, who describes the violence in socially disadvantaged immigrant neighborhoods (Méliane, 2004). After her success in France, Moroccan bookstores also displayed her book. Her call to activism was set in motion by an earlier publication of Fadéla Amara's *Ni putes, ni soumises*[5] (Neither whores nor submissive, Amara, 2003). These works are remarkable because they give minority women a voice and have a transnational reach. Themes raised in these texts reverberate with readers in Muslim countries. Certainly, the success of Méliane's book in Morocco is in part due to the fact that her parents are Moroccan.

Upon closer inspection, some troubling aspects of this genre can be observed. Occasionally, a second name appears on the cover of books by second-generation female authors, namely that of a "Français(e) de souche" co-author. *Français de souche* literary means French by roots and refers to

French who trace their ancestry to the proverbial Gauls, somewhat like the American term WASP, even though this French expression is more commonly used. The principal author's North African name is a pseudonym hidden behind a common name, whereas the actual name of the French co-author is displayed. The French co-authors presumably ensure that the text focuses on issues that make it marketable to large French audiences. The uniformity of style and content cashes in on the current fashion in books on anything associated with Islam or Muslims. Such an approach can lead to reinforcing stereotypes rather than offering fresh insights into issues affecting second-generation young women of Maghrebi origin. Few of these memoirs for instance deal with the question of employment opportunities, an issue of critical importance and one frequently raised in my conversations. Hargreaves argues that the negative images of Islam highlighted in the publishers' promotional materials seem likely to attract racists pretending to be liberal sympathizers with immigrant minorities (8). It is therefore all the more remarkable that female authors in Morocco offer a greater variety of themes and personal styles.

. . . AND IN MOROCCO

On the Moroccan side, first-person testimonies by women are a new literary genre, "littérature féminine maghrébine." First-time, non-academic authors have limited access to the nascent publishing industry in that country. Due to cultural constraints concerning writing in the first-person, female authors in Morocco often use the literary device of a novel to recount their personal stories. Notable exceptions are first-person narratives by two well-known Moroccan women, sociologist Leila Abouzeid and Fatima Mernissi. Both women hail from upper-class, prominent families. Mernissi is an internationally acclaimed sociologist and feminist and Abouzeid, a journalist who was appointed by the late King Hassan II to a commission investigating the practice of family law in Morocco. Rejecting the colonial French language, Abouzeid writes in Arabic and her books have been translated into English before French versions became available in 2006. In the preface to her autobiography *Return to Childhood. The Memoir of a Modern Moroccan Woman* (1998), she writes:

> Autobiography, until the last few years, was not respected as a literary form in Morocco. For Arabs, literature meant the lyric, the poetic, and the fantastic, whereas autobiography deals with the practice of daily life and tends to be written in common speech. . . . Perhaps even more important, a Muslim's private life is considered an *ara* (an intimate part of the body), and *sitr* (concealing it) is imperative. (3)

Abouzeid explains that the *hijab* is as much a concept as a piece of clothing, veiling women's private lives which are not to be brought into public view. This inhibition to write—or speak—about one's own life was also evident in my encounters as women often needed to be reassured of the confidentiality of these conversations and were initially hesitant about disclosing their views about private matters. Abouzeid (1998) writes:

> For me, writing an autobiography was therefore even more unusual, because I am a woman, and women in my culture do not speak in public, let alone speak about their private lives in public. When I published my first article in a Moroccan newspaper in 1962, I did not even sign it with my real name, but used the pseudonym of Aziza, and when I published my first novel, *Am al Fil* (Year of the Elephant), in 1983, I left the protagonist's hometown unnamed because it was my own. (4)

Abouzeid's coming of age memoir *Year of the Elephant*, published in English in 1989, is filled with historic references to her country's struggle for independence and her family's role in that endeavor. The great disappointment occurred when women, who bravely stood at the front line of that struggle, after independence found themselves relegated to their traditional roles in the home. Occasionally, husbands divorced their wives because they had become too independent.

In *Dreams of Trespass—Tales of a Harem Childhood* (1994) Fatima Mernissi recalls her childhood in a privileged household in the medieval, royal city of Fès, and contrasts her veiled existence in the urban harem (the separate quarters for the women of a household) with that of her summers spent in the countryside where women rode horses and freely roamed the fields. Like Abouzeid's, Mernissi's autobiography also paints a vivid picture of a specific period in Morocco's recent history and equates her countries struggle for independence from France with women's quest for emancipation.

More recently, personal narratives by less well-known authors have appeared in Morocco. Some of these texts came to North African bookstores by way of France, where they were initially published. Rachida Yacoubi, author of *Ma vie, mon cri* (My Life, my cry, 2003) recounts her difficulty as a divorced women in Morocco. Yacoubi published another installment of her memoirs in *Je dénonce* (*I Denounce*, 2002) wherein she describes how she was put in jail for having had the audacity to divorce her husband. She recalls the despicable conditions in a women's prison in Casablanca. The issue of female prisoners, as we shall see, is a particularly sensitive one.

Siham Benchekroun in *Oser Vivre* (*Daring to Live*, 1999) tells the story of a woman who rebels against her abusive husband and oppressive traditionalism in an effort to find her own identity: "Nadia would have liked to explain to her husband that she did not want to be denigrated by no matter what or who, that for her, the most important thing was to be able to choose her own truth, no matter whether it belonged to the orient or the occident or any other civilization" (Benchekroun, 1999:89). For her part, lawyer Fadéla Sebti fictionalized the story of a young French woman who marries a Moroccan man and moves to his hometown of Casablanca in *Moi, Mireille, lorsque j'étais Yasmina* (*Me, Mireille When I Was Yasmina*, 1995). The young woman becomes the victim of traditional Moroccan family law and eventually is repudiated by her husband. Because the protagonist is French and not Moroccan, the inhumane and humiliating effects of the custom of repudiation are described in detail without offending local sensibilities.

The list of female-authored books is growing and their titles reflect their content: *Une enfance marocaine* (*A Moroccan Childhood*, Touria Hadraoui, 1998), *L'Arganier des femmes égarées* (*Abandoned Women under the Argan Tree*, Damia Oumassine, 1998), *Le bonheur se chache quelque part* (*Happiness Is Hidden Somewhere*, Siham Abdellaoui, 2006) and the list could be continued.

Two memoirs stand out because they deal with a little publicized theme, namely that of female political prisoners in Morocco. One became an international bestseller, Malika Oufkir's *Stolen Lives—Twenty Years in a Desert Jail* (2001). The notoriousness of her father and her intimate connection with the palace of Hassan II, gives her story the attributes of a celebrity memoir. General Mohammed Oufkir, erstwhile head of the infamous Moroccan Security Service, masterminded the attempt to overthrow the monarch in Morocco in 1972. Oufkir was subsequently executed and Malika's entire family was imprisoned in a desert jail in a blatant case of clan liability. The tragic fate of a member of a prominent Moroccan family made the horrendous situation of political prisoners in this country known to a wider international public. Oufkir's appearance on the Oprah Winfrey show helped turn her memoir into a bestseller in the U.S. as well. The first part of the book reveals details of a lavish court life in an otherwise impoverished country which illustrate some of underlying reasons for the social tensions that threaten Morocco to this day.

The other prison memoir is a slim, discrete account of life behind bars. *Une femme nommée Rachid* (*A Woman Called Rachid*, Fatna El Bouih, 2001) tells of the ordeal of an ordinary woman who dared to oppose the political regime and was in and out of prison from 1974 until her final release in 1982. Bouih had been convicted for conspiring against the security of the state, membership in an illegal Marxist-Leninist group and distribution of political tracts and posters. Oufkir, whose book was first published in France before eventually reaching the Moroccan market, painstakingly details every measure of pain and torture she experienced, whereas Bouih is careful not to reveal too many personal details. Some of her co-defendants who add their own accounts at the end of her book speak slightly more openly for instance about sexual violence endured by female prisoners. The case of female political prisoners was fraught with such controversy that prison guards decided to assign male names to these detainees, depriving them of their identity as women—hence the title of the book.

Yet another explosive topic is addressed in a book of testimonies collected by Aïcha Ech-Channa, *Miseria-Témoignages* (Testimonies of Misery, 2004) which chronicle the despair and poverty of unwed mothers and their children. Many of the girls had been victims of sexual abuse by their employers while they worked as *petites bonnes*. Ech-Channa, a social activist now in her mid sixties, has been a constant and controversial voice in advocating family law reform. I met Ech-Channa at the women's center she founded in 1985 in Casablanca where she spoke about the difficult lives of single mothers existing on the periphery of Moroccan society. This formerly ignored organization took care of spurned women and their children and has, until recently depended entirely on foreign funding. In the wake of the Personal Status Code reform, this organization has been recognized as offering a valuable service to a marginalized group of women and now receives government support.

Further broadening the range of themes tackled by women writers in Morocco are erotic novels. Rita Khayat, a renowned scholar who has several academic titles to her name, published *La Liaison* (The Affair) in 2006 though she had written it more than a decade earlier. She felt she had to wait for the right climate in which an explicit love story between unmarried partners, told by and from a woman's perspective, could be put on Moroccan bookshelves.

Female Moroccan authors represent their life experiences in a broader spectrum than their French counterparts, who are generally reduced to their specific situation as minority women and—given the similarity of their books—are expected to speak with one voice. Narratives by women in Morocco tackle a much more extensive range of life experiences even though trials of women in a strict patriarchic and authoritarian society dominate. Despite restrictive societal norms, Moroccan women authors do not limit themselves to writing repeatedly about the same themes as is the case with female Maghrebi authors in France.

KEY ISSUES

However, in both Morocco and France, certain key issues emerge, such as motherhood and all aspects connected to marriage such as arranged marriages, free choice of a spouse, domestic abuse, rape, violence within the family and creating a life in accordance with women's ambitions and dreams. These narratives, fictionalized or not, provide useful insights into goals and challenges of women on both sides of the Mediterranean and they do so in highly personalized forms.

The fact that these narratives contain recurring subject matter can be interpreted in various ways. They can be seen as reflecting actual life stories of their protagonist and as raising issues of actual concern. Others might argue, especially in France, that once a book resonates with the audience, meaning paying customers, books with a similar theme quickly follow. And as most of these stories by and about Muslim women deal with widely popularized issues, they reflect, and possibly reinforce, existing stereotypes about this population and therefore fill a comfortable market niche.

In Morocco, reading is a privilege of a small elite. Layla Chaouni, editor-in-chief of Le Fennec, a publishing house in Casablanca, told me: "I publish books in French because in Arabic, there is even less of a tradition of reading for pleasure." She quips that Arabic is a "father tongue" due to the scarcity and inherent adversity to female authorship and the strong patriarchic structure of society. Unlike in France, book publishing in Morocco is not a revenue-generating enterprise and so Chaouni and her editor peers at other presses depend on outside funding for most of her ventures. This situation does however have the advantage that editors may publish books they consider important regardless of their commercial value, as pecuniary success is not a prime consideration. Still Chaouni laments her fellow countrymen's lack of interest in reading locally authored books. "There is no tradition of reading. It never ceases to surprise me that when people do have money, they much rather buy glossy French magazines. These actually cost more than a paperback produced right here in Morocco."

Sitting in her comfortable office in Casablanca, overlooking the grandiose Hassan II mosque and the blue waves of the Mediterranean, Chaouni is quick to point out that her editorial offices are a donation by a wealthy friend. "We could not afford such spacious premises," she explains, adding, "I don't even get a salary. This really is a labor of love." Chaouni sees it as her mission to support female writers in their effort to find a public voice.

ENTERING THE PUBLIC SPHERE

Writing a text intended for publication obviously involves a different process from simply talking without taking time to prepare. But the brief summary of contemporary women's writing in Morocco and France provides a good introduction into the popularized variation of topics in Morocco versus similar, popularized themes in France. It also shows that personal narratives may only open a very small window into the lives of a particular population group. In my meetings, I found that frequently women addressed issues that were ignored in those narratives. The public role of women, for example, was a recurring topic in our conversations. Particularly the question of female judges was of interest. Islamic Jurisprudence (*fiqh*) is linked to the study of the religion of Islam and is traditionally a male prerogative. In the Muslim world, Morocco today is at the forefront of allowing women to serve as judges. As of this writing, 20 percent of all judges in Morocco were women, and one served as Supreme Court judge. One might envision that educated, professional Moroccan women wholeheartedly support this progressive stance. Yet some women in Morocco and in France were against female judges or women in high positions of government. Some said women were "by nature ill disposed" for positions of public responsibility. Though these women were highly educated professionals themselves, they felt they did not occupy positions in which they had to make decisions that affected a great many people. One argued that women were too "emotional" and due to their menstrual cycles prone to mood swings which would not allow them to be consistently impartial as judges. One university professor maintained that in her understanding of the scripture, the position of *imam*,[6] like that of a judge, was a position reserved for men.

And yet in Morocco, in his dual role of King and Commander of the Faithful, Mohammed VI has the authority to initiate and mandate reform. In a wave to modernize the religious landscape, as mentioned in chapter 3, this country has taken a bold step and appointed fifty female preachers in May of 2006, called *murchidat* (literally: guide). In order to accommodate more dogmatic segments of society, their responsibilities differ slightly from that of an imam. Their mission is to supervise, guide, inform and raise religious awareness in line with the government's modernist approach.

In France, another facet of opposition to female leaders was raised by Ilham. She was unsure if Muslim women currently had the prerequisite professional qualifications to hold such office and did not want to see women appointed based on a notion of mandated gender or minority equality: "I don't want to see women as judges or in government and fail because they were put into those positions only to demonstrate equal opportunity. It would be disastrous if a Muslim woman was in a highly visible position for which she is not properly qualified. The way society is, it would reflect badly on all of us. Her failure would be used to justify continued discrimination." Not surprisingly, the appointment of Rachida Dati, a forty-one-year-old judge and a woman of Moroccan-Algerian parentage, to the office of Minister of Justice, was met with suspicion among the second generation. Shortly after his election in

2007 as president of France, Nicolas Sarkozy had appointed Dati to the highest position held by a member of the minority population in France. Naturally, Dati's appointment was widely discussed in the French media and Dati herself said she knew that her performance would be scrutinized more than that of any other official in a comparable position.

DOES MY OPINION MATTER?

The majority of women I spoke with believed their opinions did not matter to people who make public policy decisions. Those who believed their opinions mattered qualified their response by saying that at election time, public officials conveyed a sense that they were interested in the views of potential voters. Yet how much their views were ultimately taken into consideration by policy makers was unclear to them. Because the family law reform had enhanced their status, women in Morocco were more optimistic than their counterparts in France. There a widely shared sentiment was that the law banning the headscarf in public schools illustrated just how little the government cared about the views of ordinary Muslim citizens.

Despite the fact that Morocco is a near absolute monarchy where democratic processes are only now emerging, women felt they were part of exciting changes in their country. This gave them a sense of empowerment in this otherwise rigidly stratified society. Across the Mediterranean, in the established democracy of France, Muslim women often felt left out of the decision-making processes. As this study was concerned with individual perception, the factual basis of individual statements was not under examination. What is relevant here is how educated, professional young women with no particular access to power view the weight of their input.

As Moroccans have limited experience with democracy, most women took it for granted that people who make public policy are not interested in the views of the population at large. As an example some referred to the massive demonstrations[7] in Rabat and Casablanca for or against the family law reform that had been carefully organized and orchestrated by political parties or established Islamist movements. These mass demonstrations had not come about spontaneously or as a result of grassroots efforts. However, several women said their country was in a phase of great change and for the first time, the King and the government were somewhat open to hearing about concerns of the general population. They were quick to point out that the reasons for this new receptiveness were based on the government's fear of the rising popularity of Islamist movements and recent political gains by the Islamist party PJD (Party of Justice and Development). Support for political Islam poses a threat to the monarchy.

Another major reason as to why people in power had become more attuned to the population at large was the attack by homegrown Moroccan terrorists in May 2003 in Casablanca that killed forty-three people. This terrorist attack had become a defining moment for Moroccan public policy comparable to the effect that the September 11, 2001 attacks on the World Trade Center had on the political process in the United States. Some women said these terrorist attacks had catapulted the Moroccan political elite out of its complacency and forced it to acknowledge the existence of a potentially lethal, disenfranchised segment of the population. Having an ear on the ground had thus become a matter of national importance and crucial for the survival of the monarchy. When women spoke of the impact they felt their views had, their assessment has to be understood in this larger context.

In France, the majority of women felt their views were of little conse-quence to those in decision-making positions. They attributed this lack of in-terest in their opinions to their demographics as a marginalized cultural and religious minority. This marginalization could only be overcome with more second- and third-generation women climbing the social ladder. However, some said that with the creation of the *Conseil Français du Culte Musulman*[8] (CFCM Board of French Muslims) and similar, less prominent organizations, the French government "demonstrated that it recognizes the voice of Muslims in France," even though most did not feel personally represented by the CFCM. Zoubida, who had just attained a graduate degree in political science in Paris and was looking to become active in political life in France, said: "There are now strong advocates of Islam here in France who make their po-sitions known to a wider public, so we are no longer a voiceless minority. But we need more diversity of Muslim organizations because there is not one ho-mogenous Muslim community in France." Zoubida's mother was Moroccan, her father from Niger and she had spent time in both of her parents' countries of origin. Born and raised in France, Zoubida felt she had a good under-standing of cultural diversity and, degree in hand, she considered herself well-equipped to take her place in public life in France. Zoubida attributed some of her zest to her mixed parentage, which had made her a minority within a minority. "Though my parents are both African and Muslim, we still differentiate between people from the Maghreb and from black Africa. If I don't speak up, no one will speak for me." She also credited her mother's in-sistence on higher education with providing her with a solid base from which to launch her career.

While women were quite animated when discussing issues close to their heart, there was a noticeable reluctance among women in Morocco to engage in more general conversations about individual rights. This became evident when moving from the ban on headscarves in France to issues of religious freedom of minorities in Morocco. The majority perceived no contradiction in being critical of the French headscarf ban and being supportive of their government's stance toward religious minorities in their own country. In Morocco, the ringing of Christian church bells is not permitted, proselytizing and conversion from Islam to any other religion is illegal. In the summer of 2005, several Christians were deported after having been accused of witnessing activities.[9] When I asked if they felt authorities should have left these Christians alone, most women said they had not given much thought to the treatment of non-Muslim. Others expressed no qualms about the fact that religious freedom for non-Muslims within their borders was considerably more restricted than that of Muslims in France. And some defended their government's intervention on religious matters by arguing that Morocco was an Islamic state and therefore they had not contemplated the restrictions imposed on non-Muslims such as Jews and Christians. They perceived no contradiction between this position and demanding that the French government not interfere in religious matters, especially concerning the Muslim minority. Most evaluated government actions based on how they affected them or those they felt close to and not with regard to wider implications. An exception was Aïcha, a student in Rabat who said: "Morocco actually has a tradition of religious tolerance; we used to have a sizeable Jewish community here. I wish we would emphasize this more. On my campus there are quite a few students from other African countries and most of them are Christians. I am proud that they come to Morocco to pursue their university studies and they should be made to feel welcome here."

Aïcha came from a Berber family in the Middle Atlas and was proud to tell me of her grandfather's role in fighting against French colonialists. She also explained the relationship between religious rights for minorities and the Berber Cultural Movement. With the rise of the Berber Culture Movement, awareness of disenfranchisement of ethnic groups is beginning to enter public discourse. Interestingly, the Amazigh Movement is using secularism as its battle cry because this position allows for de-sacralizing and therefore questioning the pre-eminence of the Arabic language.[10] If Amazigh languages can be recognized on equal footing with Arabic, this will have larger consequences for public policies. It can be expected that in the wake of the assertion of Berber culture, religious freedoms may in time also be tackled. Aware of the rise of Islamism, the palace has lent support to the Berber movement in hopes of stemming the tide of Islamism.

In Morocco public discourse has to be understood within the context of the monarchy. The role of government is often seen as synonymous with the authority of the monarch. In the past, people were at the mercy of the King's whims, especially during Hassan II's iron rule (1961–1999). After two failed coup attempts in the 1970s, Morocco plunged into what is now referred to as "the leaden years"—*les années de plomb*. During this period, opponents of the King were routinely rounded up, jailed and often tortured. Speaking out in public without having to fear severe repercussions is a relatively recent phenomenon in Morocco. Women in particular have come a long way in staking new ground and therefore it might be asking too much to expect them to raise their voices in defense of causes unrelated to their immediate circumstances. Instead of offering her personal view, one woman referred to a cartoon in a weekly magazine that depicted someone bowing to kiss the king's hand, asking: "How long will we be subjects? I want to be a citizen!"[11] This kind of provocative cartoon would have been unimaginable under the previous king.

In France, our discussions often returned to the theme of separation of church and state. Because the concept of *laïcité* was invoked when introducing the ban on religious symbols in public schools, women were baffled by the fact that this separation was selectively implemented. Mouna in Paris zeroed in on public holidays to make her point: "Offices, schools, and most shops are closed on Christmas, Easter, Pentecost, and Ascension for all citizens, Christians, Muslims, Jews and atheists. Of course, there is no public holiday for *Aid al Kbir* even though ten percent of the French population is Muslim. So for us to succeed in our jobs, we have to abandon certain religious practices. I cannot walk around the office wishing people a Merry Aid, yet I [I] feel have to say Merry Christmas if I want to fit in. That does make me uncomfortable but I think it is better if I don't speak out about it." Mouna was quick to add that she felt her rights were better protected in France than in Morocco because she could practice her religion according to her personal understanding and free from government-mandated religious practices as is the case in Morocco. "How can a government demand that you fast?" asked another woman. She felt liberated by the fact that in France she could question any aspect of her religion without having to fear repercussions. "I feel I can actually be a better Muslim here than in Morocco because I live according to what I believe. Nobody at my place of work has ever asked me anything about my religion or what I do or do not practice. I am not sure I would have the same freedom in Morocco" she said. Among her colleagues at a radio station in Paris, religion was never an issue. "Of course my name gives me away. Everyone knows I have Maghrebi parents and that I am Muslim."

Several women said the French legal system protected them from certain customs their parents had brought with them to France. If it had not been for French laws, they might have been married off by their families to someone they did not know or did not like or they might not have been able to pursue their professional ambitions against the will or without the support of their parents.

Samia, one of the youngest women I met and who not long ago had passed her baccalauréate, said she was grateful for the French public school system because her parents could not have afforded a private school. From her yearly summer visits to Morocco, she understood that her cousins there did not have the same educational opportunities. Samia said that once students enter public schools, they are not considered Catholic, Jewish or Muslim, they are just students. "We are all citizens of the French Republic where religion is a private matter. And that is a very good thing. I am glad the government insists that religion is kept out of the schools because it is an issue that causes friction and conflict."

One woman, Fouzia, who works for a publicly funded agency investigating claims of discrimination in the workplace said she could not imagine the existence of a comparable organization in Morocco. "In my work I see that there are serious attempts at addressing discrimination. The headscarf certainly leads to discrimination. I remember that from the time I was at school. Teachers often treated the veiled girls differently or made comments about them. My sister had briefly put on the headscarf while still at school but then took it off because she could not handle the consequences. Now that she is married, she wears it again." But Fouzia also pointed out that discrimination was a much larger issue and could not be limited to discussions about the Muslim headscarf. As she leaned over, she whispered, "I and my female colleagues get paid less than our male colleagues, even in our anti-discrimination agency. We have talked about it among ourselves but nobody has had the nerve to bring it up with our boss."

SOCIAL CLASS

Most young women of Moroccan background in France felt they did not have sufficient professional opportunities. Educated women in Morocco did not by and large feel this way. This difference can be attributed to one significant difference between educated, professional Moroccan women and French women of Moroccan origin: social class. Moroccan women who considered their professional opportunities sufficient generally came from middle- or upper-class families. Women with this background were confident they could obtain professional positions in line with their qualifications. However those from modest milieus in Morocco overwhelmingly said they did not have sufficient professional opportunities.

In Morocco, "connections," *coup de piston*, was cited as a major factor in securing a professional position. Women with a university education who hailed from a rural background or came from poorer families felt their professional

opportunities were not commensurate with their education. Rachida, an elementary school teacher in the picturesque Middle Atlas town of Azrou, explained: "I
was the first and am the only one in my family to get a university education.
Even my two older brothers did not go to university. My mother married when
she was fourteen; of course she never went to school. She wanted a different life
for me so she really supported me in getting a good education. And my father
agreed. But now I am thirty-one years old, unmarried and work as a substitute
kindergarten teacher. Most of the money I earn comes from giving private les-
sons in the evenings and on weekends. My family does not have any connections; we don't know anyone in high places. I am here with my mother and I am
supporting her on my small salary. I wish I could get a better job."

Rachida's father lived far away with her oldest brother, who had been hand-
icapped as a result of a car accident and had since been unable to work. The
father had moved in with his son, and supported him and his family with his
income. Rachida lamented the fact that she rarely left the house apart from going to work because she did not want to leave her mother alone. "My mother
only leaves the house to go to the market or to the *hammam*."[12] Rachida said
she would like to start her own family: "There have been a few men who asked
my mother if they could marry me, but most of them were older men who were
either divorced or widowers with children. Though they could offer financial
security, my mother did not encourage me to marry any of them. She thinks I
should marry someone closer in age to me and someone I like." I asked if she
felt her mother was unhappy as a result of having been in an arranged marriage. Rachida disagreed: "My mother was still a child when she got married.
It was very flattering to her when the parents of this handsome man came to
ask for her hand. Over the years, she learned to love my father. He is a good
man; he always provided for us and never mistreated my mother. But times
have changed and she wants me to make my own decisions." We sat in
Rachida's living room in an unfinished house without heating and only cold
water. In the Atlas Mountains winters are long and cold. Like so many houses
in Morocco, theirs got build as the family had money to pay for construction.
It is a common sight throughout Morocco, especially outside the major urban
areas, to see already inhabited houses that are still under construction. Because
of restrictive lending procedures by local banks, many of these private houses
are paid for by repatriated money from Moroccans working abroad. Remis-
sions in recent years have steadily decreased as immigrants retire in Europe instead of returning to their home country and second-generation ties to Morocco become more and more feeble.

It may be instructive to take a small detour here and note that decreasing loyalty of children of immigrants to Morocco is an issue of concern for the Moroccan government because it stands to lose significant foreign income. Though

there are no accurate figures available, immigrants contribute substantially to foreign income and development, especially in rural areas. Expatriate Moroccans also retain their right to vote in Morocco. It is commonly held that Moroccans residing in a Western country do not favor Islamist parties but support government efforts at modernizing their country of origin. With the aim of maintaining and nourishing ties between immigrant families and their country of origin, the Moroccan government in 2003 initiated a Ministry in charge of the Moroccan expatriate community,[13] upgrading a previously much smaller bureau. The mission of this Ministry is based on recognizing "the numerical importance, diversity and strategic roles of the Moroccan community which resides in foreign countries." Part of its mission is to create a database of Moroccan professionals abroad and to "encourage them to support and participate in the economic development of their home country."[14]

But Rachida in her small Atlas Mountain town does not have a relative in France, Belgium or anywhere else in the world and so her house takes a lot longer to get finished than those of her neighbors whose homes I saw built from beginning to end within two to three years. She also lacks connections which would help her get a better-paying job and does not want to enter into a financially secure, but loveless, marriage. She told me that several of her friends were in a similar situation. "Imagine, one agreed to become the second wife to an old man. She says she's happy but I know she is not. At least, she does not have to worry about her bills anymore." For the time being Rachida, a beautiful, young woman with an easy smile, stays at home with her mother in the one completed room in her halfway built house and dreamed of better days to come.

Nowhere is pulling strings more important than in countries of the developing world where a closely connected upper class takes care of its own. Social class often outweighs all other factors with regard to a person's personal and professional opportunities. A glance at political leadership in some Muslim and developing world countries illustrates this point.

MUSLIM WOMEN AS WORLD LEADERS

Benazir Bhutto was the first woman to lead a post-colonial Muslim state. She was elected prime minister of Pakistan in 1988 but was ousted twenty months later. Benazir Bhutto is the daughter of deposed Pakistani premier Zulfikar Ali Bhutto. Her paternal grandfather was Sir Shahnawaz Bhutto, a key figure in Pakistan's independence movement. The country with the largest Muslim population worldwide, Indonesia, has had a female president since 2001, Megawati Sukarnoputri, daughter of former President Sukarno who led Indonesia to independence after World War II. In Bangladesh, Khaleda Zia, also a Muslim, became the first female prime minister of this East Asian country in 1991. She governed until 1996 and became premier again from 2001–2006, remaining in office as of this writing. Khaleda Zia is the widow of assassinated President Ziaur Rahman. India was headed for decades by Indira Gandhi (not a Muslim) who was prime minister from 1966 to 1977, and again from 1980 until her assassination in 1984. Indira Gandhi was the daughter of India's first prime minister, Jawaharlal Nehru, and mother of another, Rajiv Gandhi. In Sri Lanka Chandrika Kumaratunga has been president since 1994. She too comes from a politically powerful family. Both her parents had been prime ministers of Sri Lanka: her mother, Sirimavoh Bandaranaike, became the world's first premier after her husband and predecessor Solomon Bandaranaike was assassinated in 1959, holding the post three times.

More than anything else, these examples show the overwhelming importance of social class and family connections in developing world countries. All of the above women were or are part of the ruling elite and rose to power owing largely to family relations, in countries where women are often treated as second-class citizens. In Morocco too, women traditionally rise because of their connections to the royal family or the *makhzen*, the extended network of the palace that includes royal notables, businessmen, wealthy landowners, ethnic leaders, top-ranking military personnel and security service chiefs.

Given this context, it is to be expected that Moroccan professional women do not consider gender a major hindrance in their careers. In her dissertation, Souad Eddouada[15] observes that gender is not one of the most important determinants for professional opportunities—instead it is social class. Professional opportunities for educated women from the urban middle or upper class are superior to those of rural men or women from a lower socio-economic background, she writes, adding that female solidarity is often limited to those with similar economic standing. Moroccan feminists, "by seemingly arguing for the rights of women, treat Moroccan women as a homogeneous entity, neglecting the disparities among women from rural and urban areas as well as different classes," Eddouada writes. Her findings are based on her work with various prominent women's organizations in Morocco:

> My experience within the administration of these organizations demonstrated to me that patriarchy not only concerns the domination of men by women since we find hierarchy among women themselves. The absence of the young generation, the survival of hierarchical relationships of power within these supposedly feminist and alternative to male structures, in addition to the gap between the grassroots and their representations by the egalitarian discourses of these feminists' activism are due to the absence of free and open reflection within these organizations.

Educated women from well-connected families were indeed quick to admit to me that they had come by their jobs not only based on merit, but because family ties had opened doors that otherwise would have been closed to them. Lamiae who upon graduating with a degree in business administration had soon found a job in a prestigious international firm in Casablanca, said over lunch in an upscale restaurant: "I know I would not have found this job without my father's connection. Still, I have to prove to my employer that I deserve this opportunity. I also want to go abroad, get a graduate degree and maybe find a job in France or Belgium. I want to show that I can make it on my own." In Rabat, Mina who holds an upper management position, confirmed: "Of course my name opens doors but I am qualified for my job and have earned every promotion. I feel at home and comfortable here and want to contribute to the development of my country. I feel I can make a difference."

Women of the second generation in France who want to "make a difference" face different kinds of problems than women in Morocco. My French respondents felt that discrimination was more important than a lack of family connections or gender in preventing them from moving up the social ladder. A Maghrebi name closes rather than opens doors. The social exclusion of North African immigrant communities has been well-documented, and in 2003, some in the French government called for a policy of "positive discrimination," a phrase used in France to denote what in the U.S. is known as "affirmative action."[16]

Mouna, a lawyer in Paris, talked about the problems she had faced: "In France it is not so much a matter of personal or family relations, even though they help of course in getting a good job. It is more important to be part of the French system. As children of immigrants, we have nothing going for us but our education, and this is often not enough when competing with candidates who have the advantage of being part of mainstream French society." By "mainstream French society" Mouna referred to the majority culture of *Français de souche*. Even though she insisted that she shared most of the cultural and political values of her French peers, she was perceived as being fundamentally different because of her Muslim religion and immigrant background. This eloquent young woman also raised the issue of sexism. "It is not true that in the Western world women are treated equally in the workplace. When I was growing up, I always thought things worked differently in French society from *chez nous*, but now that I am part of the French professional work force, I am quite appalled by what I see going on in the office. Women most definitely are treated differently and do not have the same opportunities as men." And she added: "It took me a while to figure this out. Initially I thought I was the only one with a lower salary and, because I felt so lucky to have landed this job, said nothing. It was only later that I found out that the other women were in a similar situation."

LIVING ALONE

Since Mouna had taken a job in a law firm in Paris, she had moved out of her parents' home and lived by herself in a small apartment. For her to live alone was as big a step as embarking on a professional career. "It just is not done in our culture. I was supposed to live with my parents until I got married. My mother was worried when I told her that I was moving out and getting an apartment for myself."

Even in the Western world, the phenomenon of young women living alone is relatively recent and linked directly to increasing affluence. In times past, economic conditions often dictated that young women—and men for that matter—lived with their families until they got married and started a family of their own.

In Moroccan culture, it is still the norm for young people to live with their parents or relatives until they start their own families. Under the old family law, a woman always remained under the tutelage of a *wali* (guardian), first her father or an older male member of the family and later her husband, who was responsible for her upkeep and safety. A woman could not open a bank account, own a business or obtain a passport without the guardian's permission. Given this context, women who merely considered living alone clearly broke new ground.

For Moroccan women and women of Moroccan origin in France, living alone is such a recent phenomenon that they still have to come to terms with it emotionally. When I asked my respondents whether their mothers had ever lived by themselves, the answer was "no" without a single exception. Speaking about why they had not followed the example of their mothers unleashed a torrent of emotions. Women in both countries were at pains to explain why they lived alone. None of the women simply said, "I live by myself" and moved on with the conversation. Instead, they felt compelled to offer lengthy explanations as to the circumstances that led them to live alone.

In France, women had most often decided to live alone after a painful break with one or both of their parents who disapproved of their personal or professional choices. Some had also escaped from an impending arranged marriage. An illustration of just how complex and conflictual it is for such women to live by themselves can be found in my conversations with Latifa. She had a tiny apartment in Paris the address of which her parents did not know. She however remained in close contact with her older sister, who was married and kept quiet about Latifa's whereabouts.

Latifa said she had moved out of her parents' home because she had started to date a French man. "My father would not accept that I marry a non-Muslim. I am not a child, I am 26 years old and should be able to make my own decisions. It is horrible that I am so separated from my parents. My sister is properly married and everything is fine between her and our parents." Latifa had invited me to her one room studio and was eager to discuss her personal situation. She was disappointed but did not express anger toward her parents. "I thought at least my mother would support me, but she said my father would never condone my relationship with this man and so I had no choice but to move out." Latifa introduced me to a friend of hers, a young, divorced woman with a child who also lived without much contact with her family.

In France, whenever I met a divorced woman who had a child or children, she invariably invited me to her home. Each time I was given a tour of their small but immaculately clean apartments. As in most Moroccan homes I had visited, there were no visible signs that children were present in the household, such as toys, children's books, crayons, little shoes, or some such items that would customarily be found in a Western home with small children. The exceedingly neat living rooms were in keeping with a cultural tradition that greatly values hospitality. Guests are offered tea and cookies and there is much emphasis on making a visitor feel special—yet at the same time distant from the real goings-on in the home. It seems that divorced women were keen on showing me that they led a decent life and managed to keep up a nice home.

While in France, women often lived alone as the result of family strife arising from cultural conflicts; in Morocco women frequently found themselves in this "unnatural" situation because their place of employment was far away from where their family or relatives lived. This was most often the case among women who came from small towns, had received higher education and subsequently found jobs in the capital city of Rabat or the commercial center of Casablanca. Living alone was also often a matter of social class. Women from more affluent backgrounds often had relatives in the large urban areas with whom they could live whereas women from modest, rural homes had no such relations in the cities. Said Samira, a medical doctor in Rabat: "I have colleagues who think I am a loose woman because I live alone. They think a woman should either live with her parents or her husband. They don't hesitate to tell me that they think what I am doing is wrong. It is none of their business, I never asked for their opinion, but they tell me anyway. My family would of course prefer that I was married but they respect my choices and they are glad I have a good job and can support myself."

Interestingly, none of the women wearing a headscarf in France lived alone whereas in Morocco there was no difference between veiled and unveiled women with regard to their living situations. Veiled women in France considered it "impossible" or "improper" to live by themselves, whereas veiled women in Morocco made no such connection between personal religious commitment and living situation. Otherwise, no significant difference could be discerned between women living alone in the two countries. None of the women, for instance, said they shared a place with a friend or friends of the same gender and none said they lived with a boyfriend. It is certainly conceivable that some in fact did, but nobody admitted as much.

The story of Halima, a radio journalist in Paris, illustrates the family dilemmas faced by young, educated women of Moroccan origin in France. Halima, twenty-six years old, did well in school and was encouraged by her teachers to continue her education at a university. Her brothers were less successful at school and were currently unemployed. Her father had wanted his only daughter to get married and to raise children, while her mother supported her plans for a career. Eventually, conflict within the family grew so intense that Halima moved out. "In my experience, it is not just French society that causes us problems. It is our immediate environment in the family that is a problem. They exert such pressure on us [girls] by insisting on culture and traditions. These traditions are not Moroccan or Muslim, they are the customs of the backward, uneducated Moroccan countryside. I know, because I went to the village where my parents came from every summer while I was growing up. It was like traveling back in time."

Almost in tears as she recounted her story, she went on: "Because of where they come from, my parents can't change. So I have to separate from them for a while until I have established myself. When they can see what I have accomplished, things will be easier, I hope." Since moving to Paris nine months earlier, she had not been in touch with her family. She said she was wary of making friends with other second-generation women for fear that someone might know her family and reveal her whereabouts. She felt equally ill at ease befriending French women because of her complicated family situation. She felt ashamed of her family situation and thought French women would not be able to relate.

For our first meeting Halima suggested a bench next to a pricey café near the Eiffel Tower. After we got to know each other better, I asked why she had wanted to meet in one of the most expensive, touristy parts of town, far from where she lived. She said she had wanted to make me feel comfortable. Learning that I was not French she thought the Eiffel Tower would be a venue a foreigner such as I would appreciate. But it is also possible that she chose a location where she was not likely to be seen by anyone she knew. Halima consistently rejected my invitationa to lunch, dinner, or even a snack. Despite her urban existence, she had never eaten in a restaurant and said she did not trust food in such places. And so each time we met, we walked the streets and parks of Paris for hours, never consuming anything but bottled water. Halima, of Berber origins with light brown hair and green eyes, was obviously lonely, missing her family and friends she had not yet adjusted to life in the big city.

Despite her shyness and social awkwardness, she tackled her professional ambition with tenacity, determined to develop her potential and break out of the socially disadvantaged milieu she had been born into.

Halima felt there was no turning back for her. "My family comes from a village in the Rif Mountains in northern Morocco. They were not into the drug business so they would have stayed poor forever."[17] Halima knew that climbing the social ladder was going to be a formidable challenge, but she felt prepared to tackle it: "There is nothing for me in Morocco and there is nothing for me in the *banlieues*. I have to make it on my own, no matter how difficult." Halima worked for a small radio station and had applied for a position at a large French publishing house. One evening, before we parted, she said with tears in her eyes: "I hope one day my parents will be proud of me."

Living alone in France was usually linked to complications within the family, but in Morocco it was more a matter of social class. My conversations with women in Morocco also revealed a difficult family-related subject: trust. Touria, thirty-three, is an independent and successful professional woman in Rabat. She owned a car, dressed in fashionable Western clothes and has experience of living abroad in the West while growing up, but said she could not envision herself living by herself, the way women did in Europe. "I need to know someone is in the house when I come home and since I am not married that someone is my mother." When I asked Touria if she had considered sharing a place with a friend her age, she said she could not trust even her best friends, so this would be out of the question. She said she could only trust her family. As with the issue of fear which had been raised before, my ears perked up when Touria started talking about trust. I subsequently asked other women about their thoughts on trust.

Complete trust, I was told, existed only within the family, nuclear and extended. Some asserted that the absence of trust was a major obstacle to economic development. People were apprehensive about going into business with someone who was not a family member. Therefore, positions were often not filled by the best qualified people but by trusted ones, that is, people who were part of the family. The issue of trust also entered into discussions on marriage. Women in Morocco and in France described marriage as an agreement between two families, not just an affair involving two people. Trust between the families joined through marriage was of major concern.

Once I waited in a busy coffee shop in the center of Rabat for Nadia, a veiled woman whom I had not seen for a year. When she spotted me, she rushed to my table and announced with a big smile: "I am in love!" I asked if her family knew her beloved, to which she replied emphatically: "No, not yet. I want to make sure that we have a solid relationship. If we appear unsure in front of our parents, they will take over the process and start making decisions for us. This is something between me and him." All through our conversation she avoided the term boyfriend. "We need to trust each other. That is what matters. And we can best develop this trust if there is no interference from our families. Here, marriage is an affair between two families, but the Qur'an does not say parents must chose a spouse for their children. I am going to do what is my right and he sees it the same way."

MARRIAGE

Marriage was considered an essential part of life despite the fact that most of the women I met in Morocco and France were not married. They had invested years pursuing higher education and/or professional training and were busy establishing themselves in their professional careers. In France, the average marriage age for women is 28.5 years (for men 30.6) while in Morocco the average marriage age for women is 20.5 (for men 22.6).[18] The rural/urban dichotomy in Morocco skews this figure as girls in the rural areas tend to get married in their teens whereas urban women often do not marry until their twenties.

Most women in both countries said they did consider marriage an essential part of life. They emphasized that marriage was a choice and not an obligation, even though it had been presented to them as such during their upbringing. One, a medical doctor in Morocco, felt that marriage would not allow her to pursue her career the way she wanted. She also felt that because she was already over thirty, she would not be considered a suitable marriage partner for most Moroccan men. In France, some women told me that their experience growing up with parents who had been obliged to marry by their families, and the high divorce rate of French couples who had married for love, made them apprehensive about marriage.

When I was living in Morocco, women sometimes asked if I knew someone in America or in Europe whom they could marry. Most of these requests were made in establishments that doubled as a beauty salon and meeting place for women. As places where women can meet in public are limited outside the major urban centers, the *hammam*—the traditional public bath—and the beauty salon take on that function in smaller towns. I developed the habit of going to the hairdresser once a week, ostensibly to get my hair worked over with henna or some local potion made with olive oil, but the real reason was to spend time with women. My favorite salon cum hang-out was furnished with a large comfortable couch and sofa chairs with women constantly coming and going, chatting and drinking tea. Often there were more women just sitting around and talking than customers getting their hair or nails done. As

I became a regular fixture at the salon, women included me in their conversations more and more. After a few months, one of the hairdressers mustered the courage to break the question: "Do you know someone who would want to marry me?" This attractive young woman feared she would have to marry someone her father had chosen. He had already introduced her to several men, all of whom she rejected because they either were much older than her, were widowers or she would become their second wife. Fatima Zhora understood that her father was looking out for her financial security, but she dreamed of love. One day, she showed me a French brochure with passport size pictures in a "men seeking women" section. She had put a cross next to two photos. "Could you write them a letter for me?" she asked as she considered her written French insufficient. I told her that I thought organizations distributing such dating brochures in developing world countries were suspect and advised her not to get involved. Fatima Zhora was clearly distraught. "You just don't want me to be happy. I would be careful, I am not stupid. If they would try any tricks, I would just run away." This hairdresser was more insistent than her colleagues who also asked me to find them husbands. When I inquired whether it did not matter to them that these foreign men were not Muslim, they laughed and responded almost in unison: "That would be an advantage. I am sure they would not treat women as bad as our men here do." In time, Fatima Zhora gave up and did not repeat her request, but she was clearly disappointed that her one connection with a foreigner did not lead to some tangible result for her. As arranged marriages are a common practice in Morocco, and meeting men was not easy in smaller towns, it was not unusual to draw on acquaintances for suggestions for possible partners.

Marriage was an issue of considerable personal agony for unmarried women in both Morocco and France. Because women placed such high value on matrimony, they feared that their educational and professional choices would prevent them from finding husbands. In looking for a potential spouse, most—but not all—maintained that having the same religion was an important factor, mostly with regard to raising children. Another criterion mentioned frequently was approval of a spouse by parents. I was told over and over again that marriage involved two families rather than just two people. Several women in Morocco and France also spoke of the need for financial security. This was especially the case among those who had grown up in difficult economic circumstances and where the father had barely been able to provide for the family. Open-mindedness and intellectual compatibility were cherished qualities too. Said Lamiae in Casablanca: "We need to understand each other. We need to have the same intellectual level. I also think it is more difficult to be married to someone who does not come from the same culture. I do not insist on marrying a Muslim, but I think it is easier if both spouses come from a similar cultural and religious background. To me this is not a religious mandate but I believe we will have similar ideas about raising children." Though Lamiae said that her preference for a Muslim husband was her personal choice, her sentiments are in accordance with Islamic dogma, which stipulates that a Muslim woman is not allowed to marry a non-Muslim. In France, women expressed the same desire for marrying a Muslim, but several were open to the possibility of marrying a French man.

While women fantasized about husbands, they also feared the changes that marriage would bring. Hind, a twenty-nine-year-old woman in Rabat, said: "Of course, I would like to have a family and children. But now that I have a graduate degree and started a new job, I feel I need to establish myself professionally first. My mother who cannot even read or write is so proud of me. Even if I wanted to, I could not just marry and do pretty much the same things my illiterate mother did. Raising children is not considered a job in Morocco. The life of a married woman is still very traditional, you have to put your husband first, serve your mother-in-law and raise children. For many married women, life revolves around the home and the *hammam*." Hind came from a blue-collar family, and was keenly aware of the pronounced class differences that divide Moroccan society.

"Though I am a very educated woman now, I don't want to lead the life of a typical middle-class woman. Here, middle-class families have maids and servants and nannies. My mother worked as a maid most of her life. It is such a hard job. If possible, I don't want to have a maid but we don't yet have all the amenities common in Europe and so it is almost impossible to have a family where both parents work without domestic help. Though I would like to get married and have children, at this point this is not a realistic option." As was the case with other women, Hind half-jokingly asked if I knew of a young man who might be compatible with her.

Laatifa, another professional woman in her late twenties in Morocco, who also came from a family of limited means, spoke about the expectations she had of a future husband: "First and foremost, I want him to be a responsible person. And we must communicate well with each other. Often, it is the small things that make a marriage fail. I think I would like to have a practicing Muslim as a husband, one who observes the daily prayers, who does not drink or smoke. He must be honest, too. I am not sure what I would do if I were presented with the choice of a non-Muslim who has these qualities and a Muslim who falls short of my expectation. I hope I won't ever be faced with that dilemma."

Another woman painted a rather negative picture of a married woman's life, saying she had no time of her own: "I get very upset when certain customs are justified by religion. For example when a husband beats his wife or when a brother makes decisions for his sister. I have a much better education and job than my brother, but he feels he can tell me what to do because that is what the Qur'an allows him to do. I know that the Qur'an says some of those things and I am really struggling with that because I am a devout Muslim. Also, here you don't just marry a man; you marry a family. Women are supposed to serve their mother-in-law. As a woman, you are not the master of your own time. Let me tell you: I live here in Rabat by myself and when someone wants to visit me, I want them to call ahead of time and not just show up around dinner time. When I am at home at my mother's house, there are all these relatives who stop by any time they want and my mother has to put everything she was doing aside to prepare a meal for them. I always fight with my uncles and tell them, 'you should call before you come; my mother has things to do other than to feed you.' But then my mother scolds me and says I can live this modern city life when I am in Rabat. She says there I can insist on these new ways of going about things, but when I am at home I have to abide by traditions and customs which include welcoming visitors at any time and serving them food. Of course, my brother has no such obligations. My mother says even if you don't like it, this is the way it is in Morocco. She does not want me to come in and upset our relatives just because I am an educated woman who has a good job in the capital. So as for marriage, I don't know. It will not be easy for me to find a husband."

The conflict between the traditional way of life and the new life of educated, professional women was a recurring theme in Morocco. Zhour, an accountant, said: "For me it is important that my husband has studied or lived abroad. I am a practicing Muslim and I want my husband to understand the difference between religion and some of the cultural practices and traditions in Morocco." Naima, a journalist in her thirties, said she could not even imagine marrying a Moroccan: "I really have a hard time putting up with Moroccan mentality. Mixed marriages are the way to go but I know there will be difficulties. In my profession, I have the opportunity to meet foreign men and I have dated a few. I think my family would be OK with this but unfortunately, the relationships never worked out. Most foreign men are here on limited assignments. I am not sure if I can find a job in my area in another country. At the moment, my work is very important to me. But at least I am free to pursue my professional goals. How to find a man, I don't know. I am thirty-three and still single."

There are some voices in Morocco that caution against such strong emphasis on marriage. One of them is Aïcha Ech-Channa, the founder of the *Association Solidarité Féminine* in Casablanca, an organization helping unwed mothers that was mentioned earlier. Ech-Channa felt the ideal of marriage is used to justify neglect, rejection and abuse of single mothers.

"They are pariahs in Moroccan society," she told me. "They cannot find jobs, no self-respecting man will marry them, and often they are cast out by their families." Ech-Channa herself was never an unwed mother, but a personal experience led her to feeling called to assist such women. She described an event she witnessed shortly after giving birth herself. She saw how the newborn baby of a single mother was yanked out of her arms by hospital staff, milk still dripping from the women's breast. The baby was to be taken to an orphanage. Her look of horror, fear and despair left such a deep impression on Ech-Channa that she decided to act. This social worker feared that the current rise of Islamism in her country would aggravate the situation of unwed mothers by dismissing them as "prostitutes." The negative view of single motherhood also has consequences for educated professional women because it limited their options. Having children without getting married was entirely out of the question for the women I spoke with. In fact, most were offended when I broached the subject.

Breaking with customs, the law even, was not a problem for women who faced another kind of dilemma in France, namely that of acquiring citizenship. Women accepted an unconventional arrangement that allowed them to get around this problem: *mariage blanc*. A "white marriage" exists on paper only and is entered into for the purpose of gaining a work permit or citizenship. Some of the women in such marriages were French citizens married to Moroccan relatives in an attempt to enable them to live in France. They said they had accepted the arrangement to help their families out and because it was financially beneficial. Other women, though born and raised in France, had missed the deadline for applying for French citizenship and married French citizens to legalize their situation. Some had gone into considerable debt to contract such a marriage with a French national.

Muslim women in France generally aspired toward marriage like the women in Morocco, and faced the same choices between career and marriage. There was one striking difference. Women in France frequently invoked *l'amour*—love—when speaking about marriage, while in Morocco the word was rarely mentioned. It would not be correct to infer that love was unimportant in Moroccan marriages; the difference in emphasis rather suggests that the concept is not understood in quite the same way.

In France love was described as a kind of romantic feeling, a feeling that was important to women. It was associated with free choice of a spouse and mutual respect and affection. In Morocco, on the other hand, love is not regarded as a stand-alone value but was associated with additional aspects such as compatibility of ideas and character, same religious or spiritual values, honesty. Women in Morocco were also more inclined to perceive provision of financial security as a sign of love which is not surprising in a developing country where everyday survival can be a struggle. The fact that a man was capable and willing to provide for his family was therefore an important criterion. Even professional women understood that their situation was new and precarious and that they could not necessarily rely on their own means for raising a family.

Among women in France who were contemplating marriage, the conflict over possibly choosing a non-Muslim husband was naturally more acute than in Morocco. This became apparent in my conversations with Wafaa and Khadija.

In her early thirties, divorced and with a son, Wafaa lived in a small apartment in Paris. "I am looking for someone with an open mind. Of course loyalty and trust are important but unfortunately they rarely exist. My father had several wives but he never divorced my mother before he moved in with another woman and after that with another one. So my mother could never remarry and my father did not have to pay child support, not for the children from his first marriage nor from any subsequent relationships. It was a really difficult situation for us. When my sisters and I were old enough to live alone, my mother moved back to Morocco. Life in France had become too difficult for her; she needed the support of her family back there. By the time I got divorced myself, I had a child. Now my mother raises my son in Morocco and I only get to see him once a year. As a single mother, I could not pursue my education but had to find job. In Paris everything is so expensive." Wafaa went on while preparing traditional mint tea which she served in small, gold-rimmed glasses. It would be difficult for her to attract a man, she explained, if her young son lived with her.

I was amazed how easily the term "single mother" had crossed Wafaa's lips, given how controversial and problematic single motherhood is in the country where her son is being raised. But as a divorced woman, she did not have her son out of wedlock and therefore her situation was legitimate. She continued: "Actually, I am dating a Portuguese man right now. He is Catholic. I don't know what to do. How would we raise our children if we married? I am really afraid. If he converts to Islam, he may become like most Muslim men and think he can have more than one wife, or do all sorts of things common for Muslim men. He may think it is OK for him to beat his wife. But if he does not convert, it is not right for me to marry him and it will be difficult for my family to accept him. I don't want to live in fear again. Fear is so much part of our life as Muslims and Moroccans. I am studying the Qur'an right now to see what exactly it says about a Muslim woman marrying a non-Muslim."

Khadija was struggling with somewhat similar issues. We met at a fancy American ice cream parlor on the Champs-Elysées. Like some other women, she chose a meeting place which she thought would make me feel comfortable.

This heightened awareness of cultural difference was a noticeable trait among women I got to know in France. In Morocco, women generally chose a meeting place based on convenience; their home, their place of work or a coffee shop within easy reach for both of us.

When Khadija spoke about her impending marriage, her voice became almost inaudible. "This is difficult to talk about. I lived in England for two years and I met a wonderful British guy whom I hoped to marry. Then I got pregnant. It was terrible. My mother arranged for an abortion, and my family insisted that I marry a man they had chosen. I could not refuse, after all the shame I had brought to them. Even my best friends don't know about the abortion. I did not tell them that this is an arranged marriage. It looks so old fashioned. We Moroccans in France think we are different from the people in the *bled*.[19] I mean my friends know that my parents introduced me to this man but I told them I was in love with him. I just cannot cause my parents any more trouble. I am determined to learn to love this man. He is a practicing Muslim. He is from a good family, of Moroccan origin like me." Khadija was unsure what her marriage, which was scheduled to take place within a few weeks of our meeting, might mean for her professional career. But as life in Paris was expensive she trusted that she would continue to work even after she got married or had children.

Another woman, Hassiba, made it clear that she wanted a Muslim husband. This young divorcée lived with her daughter in one of the few well-maintained public housing projects in the heart of the city and dreamed of marrying again. "Most important is that my husband is Muslim." Hassiba had said earlier that she was not a practicing Muslim; she smoked and on her kitchen counter was a rack with wine bottles. I asked why she insisted on a Muslim husband. After some hesitation, she finally said it was because she could not marry a man who was not circumcised. Sex with an uncircumcised man was not "hygienic," she had been told. She knew that circumcision was only required of Muslim and Jewish men but Jewish partners were out of the question for other reasons. Hassiba also believed that Muslims were by definition "cleaner" than men of other religions because there are numerous prescriptions concerning personal hygiene in the Qur'an, for example the insistence on ritual cleansing before entering a mosque for prayers. As our conversation continued, I noticed that Hassiba did not question her own prejudices. In the Moroccan countryside, I had encountered similar assertions about the perceived superior cleanliness of Muslims versus the lax hygienic standards of *Nazrines* (Christians) but I had not expected to hear such a statement from a non-practicing Muslim in Paris.

Hassiba lived near Montmartre, in an apartment with distinct Moroccan décor. Banquettes with red and gold tasseled cushions lined the walls, and the customary round table was graced with a shiny brass teapot. She went on to talk about other issues that came to her mind, asserting that the law banning the Muslim headscarf was a Jewish-French conspiracy against Muslims. Though she had lived all her life in Paris and had French colleagues at work, she had never befriended anyone outside of the North African immigrant community. Hassiba can be regarded as an example of someone living in a parallel society.

The concept of parallel society entered public discourse in Europe in the late 1990s. It refers to self-contained minorities which are not part of main-stream society and often reject the norms imposed by the majority culture. As the mathematical concept of parallelism indicates, the two strands of society meet only in infinity. The concept of parallel society denotes an unbridgeable gap between population groups, which in turn is attributed to the failure of in-tegration.

The majority of women in Morocco and France had at one time or another thought about marrying a non-Muslim. For the most part, they had ambiva-lent feelings about it. On one side, they felt such a union might be better suited to accommodate their professional ambition with family life and would allow them to leave some of the customs and traditions they had come to re-ject behind. But the prospect also frightened them, especially as they thought about raising children. Willingness to consider a non-Muslim husband was also the result of their advancing age and with this the diminished prospects of finding a Moroccan husband. There was a direct correlation of age with the consideration of a non-Muslim husband. Most women under the age of twenty-five said they did not consider it possible to marry someone from a different culture or religion. But as they advanced in age, their prospects of attracting someone from their own culture diminished, and consequently, the idea of marrying a non-Muslim was more readily considered.

FRIENDS

Aside from marrying a non-Muslim, socializing across religious boundaries was not uncommon. In France the overwhelming majority said they had friends who were not Muslim. In Morocco, where exposure to people from different religions is much less prevalent, a considerable number of women still said they either currently have or have had such friends in the past when they lived abroad. It is certainly not easy to determine what constitutes "friendship." One criterion might be to consider whether women met with non-Muslims outside of school or work and spent part of their leisure time with them. In the workplace, relationships are not freely chosen whereas in one's leisure time, contacts are voluntary. A number of women in both countries said they did spend off-work time with people who were not Muslim.

Self-segregation in one's private life is a common phenomenon; thus the fact that the majority of the women in France and some in Morocco said they had friends from a different cultural and religious background suggests a strong appreciation for these contacts. This also shows that the majority of Muslim women in France are not inclined toward living in a parallel society. Quite the contrary, they actively seek to integrate and to become part of French society. In Morocco an appreciation for cross-cultural relationships shows that educated, professional women see an international orientation as desirable and as no threat to their cultural or religious identity.

TRAVELING WITHOUT A GUIDE

Young, educated professional Muslim women in Morocco and in France do not have a plethora of role models for their lives. They embark on journeys without a guide. They often told me that despite conflicts with their families, they loved and appreciated them. At the same time many said their families were the biggest obstacles to achieving their personal and professional goals. One woman in France blurted out: "The biggest problem is our families. They have their ways and want to impose those on us. They brought the customs of long ago with them to France. Even in Morocco things have changed but our parents don't know that." In Morocco, responses were similar but less harshly formulated. Said one woman: "Our lives are so different from those of our mothers. Even if they support us they can't understand all the things we do and want for ourselves. There are many things I don't do because I don't want to hurt my mother. For example, I rarely go out on weekends. Every day after work, I come straight home. How am I supposed to meet a man under these circumstances?"

Another woman in Morocco put it this way: "After I finish my studies, I need to find a good job and help my parents financially. They have sacrificed a lot to allow me to get a university education, so I need to take care of them. Of course, I would like to marry but I don't see that happening because a husband may not want me to send money to my family."

Halima struck a slightly more optimistic tone: "In a Muslim society, it is very hard to succeed both professionally and in your personal life. This is because succeeding in your private life is measured by the time and effort you give to your husband and children. But I believe that where there is a will, there is a way. Within the next ten years, I hope I will find a husband who believes that as a husband and wife, we can have common goals and also accomplish our own individual goals. For example, I want to pursue a doctorate and so I need a husband who can be supportive of this ambition. For the moment, my education and profession comes first, even if that means that I may not ever marry."

In France, some women's struggles were different because they did not come from typical immigrant families. One woman said her father had come to Paris as a professional, working for an international company. She had attended private schools in Morocco and France, and knew both societies from the vantage point of her upper-middle-class family. When I told her that I was interested in meeting women of Moroccan origin in France, she responded right away that most immigrants from the Maghreb were "uneducated folks from the countryside" with whom she had little in common. "They import their ignorant ways to France. It is a question of traditions, not religion. I do not socialize with these people just because they are fellow Moroccans. We do not come from the same background. I don't have much in common with them." Again, the issue of social class became apparent. As we picnicked on the banks of the Seine, this woman talked about her upbringing and how she had moved back and forth between France and Morocco. Due to her father's connections, she said she could easily get a good position in Morocco while in France her father's clout was limited. Torn between two worlds, she knew she could never live in the small Moroccan town where most of her family resided, but she also was unsure about how to pursue her professional goals in France, and consequently had switched jobs several times. "I don't belong there. And I am not sure where I belong here." She continued: "Basically, I want to lead a normal life, have a house, marry, have children and be financially secure." "Normal" for her meant marrying a fellow Muslim and securing her middle-class lifestyle.

Women in Morocco and France felt uncertain about having to pave a way that had not been trodden before. They were proud of their education and potential and eager to apply their skills—even against the will of their parents. None of the women however, took lightly the conflict their ambitions presented to their families. Remarkably though, I did not hear women speak ill of their parents even in cases where there was severe disagreement, to the point of physical abuse. The level of respect, compassion and love expressed by these women was astonishing. It is possible that criticizing ones' parents is such a taboo, that those feelings may be repressed. This would explain that women could not allow themselves to voice their anger to an outsider.

The above testimonies show that women on both sides of the Mediterranean had traits in common concerning their personal and professional ambitions and challenges. They pursued professional goals at the cost of postponing marriage and were aware of the risk of not finding a husband. The difficulty in attracting a potential spouse was a particularly sensitive and difficult issue for women to discuss, especially since the majority considered marriage an essential part of life. Family ties were important to most women, even if considerable difficulties arose within the family as a result of their decision to pursue higher education and professional careers. Instead, most understood that their parents' generation was bound by customs and traditions they were not equipped to critically evaluate. Adding to their personal dilemma was the difficulty in finding the kind of jobs they had gone to great length preparing for. In Morocco, professional limitations were often imposed by social class and lack of connections while women with higher social standing were satisfied with their professional opportunities. In France, discrimination and a sense of not being part of the established system were cited most frequently as obstacles in the professional path. These women displayed great tenacity in claiming a new private and public role. As Rumi said eight centuries ago: "If anyone goes traveling without a guide, every two days' journey becomes a journey of a hundred years."[20]

Despite the differences in circumstances in Morocco and France, the challenges of young, educated, professional Muslim women are similar. In both countries, women expressed a need to overcome traditions and customs that impede choices in the private and public sphere.

NOTES

1. I am using the term minority here in the sense described by Leila Ahmed and explained in chapter 3.

2. The term Beur, referring to second-generation North Africans, was formed by inverting the syllables which make up the word "Arabe."

3. The sultan spares Sherazade's life because she ends every evening's story with such a cliffhanger that he cannot bring himself to have her killed but waits to the following night to hear the end of the story. Yet for a 1001 nights, she ends the evening without giving away the conclusion until the Sultan finally sets her free.

4. Beurette is the feminized version of Beur.

5. "Ni putes, ni soumises" is also the name of a highly mediatized organization fighting for the rights of minority ethnic women.

6. "Leader" or "exemplar," in Sunni Islam, leader of Friday prayers in a mosque.

7. In the spring of 2000, tens of thousands took to the streets in Casablanca and Rabat demonstrating both for and against a government proposal to improve women's rights within the personal status code, *moudawana*.

8. The CFCM was initiated in 1999 as the first publicly recognized organization to represent the views of Muslims in France.

9. See "Percée protestante au Maghreb" in *Le Monde*, *Dossiers and Documents*, No. 343, June 2005, 6.

10. This point was argued in detail by Samir Ben-Layashi in his article "Secularism in the Moroccan Amazigh Discourse" published by the *Journal of North African Studies*, vol. 12, no. 2, June 2007.

11. *TelQuel*, April 18, 2005.

12. A *hammam* is a public bathhouse, much like a Turkish steam bath.

13. Ministère Délégué Chargé de la Communauté Marocaine Résidant à l'Etranger.

14. Broschure of Ministère des Affaires Etrangères et de la Coopération outlining the Stratégie du Ministère Délégué Chargé de la Coomunaute Marocaine Résident à l'Etranger.

15. Souad Eddouada, *Women, Gender and the State in Morocco: Contradictions, Constraints and Prospects,* Ph.D. Dissertation, Mohammed V University, Rabat, 2003.

16. According to statistics provided by INSEE (National Institute for Statistics and Economic Studies): 9.2 percent unemployment rate for people of French origin, 14 percent unemployment for people of foreign origin (adjusted for education), 5 percent overall unemployment for university graduates, 26.5 percent unemployment for "North African" university graduates.

17. The Rif Mountains in Morocco is the largest cannabis producing region in the world and a major drug supplier for the European market.

18. UNICEF country statistics, 2004.

19. *Bled*, Arabic for land, place, often used in a somewhat derogatory sense to refer to underdeveloped regions of North Africa.

20. Jalal ad-Din Muhammad Rumi was a thirteenth-century Persian poet, jurist, theologian and teacher of Sufism.

6

Conclusions

In this book, I set out to compare attitudes on important life issues of young, educated, professional and urban Moroccan women and young, educated, professional women of Moroccan origin in France. Individual opinions were set within the larger context of scholarly works and personal narratives concerning these two population groups. The purpose of the study was to ascertain similarities and differences with regard to attitudes toward Islam, legal changes affecting women in both countries and personal and professional goals and challenges. In-depth interviews conducted in Morocco and in France allowed for a comparative look at population groups that to date have not been compared in this way. The reason for choosing these two particular groups lies in the fact that France is host country to the largest number of Moroccan immigrants. Today, sons and daughters of these immigrants are of an age where they are entering public life in France. Moroccans are part of the Muslim population which makes up the single largest minority in France, estimated to be 10 percent of the population. In an effort to gain a deeper understanding of this growing minority that is changing the cultural and social fabric not only of France but of Western Europe, it is instructive to get a sense of the country, or countries, from which immigrants emanate. Morocco too is undergoing substantial changes at this time especially with regard to women. Thus, we witness two societies in motion with changes in one country reverberating in another and vice versa. Because changes in the Muslim world and in Muslim communities in the West largely hinge on the question of the status and the role of women, this study is relevant beyond France and Morocco.

Europe is at the threshold of a new era in which new cultural identities are emerging as a result of large Muslim minorities in several major European countries. Discussions about the entrance of Turkey into the European Union make it all the more important to gain a deeper understanding of Muslims in the Western hemisphere. To recognize issues affecting Muslim women in a Western country, it is instructive to gain insights into the traditions and cultures of the countries from which they originate. The results of this inquiry are intended to contribute to a better understanding of Muslim women and the degree to which their particular circumstances are similar or different in a European country on the one hand and a North African, Islamic country on the other. Improved understanding is a vital prerequisite for policies which aim at greater inclusion and for unlocking human potential with regard to national development.

The comparative nature of this study allowed for an examination of attitudes and viewpoints that are not commonly looked at in this fashion. Conventionally, a hard and fast demarcation line between the West and the Arabic or Muslim world is an accepted fact. Morocco, though an African country, is most often placed within the context of the Middle East or the Arab world. Taking Morocco out of its African context belies the fact that nearly half of its population is of Berber and not Arab origin. Commonly it is said, if you scratch a Moroccan, you find a Berber. Furthermore, most inquiries focus either on the Muslim world or the West. An exception to this is research by Olivier Roy who has investigated trends among and within Muslim communities regardless of geographical boundaries. His conclusions about a changing conception of Islam that is no longer bound to a particular geographical region, a local authority, or particular dogma confirms my own findings, most notably that differences and similarities were more prevalent within country-based groups than between them. Roy further observes that re-Islamization is a global phenomenon that is occuring within Muslim communities in the Arab/Muslim world as much as in Muslim populations in the Western world. This newly emerging globalized Islam is shaped by two major trends: individualization and deterritorialization, that is, the fact of not being bound by cultural practices and norms of a specific country or region. Thus, Roy argues against the perceptions of a dichotomy between the Islam of the Muslim world and that of the West. Instead, the fault-lines occur within Muslim populations regardless of their places of residence. In my own conversations with women I found that what Roy writes about conceptions of Islam also applies to other areas such as interpretation of legal changes and personal and professional aspirations and challenges. Regardless of their place of residence, women in Morocco and in France distinguished between the religion of Islam and common cultural practices in their country or their families. They filtered out aspects of the latter with which they disagreed, emphasizing instead aspects of their religion that supported their personal and professional aspirations.

In an effort to uncover issues important to a certain segment of Muslim women, it was essential to be open for themes and issues raised by them. I met with a range of women in France and in Morocco over a period of three years, beginning in the summer of 2004, which made it possible to ascertain recurring themes. The information presented in this book is based largely on the views shared by a particular group of women, namely young, educated professionals. Though this is a minority of a minority, this population group is at the center of social and cultural changes and acts as a driving force in their respective locations.

The views expressed by these women are based on their personal life stories. They have embarked on personal and professional paths that are significantly different from those of their mothers. As they have few role models to follow, these women are indeed trailblazers in their own right. Their approaches to life are indicators of larger cultural and societal trends. These women are agents of change in the societies in which they reside.

One issue that stood out among all others was the women's insistence on individual choice with regard to their personal and professional lives. This insistence included their right to a personal interpretation of the Qur'an and the religion of Islam. Individual choice is commonly regarded a characteristic of highly industrialized Western countries, therefore it may not be surprising that Muslim women in France felt strongly about this. The fact that women in Morocco also emphasized individual choice and responsibility over conformity to the collective stands out. Another major topic of concern was the distinction between culture, customs, traditions and religion. Most women pointed out that the religion of Islam was not what held them back or restricted their personal or professional ambitions but it was the blend of local cultures and customs, the combination of pre-Islamic habits, the mixing of Berber and Arab traditions and centuries of male dominated Islamic exegesis that supported a patriarchic and authoritarian system.

Because Muslims constitute the single largest ethnic minority in France, they pose the greatest challenge in terms of national identity, social cohesion and economic parity. The research on which this book is based shows that young, educated, professional women, who have grown up in immigrant families of low-skilled workers and often illiterate mothers, demonstrate remarkable determination to climb the social ladder. They desire to become part of the French mainstream while retaining their religious identity as Muslims. Discrimination and social exclusion notwithstanding, they felt strongly attached to France and expressed no desire to leave this country. Their counterparts in Morocco felt equally loyal to their country in spite of piercing criticism of social injustices, corruption, and lack of professional opportunities. They displayed a sense of empowerment and previously unheard of upward

mobility. Women in these two very different countries were equally determined to take part in public life.

Though women in Morocco and France are exposed to greatly differing influences on a daily basis and their resources for approaching issues vary, similarities were found in attitudes toward Islam, legal changes, and views on personal and professional challenges. Differences occurred mainly within each
group and not between the two country-based groups. Similarities can certainly
be attributed in part to the particularities of the two groups, namely high educational levels and professional ambition. Moroccan women echoed French
women's more advanced struggle against traditional patriarchal structures. The
roots of these small samples represent two groups of women who are moving
out of the authoritarian structures of their society (in Morocco) or families (in
France) and therefore contribute to nothing short of a quiet revolution.

Insistence on the right to interpret the Qur'an according to their own understanding was coupled with rejection of the right of others to stand in judgment of their choices. This personalized interpretation led women in both
countries to basically two different conceptions of Islam. One was a more liberal understanding of religion, the other more in line with Islamist readings.
The more liberal understanding resulted in an emphasis on ethical behavior
freed from obvious adherence to religious dogma and treating faith or religious belief as a private affair. Still, this group of women emphasized their
support for those who opted for more rigorous religious observance, even
though they had chosen a different path for themselves. They stressed that a
professional career whether in Morocco or France, often required less overt
devotion. The approach more in line with Islamist views emphasized explicit
observance of certain practices, such as wearing the headscarf, and viewing
Islam as the basis for all aspects of life, personal and public, which includes
an understanding that, ideally, laws should be scripturally based. I should reiterate that I only met with Islamists who embraced a decidedly non-violence
stance. These Islamists supported women's right to assume public responsibilities. This is in contrast to some other Islamist groupings and an important
reminder that Islamism is not a homogenous, coherent movement but that
various strands can and do disagree with each other. The Islamist women I
met insisted on their right to freely choose their path, but they were sometimes skeptical of co-religionists who professed to be Muslims but did not in
any obvious way show their adherence. And yet even devout Muslims said
that their practice was based on personal choice. "Submission" as the term Islam indicates, was understood as a voluntary act and not one that could simply be passed on from one generation to the next, nor could it be mandated.
They emphasized that "submission" referred to God even though in everyday
reality, submission of women to men is expected. Because certain practices

are required and not optional from a dogmatic point of view, insistence on the right to personal choice concerning religious interpretation marks a significant shift in attitudes.

One possible reason for these diverging conceptions of Islam is suggested by prominent scholar Tariq Ramadan (2004), who writes:

> It can never be said enough that intracommunal dialogue between Muslims is virtually non-existent. Groups know one another, know how to identify one another, and work out where they are in relation to one another, but then they immediately ignore one another, exclude one another, or insult one another, without any attempt at discussion. . . . The culture of dialogue has practically abandoned Muslim communities and the respect for diversity, which always has been and should have continued to be their source of richness, has been replaced by dueling disagreements that contribute to the division, which causes their weakness. (210)

Incidentally, Ramadan is often referred to as a Muslim intellectual not merely as an intellectual or a scholar of Islam. One would not speak with the same ease of a Jewish intellectual or a Christian intellectual, a fact indicative of the continued "otherness" with which Muslims are treated.

Another reason for the emergence of new religious understanding has been suggested by one of the leading experts on Islam in the West, Joycelyne Cesari, who states that to be a Muslim in Europe or the United States involves a removal from Islamic society and of its cultural and social context and enters into a sphere of individual choice and by extension the domain of questioning (Cesari 2004: 72). Cesari's research, however, does not take into account the fact that similar changes in attitude occur among Muslims who continue to live in Islamic societies. In addition, Western influence that results in a critical evaluation of Islam does not necessarily lead to a distancing from it but rather to a new, invigorated understanding that tries to shake off certain cultural norms and practices by replacing individual choice with previously highly valued conformity. To cite Ramadan once more: "The West is therefore permeated by a new religiously based citizenship dynamic based on the fact that there are individuals who consider themselves both Muslims and completely European or American" (2004: 68).

Personal choice, individual assessment of their religion, and critically evaluating the difference between local culture and tradition and the religion of Islam were common traits of women in Morocco and France. A cover story of a Moroccan weekly magazine cried out: "What kind of Islam do we want?"[1] The article argued that it will be necessary in Morocco to accept free choice of individuals. Economic development frequently goes hand in hand with more individualism. Like many of the women I spoke with, the article predicted that with economic development, Moroccan society will have to become more flexible.

Continued insistence on a simplistic dichotomy between the West and the Islamic world should be considered obsolete. In fact, the term Islamic world itself is problematic. We do not speak of the Christian world but rather employ the more neutral geographical term Western world. I would contend that a more appropriate term for public discourse—as long as such designations are required—is Muslim world. This encompasses countries primarily inhabited by Muslims who create cultural patterns and whose views and practices change according to time and place. This term more accurately reflects that current challenges are posed to Muslims and not to Islam as a creed.

Thinking in terms of "us" versus "them" is still a widespread perspective in the West as well as in Muslim societies. It is commonly held that Moroccan culture and Islamic laws are intrinsically different from and incompatible with French culture and laws. With regard to the law, this difference is based on the belief among conventional interpreters that Islamic law is divinely inspired and therefore superior to any man-made law. Throughout history however, divine law has been corrupted in the process of human application and there is no country in the world that has to date successfully achieved the ideal of the Muslim *umma,* the community of the faithful as envisioned by the Prophet. By the same token, French law is at some level inspired by Christian doctrine no matter how much the separation of the religious from the secular is emphasized. It could be argued that the difference between France and Morocco is not as large as it seems.

Dualistic thinking is the hallmark of the three Abrahamic religions and resulting worldviews. The cosmology of these faiths is based on a belief in the duality of heaven and hell, good and evil, salvation and damnation, God and Satan, life on earth and in the hereafter, superiority and inferiority. In this, the Muslim world and the Western world with its marked Judeo-Christian heritage are more similar than dissimilar. Thus one could argue that some of the conflict between the Western and the Muslim world is founded more in this likeness than in their differences. One example relevant to this discussion is the fact that the mother of Saint Augustine (354–430), one of the Christian fathers of faith, was an Amazigh (Berber) woman. Augustine, Bishop of Hippo, was born and died in what is now Algeria. His mother Monica was a devout Christian married to a wealthy, pagan Roman landowner. She is believed to be the inspiration behind Saint Augustine's spiritual quest. This important figure in the development of Western Christianity has his roots in the Berber cultures of the Maghreb.[2]

An encrusted dualistic *Weltanschauung* has little to offer in terms of bridging gaps and ultimately does not hold the promise of peace and security. In a conflict of competing worldviews, proponents on each side insist on the superiority of theirs. This is particularly the case when religion is part of the discourse. From the viewpoint of a dogmatic believer, there can be no equality among messianic faiths. The women who contributed to this study are living examples of another way: they saw no inherent conflict between being a Muslim and a good citizen of a Western country. They felt loyal to France, a country that offered them educational, personal and, to a certain degree, professional opportunities they felt they would not have had had their parents remained in Morocco. Most of my respondents perceived Islam and Christianity as religions of equal value. In Morocco, upwardly mobile women professed to be Muslims and in favor of significant social changes that lead to a more democratic, open society. Morocco and France stand to gain much by making a deliberate effort to put policies into place that promote this generation of women.

And yet, the growing importance of Islamist movements that seek to turn societies into theocratic states should not be underestimated. This type of fundamentalism is incompatible with democratic values. The increasing appeal of these types of movements is directly related to issues of social exclusion and alienation, pervasive discrimination, injustice and corruption.

My findings shed doubt on the continued belief in the perceived divergence between Western European and Muslim worldviews as exemplified in the two groups of women. They are more in line with Mohammed Arkoun's assertion that the cultures that have developed along the Mediterranean coastline were shaped up until modern times by the same historical forces. Arkoun rightfully challenges the notion that the Christian West and the Islamic East are innate opposites with few, if any, social and cultural commonalities (Arkoun, 1994). Islam needs to be treated as a part of the European religious and cultural fabric.

My respondents were often critical of changes that restricted their freedoms, such as the headscarf ban in France. They questioned the motive for passing this law despite the fact that some women actually supported the notion of unveiling school girls. All affirmed that laws needed to be obeyed regardless of whether one agreed or disagreed with them and thus demonstrated a keen desire to work within the system. Few women displayed revolutionary zeal despite the fact that in their own ways they were contributing to a significant transformation in their respective societies.

Attitudes transcended national boundaries even though the actual status of women in France and in Morocco is unquestionably very different. In both countries, women who participated in this project displayed a notable eagerness to contribute to transformations within their respective communities and societies at large. They viewed existing societal or familial structures as being in contradiction to their desire for personal choice and professional advancement.

At the same time, they were not willing to sacrifice hopes for marriage and family, in fact most were troubled by the fact that they were still single.

There was a strong link between the insistence on individual rights, choice and education. All women who contributed to this study had received their formal education in educational institutions modeled after Western schools and universities. With attainment of this type of higher educational qualifications came a desire to break out of conventional gender roles and to seek a place in the public sphere. Women in both countries credited higher education as an important factor in their transformed sense of self and with that the potential of crossing over the divide imposed by social class.

In addition to academic training, another major factor in shaping individuals' perceptions was the degree of exposure to people from different countries. International travel had a marked effect. A comparison of responses revealed that an extended stay in Saudi Arabia, for example, led to consequences comparable to a trip to the United States in that it brought to the traveler an awareness of the difference between religion and culture. It also allowed for a re-examination of interviewees' understanding of the status of women. Even when international exposure occurred within Morocco by attending a university with a strong international exchange program, the result was an appreciation of difference rather than a rejection thereof. Women with close international or intercultural contacts often said Islam was one religion among others but it happened to be theirs. In France, international travel was limited, yet the very fact of growing up in France necessitated negotiating and evaluating matters of culture and religion. The women I met took their cues from a variety of sources and followed with interest how women from different cultural and religious backgrounds approached major life issues. In France young women were surrounded by the values of mainstream secular French society which often were seen in contrast with those of their families. Those women critically, evaluated the totality of their experiences and incorporated the various influences to forge a new sense of identity. Their attitudes did not reflect a dualistic worldview, but one in which Western values of individualism, choice, rights and freedoms go hand in glove with a life of faith guided by the Qur'an.

Young, educated and professional women arrived at an understanding of the Qur'an that differed from conventional interpretations because in their reading, the divinely intended status of women was equal to that of men. This understanding is not to be confused with secular, Western feminism but affirms femininity in all its expressions. To be a wife, a mother, a spiritual person and a professional are all worthy elements of a woman's life. A woman's success is to be measured on its own merit and not by using men as the standard. Education and professional ambitions were in their view supported by the scriptures. The public domain was not understood as being reserved for men. On this point women in Morocco and in France agreed almost unanimously and regardless of their conception of Islam. Though some with Islamist leanings were hesitant about the extent of the public role of women, in general they strongly disagreed with patriarchic, autocratic readings.

As stated earlier, gender was only one factor impacting on women's perceptions of their personal and professional opportunities. Social class surfaced as a recurrent issue in France and even more so in Morocco. Educated women felt that crossing social divides posed a larger hurdle than overcoming disparities based on gender. Certainly, in a developing world country such as Morocco, class divisions are more pronounced than in a highly industrialized Western country such as France. In Morocco a substantial middle class is only now emerging; historically there has been a very small elite upper class while large segments of the population hovered on the edges of poverty. The women in France did not speak as much about social class as about the distinction between majority and minority cultures. Yet as minorities in France find themselves at the lower end of the social ladder, this division also amounts to a class issue. In France it is the majority culture that discriminates against an ethnic and religious minority whereas in Morocco it is a social minority that limits the advancement of the majority of the population.

Unemployment in Morocco is officially at 19 percent[3] but in reality is estimated to be much higher, therefore employment in line with educational qualifications is limited. Unemployment figures for the French *banlieues*[4] may be comparable to those of Morocco, creating a similar environment of uncertainty. A study investigating unemployment in the French *banlieues* and comparing this with unemployment in Morocco could yield interesting results.

Women treasured their educational opportunities as a means which offered them an altered sense of self. Barriers imposed by social class or the majority/minority divide filled women in Morocco and France with resentment and frustration. This is not necessarily because of some heightened sense of social justice or support for an egalitarian system but because of their personal experience of exclusion. Very few women displayed a particular interest in political ideologies. Yet, being denied access to opportunities for which they were well qualified can lead to a degree of anger, resentment and alienation that should not be underestimated. Neither the government of France nor that of Morocco should halt the momentum of women who are keen and willing to overcome current obstacles. If large numbers of women in the end remain unsuccessful as a result of lack of opportunities, discrimination or old class divisions, both nations stand to waste tremendous human and economic potential. Regardless of substantial hurdles, young, educated women on both sides of the Mediterranean had already made remarkable strides. Those who had secured good professional positions said they saw education as an important factor in overcoming boundaries imposed by social class. Higher education allowed them entry into a work environment in which they interacted with people of similar educational backgrounds, regardless of social class.

Nonetheless, professional ambitions and achievements came at a high cost: marriage. The majority of the women I met were single, most in their late twenties, some in their thirties. Marriage was seen as an integral part of life and the fact that they had not yet been successful in finding a husband was a source of great concern, even agony. Most were hopeful that by some miraculous turn of events they would come by a partner who respected their personal and professional choices, supported their careers and would be willing to disregard their age. By any standards, these women had embarked on extraordinary life journeys and were willing to postpone marriage at the risk of possibly never attaining it.

Certainly, no society can afford to have a generation of educated, professional young women rejected by the male population. King Mohammed VI provoked a national discussion about marriage and gender roles when he married Salma Bennani, a young, professional information technology engineer. Though there was a considerable age difference between the then thirty-eight-year-old King and his twenty-four-year-old bride, the fact that the monarch chose a professional woman and married her in a public ceremony in July 2002 struck a new chord. The King had invited two hundred couples from across the nation to get married at the same time, thereby ensuring that this wedding was an affair that resonated with varying local populations and was to be remembered. By contrast, the marriage—or marriages—of his father, King Hassan II, had been kept out of the public eye. In a country where societal change is initiated from the top down, Mohammed VI's choice of spouse carried a personal message of change.

Postponing marriage by the women in question can be viewed as a courageous, risky, or desperate decision. Courageous because women intentionally prioritize education and career ambitions over fulfillment found in marriage and family life; risky because they might end up not getting married at all or desperate because education is the only avenue that affords women a degree of self-determination and independence unheard of in their mother's generation. Some might argue that Berber populations in the rural areas have traditionally granted women a measure of independence unknown to urban women, such as working outside the house in the fields or tending to livestock, thereby having an opportunity to meet men and marry someone of their own choosing, owning property or learning a skill such as carpet weaving. Even though these are by current standards limited choices, they still serve as a reminder that women's freedom and right to choose are not an entirely new, Western invention.

Women in both countries insisted that changes in mentality and behavior are even more important than legal changes such as the family law reform in Morocco. While respondents in Morocco felt that a change of mentality fell mostly on the shoulders of men, their counterparts in France saw that men and women both needed to change their mentality, thrust aside habits and discard traditions that for generations supported a patriarchic, authoritarian system. Women cited archaic mentalities as one of the main obstacles on their path to personal and professional fulfillment. They said a mentality that supported authoritarian, patriarchic systems was based in pre-Islamic, Arab culture and was not justified by the religion of Islam.

Limited professional opportunities, precarious social status as emancipated women, insistence on personal choices in all spheres of their personal and professional lives were traits the women I spoke with shared. In Morocco and France, women were striving to expand the range of their rights and freedoms in the face of tremendous obstacles. In general, disenfranchised groups display similar traits owing to their particular situation of "oppression." It is upon achieving relative equality that differences between them may come more sharply into focus. Thus, broad similarities between the groups of women in Morocco and in France may disappear as women attain their personal and professional goals and are able to focus on bringing their individual talents to bear on their respective societies.

As there seems no end in sight to the conflict between the West and the Muslim world, it is all the more important to focus more attention on population groups that can and—more importantly—are willing to lend their backing to peaceful transitions in their respective societies. Increased public support for women would allow France and Morocco to tap into the vast potential of women who aspire to offer their contributions to the private and public spheres.

NOTES

1. *Telquel* No. 99, November 7, 2003.

2. For a comprenesive description of prominent Berbers in world history, see: M.A. Haddadou, *Les Berbères célèbres*. Algiers, Berti Editions, 2003.

3. World Bank Country Statistics, www.theworldbank.com. Last accessed April, 2005.

4. Unemployment among young people is estimated at 25 percent in the socially disadvantaged *banlieues* according to "Es beginnt in den Banlieues," *Frankurter Allgmeine Zeitung*, July 19, 2005, 5.

Appendix A: Glossary of Arabic Terms

Aid   Festival, holy day

Aid al-Adha   The Feast of Sacrifice. Takes place during the traditional time of pilgrimage to Mecca. It is celebrated by pilgrims in Mecca and by those who remain at home. It commemorates Abraham's obedience to God by being willing to sacrifice his son. Each family is supposed to kill a sheep and prepare a feast using the meat.

Aid al-Fitr   The day of celebration that marks the end of *Ramadan*. Children receive gifts or money from their relatives.

Al Adl wa Ihsane   Justice and Benevolence, name of the largest Islamist movement in Morocco

Allahu akbar   God is great

Al Qur'an   Literally "the recitation," also spelled Quran, Koran; central religious text of Islam. Muslims believe the Qur'an to be the literal word of God as revealed to Muhammad over a period of twenty-three years by the angel Gabriel. It is understood as God's final revelation to mankind.

Amazigh   Amazigh people, Berber people, pl. *Imazhigen*

Amir al Moumine   Commander of the Faithful, one of the dual titles held by the King of Morocco which makes him the highest religious authority in the country

Ayat   Verses in a *sura* (chapter) of the Qur'an.

Baraka   Holiness, special blessing, good fortune

Bismi'll-ah   Opening phrase of all Qur'anic *suras* except one

Bled   *Bilad (or bled) -al siba*, lit.: place (city) of youth, meaning "Lands of Dissidence" (until 1930s, Berber-dominated

	Rif, Atlas and Sahara); today often used by French to refer to countryside or Morocco
Chorfa	Elevated place in the mosque for the imam
Dereja	Dialectical Arabic spoken in Morocco, containing Berber and French words and expressions
Dhikr	Remember, collect. Spiritual exercise designed to render God's presence throughout one's being
Djellaba	Floor-length, loose-fitting hooded garment, worn by men and women in Morocco
Fatwa	Legal opinion rendered by an Islamic scholar
Fiqh	Religious law
Ftour	(Or *iftar*), the festive meal after sunset that breaks the daily fast
Habous	Religious foundation, in Morocco there is a Minister for Islamic Affairs and *Habous*
Hadith	Collection of customs, sayings of the prophet
Hajj	Ritual pilgrimage to Mecca, *hajja*, honorific title of a woman who has performed the pilgrimage
Halal	Permissible. In French and English this term refers mostly to food. In Arabic it refers to all that is permissible under Islam.
Hijab	Muslim headscarf
Hshuma	Forbidden, shameful, common expression in Morocco
Ijtihad	Rightful interpretation of sacred texts
Imam	Leader in public worship
Imazighen	Pl., the free people, original name for Berbers, original inhabitants of North Africa, sing. Amazigh
Jihad	Striving along the mysterious path, also used in the sense of holy warfare
Jinn	Category of spirits, common belief in Morocco
Kabyle	Ethnic (Berber) group in Algeria; the *Kabyle* language
Lalla	In Morocco a respectful way to address a woman
Maghreb	The West, Al Maghrib also meaning Morocco
Marabout	French version of *Murabit*, in North Africa a general term for any kind of professional religious man
Mashriq	The East, region of Arabic-speaking countries in the Eastern hemisphere
Mirhab	A niche in the wall of a mosque indicating the direction of prayer
Muqqadam	Sectional leader in a Sufi order

Murchidat	Guide, leader, new title given to female religious leaders in Morocco
Murshid	Sufi guide
Nafs	Soul, in Islam used to describe the lower self
Ribat	Strong point, frontier post, also walled–in city, origin of Rabat, the capital city of Morocco
Shahada	Testimony, the profession of faith
Shari'a	The path to be followed, Islamic jurisprudence
Sharif	One who claims to be a descendant of the prophets
Sheikh	Master, head
Sidi	Mister, in Morocco respectful way to address a man
Suf	Wool
Sufi	A Muslim mystic
Sunna	Custom, tradition of a custom of the prophet
Sura	Chapter of the Qur'an
Tafasir	Exegetical works
Talaq	The right of a man to single-handedly repudiate (divorce) his wife
Tachelhit	Berber language spoken in Morocco
Talib	(Law) student, candidate
Ta'lim	Teaching, instruction
Tamazight	Berber language(s)
Tarifit	Berber language spoken in Morocco
Ulema	Singular *alim*, those who are trained in the religious sciences
Umma	Community or nation (often spelled *ummah*) is used to mean the community of the believers (*ummat al-mu'minin*)
Wali	Guardian
Waqf	Religious foundation, in Morocco called *Habous*
Zawija	In Morocco from French: *zaouia,* small mosque, saint's tomb

The five pillars of Islam: 1. *Shahada*: profession of faith (there is no God but God and Mohammed is His prophet); 2. *Salat*: daily prayers; 3. *Zakat*: giving of alms or charity; 4. *Swam*: fast during the month of *Ramadan* in commemoration of the revelation of the Qur'an completed with the feast of *Id-al-Fitr*; 5. *Hajj*: pilgrimage of every physically and economically able Muslim to Mecca.

Appendix B: Glossary of French Terms

Banlieue	Lit. suburbs, in contemporary French context commonly understood as neighborhoods marked by social disadvantage, ethnic alterity and criminality of the kind associated with "inner-city ghettoes" in the English-speaking world.
Beur	The term "Beur" was coined by inverting the syllables of the word "Arabe" which often carries a pejorative connotation in French. *Marche de Beurs* refers to a major political demonstration held in 1983 by younger members of the immigrant Maghrebi community. Its official title was *la marche pour l'égalité et contre le racisme*.
Chez nous	Lit. "at our place," the way things are done in our place
coup de piston	Pulling strings, having connections
Harki	Algerian Muslim soldiers who fought on the side of the French during the Algerian war of Independence and who were at the end "repatriated" to France
HLM	Habitation à loyer moderé (Housing for low rent) equivalent of public housing.
Liberté, égalité, fraternité	"Liberty, equality, fraternity (brotherhood)" is the motto of the French Republic dating back to the French Revolution (1789). The original slogan was *Liberté, égalité, fraternité, ou la mort!*

(Freedom, equality, fraternity, or death!). This slogan outlived the revolution, later becoming the rallying cry of activists, both militant and non-violent, who promote democracy or overthrow of oppressive governments.

Ni putes, ni soumises   Roughly translated as "neither whores nor submissive" the name of a highly mediatized organization fighting for the rights of minority ethnic women. French feminist movement, founded in 2002, which has already secured the recognition of the French press and parliament. It is also the name of a book written by Fadela Amara, one of the leaders of the movement, with the help of *Le Monde* journalist Sylvia Zappi.

Ostensiblement   "Overt" is the closest rendering I can offer for the French "ostensiblement," the term used in the French law banning religious insignia in French public schools. The reason for putting it in quotation marks is because there is no precise description in the law as to what is considered "overt." The wearing of Christian crosses, for example, is not disallowed and therefore the law can be interpreted to be directed at the wearing of the Muslim headscarf.

petites bonnes   Girls as young as seven years, working as domestic servants

pieds-noirs   Lit. black feet, term used for former white settlers in North Africa, especially Algeria

Verlan   Kind of slang that functions by inverting the first and the last syllables of words. The term "Beur" is a verlan version of Arabe. The term verlan itself is the result a word play, originating in the world *l'envers,* meaning the other way around. Other common verlan words are *meuf* for *femme* (woman) or *keuf* for *flic* (policeman).

Appendix C: List of Participants

To protect their identity and assure confidentiality, names are pseudonyms. The exact date and location where the interviews took place are omitted for the same reason.

MOROCCO

Aïcha, 18–22, single, student
Amal, 18–22, single, student
Aziza, 18–22, single, student
Chaibia, 22–26, single, M.A., communications officer
Djamila, 22–26, graduate student
Farida, 22–26, single, MBA, between jobs
Fatna, 22–26, single, B.A., computer analyst
Fouzia, 22–26, single, licence, accountant
Hanane, 22–26, married, M.A., university career center
Hasna, 22–26, single, BAC, adminsitrative assistant
Halima, 22–26, single, licence, executive assistant
Hiba, 22–26, single, foreign service
Hind, 26–30, single, civil servant
Huda, 22–26, single, student
Ikram, 30–35, single, medical doctor
Jamila, 26–30, single, M.S., university staff
Kaotar, 26–30, married, licence, Human Resource administrator
Karima, 26–30, married, librarian

Khalida, 26–30, licence, teacher
Laatifa, 26–30, single, M.A., civil servant
Lamiae, 26–30, single, B.S., mid-level manager international corporation
Leila, 26–30, married, 3ième cycle, program officer
Loubna, 26–30, married, graduate student
Mina, 26–30, M.S., financial officer
Nadia, 30–35, single, M.A., civil servant
Naima, 30–35, single, licence, journalist
Nezha, 30–35, married, 3ième cycle, civil servant
Rachida, 30–35, single, licence, teacher
Rokia, 30–35, single, licence, nurse
Saadia, 30–35, single, Ph.D., university professor
Sadia, 30–35, single, works for international aid organization
Samira, 30–35, single, Ph.D., psychologist
Touria, 30–35, single, Ph.D., consultant
Youssra, 26–30, single M.A., in between jobs
Zhour, 30–35, married, licence, accountant
Zineb, 30–35, single, civil servant

FRANCE

Aïcha, 26–30, single, journalist
Amina, 30–35, single, maîtrise, assistant director, NGO
Assia, 30–35, single, maîtrise, biochemist
Farida, 30–35, divorced, director, social service organization
Fatima, 18–22, single, teacher
Fatma, 18–22, single, student
Fouzia, 26–30, single, licence, social service program development
Halima, 22–26, single, journalist
Hayat, 18–22, single, student
Imane, 18–22, single, student
Ilham, 18–22, single, student
Jihane, 18–22, single, student
Karima, 26–30, single, maîtrise, web designer
Khadija, 22– 26, single, licence, legal assistant
Khalida, 22–26, single, high school teacher
Kheira, 26–30, divorced, professional degree, nurse
Latifa, 22–26, single, BAC, in between professions
Lila, 22–26, single, licence, teacher
Malika, 22– 26, single, professional degree, assistant manager

Mariam, 22–26, single, professional degree, security officer
Mouna, 30–35, single, 3ième cycle, lawyer
Nacira, 26–30, married, accountant
Nadia, 26 –30, single, administrative assistant
Naima, 26–30, married, administrative assistant
Rabha, 18–22, single, student
Rhizzlane, 22–26, married, BAC, nursery school teacher
Sadia, 30–35, single, BAC + 3, communications specialist
Siham, 30–35, single, teacher
Smia, 20–22, single, student
Touria, 30–35, divorced, maîtrise, bank employee
Zoubida, 30–35, single, M.A., political activist

Bibliography

Abd al Malik. *Qu'Allah bénisse la France*. Paris: Albin Michel, 2004.

Abdellaoui, *Siham. Le bonheur se cache quelque part*. Casablanca: Le Fennec, 2006.

Abedin, Syed Z. and Sardar, Z. (eds.). *Muslim Minorities in the West*. Canada: Seal Books, 1995.

Abou El-Fadl, K. *Rebellion and Violence in Islamic Law*. Cambridge: Cambridge University Press, 2001.

——. Speaking in God's Name. Islamic Law, Authority and Women. Oxford: Oneworld Publications, 2001.

—— (ed.). *Islam and the Challenge of Democracy*. Princeton: Princeton University Press, 2004.

Abouzeid, Leila. *Return to Childhood—The Memoir of a Modern Moroccan Woman*. Center for Middle Eastern Studies, The University of Texas at Austin, 1998.

Abu Lughod, Leila (ed.). *Remaking Women—Feminism and Modernity in the Middle East*. Princeton, NJ: Princeton University Press, 1998.

Abun_Nasr, Jamil M. *A history of the Maghrib in the Islamic period*. Cambridge University Press, 1987.

Afsaruddin, Asma (ed.). *Hermeneutics and Honor: Negotiating Female "Public" Space in Islamic Societies*. Cambridge: Middle Eastern Monographs, 1999.

Ahmed, Leila. "Western Ethnocentrism and Perceptions of the Harem." *Feminist Studies* vol. 8, no. 3, 1987.

——. *Women and Gender in Islam: Historical Roots of a Modern Debate*. New Haven: Yale University Press, 1993.

Ahmida, Ali Abdullatif (ed.). *Beyond Colonialism and nationalism in the Maghreb: History, Culture and Politics*. New York: Palgrave, 2000.

Alami M'chichi, Houria. *Genre et politique au Maroc; les enjeux de l'égalité hommes-femmes entre islamisme et modernisme*. Paris: L'Harmattan, 2002.

Al-Ashmawwy, M. *L'islamisme contre l'islam*. Paris: La Découverte, 1989.

Allievi, Stefano. *Les Convertis à l'Islam*. Paris: L'Harmattan, 1998.

Alloula, Malek. *The Colonial Harem*. Minneapolis: University of Minnesota Press, 1986.

Al-Marouri, Abderazzak. "Regards sur la question de la femme: sur le concept de la relation," *Risalat al-Ousra*, no. 1, 1989.

Al-Qur'an. *A Contemporary Translation by Ahmed Ali*. Princeton: Princeton University Press, 1988.

Alsayyad, Nezar and Castells, Manuel (eds.). *Muslim Europe or Euro-Islam: Politics, Culture, Citizenship in the Age of Globalization*. Lanham, MD: Rowman & Littlefield, 2002.

Altavista, Maroc. 2003. Portail web Marocain. "Plan d'intégration de la femme au development." http://www.ilo.org/public/english/employment/gems/eeo/guide/maroc/topic1.htm (last accessed April 7, 2005).

Altschull, E. *Le voile contre l'école*. Paris: Seuil, 1995.

Amara, Fadela. *Ni putes, ni soumises*. Paris: La Découverte, 2003.

Amear, Sahar. "Muslim Women in France at the Turn of the Millennium," *Contemporary French Civilization*,vol. 27, no. 2, Summer/Fall 2003.

Amrani, Younès and Beaud, Stéphane. *Pays de malheur! Un jeune de cité écrit à un sociologue*. Paris: La Découverte, 2004.

Amrouche, Fadhma. *My Life Story: The Autobiography of a Berber Woman*. New Brunswick, NJ: Rutgers University Press, 1989.

Amselle, Jean-Loup and Todd, Jane Marie. *Affirmative Exclusion: Cultural Pluralism and the Rule of Custom in France*. Ithaca, NY: Cornell University Press, 2003.

Anderson, Benedict. *Imagined Communities: Reflections on the Origin and Spread of Nationalism*. London: Verso, 1991.

An-Na'im, Abdullahi. *Human Rights and Islamic Identity in France and Uzbekistan. Meditation of the Local and the Global*. Atlanta: Emory School of Law Publication, 1999.

Ardener, S. *Women and Space: Ground Rules and Social Maps*. Oxford: Berg, 1997.

Arkoun, Mohammed. *The Unthought in Contemporary Islamic Thought*. London: Saqi Books, 2002.

——. *L'islam est-il menacé par le christianisme?* Paris: Concilium, 1994.

——. *Rethinking Islam. Common Questions, Uncommon Answers*. Oxford, San Fransisco: Westview Press, 1994.

——. *Ouverture sur l'islam*. Paris: Ed J. Grancher, 1992.

Armstrong, Karen. *The Battle for God*. New York: Ballantine Books, 2000.

Asad, Talal. *Geneologies of Religion. Discipline and Reasons of Power in Christianity and Islam*. Baltimore: Johns Hopkins University, 1993.

Assouline, Florence. *Musulmanes: une chance pour la France*. Paris: Flammarion, 1992.

Auclert, Hubertine. *Les Femmes Arabes en Algérie*. n.p., 1900.

Audinel, Jacques. *Le temps du métissage*. Paris: Les Editions de l'Atelier, 1999.

Ayoun, Richard, and Cohen, Bernard. *Les Juifs d'Algérie: 2000 ans d'histoire*. Paris: Lattès, 1982.

Aziz, Philippe. *Le Paradoxe de Roubaix*. Paris: Plon, 1996.

Babès, Leïla, and Oubrou, Tareq. *Loi d'Allah, loi des hommes: liberté, égalité et femmes en islam*. Paris: Albin Michel, 2003.

Babès, Leïla. *Islam en France: Foi ou Identité*. Paris: Albouraq, 2003.

———. *L'Islam Positif. La religion des jeunes musulmans de France*. Paris: Les Editions der l'Atelier, 1997.

———. "L'Islam Pluriel au Maghreb," *Revue internationale d'action com- munautaire*, vol. 26, no. 66, Autumn 1991, pp. 119–28.

——— (ed.). *Les Nouvelles Manières de Croire. Judaïsme, christianisme, Islam, Jamal nouvelles religiosités*. Paris: Les Editions de l'Atelier, 1996.

Badawi, Jamal. *Gender Equality in Islam: Basic Principles*. Plainfield, IN: American Trust Publications, 1995.

Badinter, Elisabeth. *Fausse route: Réflexions sur 30 années de féminisme*. Paris: Odile Jacob, 2003.

Badran, Margot. "Understanding Islam, Islamism and Islamic Feminism," *Journal of Women's History*, vol. 13, no. 1, p. 47–52, 2001.

Badran, Margot and Cooke, Miriam (eds.). *Opening the Gates: A Century of Arab Feminist Writing*. London: Virago, 1990.

Bahechar, Souad. *Ni fleurs, ni couronnes*. Casablanca: La Fennec, 2002.

Baker, Alison. *Voices of Resistance: Oral Histories of Moroccan Women*. Albany, NY: State University of New York Press, 1998.

Balta, Paul. *Islam, civilisation et sociétés*. Paris: Editions du Rocher, 1991.

Barlas, Asma. *"Believing Women" in Islam: Unreading Patriarchal Interpretations of Islam*. Austin: University of Texas Press, 2002.

———. "Sex, Texts and States: A Critique of North African Discourses on Islam." In *The Arab-African and Islamic Worlds: Interdisciplinary Studies*, R. Kevon Lacey and Ralph Coury, pp. 97–116. New York: Peter Lang, 2000.

Barot, Rohit (ed.). *Ethnicity, Gender and Social Change*. Hampshire, UK: Palgrave Macmillan, 1999.

Barreau, Jean-Claude. *Tous les dieux ne sont pas égaux*. Paris: Lattès, 2001.

Barthélémy, Catherine, Laugier, Marie-Bruno and Lochon, Christian (eds.). *L'Islam en Europe*. Paris: SRI, 1996.

Baubérot, Jean. *Religions et laïcité dans l'Europe des Douze*. Paris: Syros, 1994.

Bedaham, Hussain. *Personnalité maghrébine et fonction paternelle au Maghreb*. Paris: La Pensée universelle, 1984.

Bedouelle, G. and Bedouelle, J.-P. *Les laïcités à la française*. Paris: PUF, 1998.

Begag, Azouz. *L'intégration*. Paris: Le Cavalier Bleu, 2003.

Beguigui, Yamina. *Memoires d'immigrés*. Paris: Albin Michel, 1997.

Behija, M. "Le Coran impose-t-il le voile?" *L'Action* [Tunis], 3 Février 1958.

Bekkar, Rabia. "Statut social des femmes, accès à l'espace et à la parole publique," *Espaces Publiques au Maghreb et au Mashrek*, ed. Hanna Davis Taïeb, Rabia Bekkar and Jean-Claude David. Paris: L'Harmattan, 1997.

Benaïssa, Aïcha. *Née en France*. Paris: Pocket, 2000.

Bencheikh, Soheib. *Marianne et le Prophète. L'islam dans la France laïque*. Paris: Grasset, 1998.

Benchekroun, Siham. *Oser vivre*. Casablanca: Eddif, 1999.

Benchenane, Mustapha. *Les Droits de l'Homme en Islam et en Occident*. Fondations Méditerranéene d'Etudes Stratégiques. www.Fmes-France.org (last accessed March 2005).

Ben-Layashi, Samir. "Secularism in the Moroccan Amazigh Discourse." *Journal of North African Studies*, vol. 12, no. 2, June 2007.

Benzine, Rachid. *Les Nouveaux Penseurs de l'islam*. Paris: Albin Michel, 2004.

Bennani-Chraïbi, Mounia. *Soumis et rebelles. Les jeunes au Maroc*. Casablanca: Editions Le Fennec, 1994.

———. *Nous avons tant des choses à nous dire*. Paris: Albin Michel, 1997.

Berger, Peter L. *The Sacred Canopy: Elements of a Sociological Theory of Religion*. New York: Doubleday, 1967.

Berques, Jacques. *Une cause jamais perdue: Par une Méditerranée plurielle écrits politiques (1956–1995)*. Paris: Albin Michel, 1998.

Berthoud, Jean-Marc. *Une religion sans Dieu: Droits de l'homme et parole de Dieu*. Paris: Age de l'homme, 1998.

Bessis, Sophie and Belhassen, Sohayr. *Femmes du Maghreb: L'enjeu*. Paris: J. C. Lattès, 1992.

Bhabha, Homi K. *The Location of Culture*. London: Routledge, 1994.

Bloul, Rachel. "Veiled Objects of Post-Colonial Desire: Forbidden Women Disrupt the Republican Fraternal Sphere," *Australian Journal of Anthropology*, vol. 5, nos. 1–2, pp. 112–23, 1994.

Bonn, Charles (ed.). *Littératures des immigrations: un espace littéraire emergant*. Paris: L'Harmattan, 1995.

Borrmans, Maurice. *Statut personnel et famille au Maghreb: de 1940 à nos jours*. Paris: Mouton, 1977.

Boubakeur, Amal. *Le voile de la mariée—jeunes musulmanes, voile et projet matrimonial en France*. Paris: L'Harmattan, 2004.

Boubakeur, L. (ed.). *Charte du Culte Musulman en France*. Paris: Editions Rocher, 1995.

Boudhiba, Abdelwahab. *Sexuality in Islam*. London: Routledge and Kegan Paul, 1985.

Boughali, M. *Jaques Berque ou la saveur du monde arabe*. Rabat: Editions Laporte, 1995.

Boussejra, Houria. *Le corps dérobé*. Casablanca: Afrique Orient, 1999.

Boutih, Malek. *SOS Racisme: La France aux Français? Chiche!* Paris: Mille et Une Nuit, 2001.

Bouzar, Dounia and Kada, Saïda. *L'une voilée, l'autre pas*. Paris: Albin Michel, 2003.

Bouzar, Dounia. *Etre Musulman aujourd'hui*. Paris: De La Martinière Jeunesse, 2003.

Boyer, Alain. *L'Islam en France*. Paris: PUF, 1998.

Brand, Laurie A. *Women, the State, and Political Liberalization—Middle Eastern and North African Experiences*. New York: Columbia University Press, 1998.

Brett, Michael and Fentress, Elizabeth. *The Berbers*. Oxford: Blackwell, 1996.

Brunin, Jean-Luc. *Rencontrer l'Islam*. Paris: Ed. de l'Atelier, 1993.

Butler, Judith. *Gender Trouble: Feminism and the Subversion of Identity*. New York: Routledge, 1990.

Caldwell, Christopher. "Allah Mode. France's Islam problem." *The Weekly Standard*, vol. 007, Issue 42, Washington, D.C., July 2002.

Célestine, Roger, Dal Molin, Elaine and de Courtivron, Isabelle. *Beyond French Feminisms—Debates on Women, Politics, and Culture in France 1981–2001*. New York: Palgrave, Macmillan, 2003.

Cesari, Joycelyne. *L'islam a l'épreuve de l'Occident*. Paris: La Découverte, 2003.

——. *Etre musulman en France aujourd'hui*. Paris: Hachtette, 1997.

——. *Musulmans et républicains. Les jeunes, l'islam et la France*. Paris: Editions Complexe, 1999.

Chadwick, Kay. "Education in Secular France: (Re) Defininig Laïcité," *Modern and Contemporary France*, vol. 5, no. 1, pp. 47–60. February, 1997.

Chafiq, Chala and Khosrokhvar, Farhad. *Femmes sous le voile*. Paris: Editions du Félin, 1995.

Chafiq, Nadia. *La fille du vent*. Paris: L'Harmattan, 1997.

——. *A l'ombre de Jughurta*. Paris: Paris-Méditerrané, 2000.

Charaf, Dounia. *Fatoum, la prostituée et le saint*. Paris: L'Harmattan, 1999.

Charrad, Mounira. *States and Women's Rights: The Making of Postcolonial Tunisia, Algeria and Morocco*. Berkeley: University of California Press, 2001.

Chebel, Malek . *Manifeste pour un Islam des lumières—27propositions pour réformer l'Islam*. Paris: Editions Hachette, 2004.

——. *L'esprit de sérail: Perversions et marginalités sexuelles au Maghreb*. Casablanca: Lieu Commun., 1988.

Chekir, Hafidah. *Le Statut des femmes entre les textes les résistances: Le Cas de la Tunisie*. Tunis: Chama, 2000.

Cherfi, Hanifa. "Jeunes filles voilées: des médiatrices au service de l'intégration," *Hommes et migrations*, no. 1201, September 1996.

——. "Manifestations identitaires et religieuses chez les jeunes à l'école," *Pour un Islam de Paix*. Pp. 145–50. Paris: Albin Michel, 2001.

Clarke, P.B. (ed.) *New Trends and Developments in the World of Islam*. London: Luzac Oriental, 1998.

Cohen, Shana and Jaidi, Larabi. *Morocco: Globalization and its Consequences*. New York: Routledge, 2006.

Conac, G. and Amor, A. *Islam et droits de l'homme*. Bucharest, Romania: Economica, 1994.

Conseil de l'Europe. *La religion et l'intégration des immigrés*. Strasbourg: relations intercommunautaire, 1999.

Cooke, Miriam. *Women Claim Islam*. New York: Routledge, 2001.

Couchard, Françoise. *Le fantasme de séduction dans la culture musulmane: mythes et représentations sociales*. Paris: PUF, 1994.

Crapanzano, Vincent. *The Hamadsha: A Study in Moroccan Ethnopsychiatry*. Berkeley: University of California Press, 1973.

Criscuolo, Josianne. *Femmes musulmanes. Rencontres ici et là-bas*. Lyon: Chronique Sociale, 2001.

Cross, Rita. *Feminism and Religion*. New York: Routledge, 1996.

Croutier, A.L. *Harem: The World Behind the Veil*. London: Bloombsury, 1989.

Dakhila, Jocelyne. *Islamicités*. Paris: PUF, 2005.

Daoud, Zakya. *Féminisme et politique au Maghreb: Sept décennies de lutte*. Casablanca: Eddif, 1997.

——. *Casablanca en mouvement—Des innovateurs dans la ville*. Paris: Editions Autrement, 2005.

Dassetto, Felice. *La construction de l'islam européen: Approche socio- anthropologique*. Paris: L'Harmattan, 1996.

Davies, Merryl Wynn. *Knowing One Another: Shaping an Islamic Anthropology*. London: Mansell Publishing Ltd., 1988.

Davis, Susan S. *Patience and Power*. Rochester, VT: Schenkman Books, 1993.

Debray, Régis. *Ce que nous voile le voile*. *La République et le sacré*. Paris: Gallimard, 2004.

De Certeau, Michel. *La faiblesse de croire*. Paris: Esprit/Seuil, 1987.

Déjeux, Jean. *La littérature féminine de langue française au Maghreb*. Paris: Editions Karthala, 1994.

Delcambre, Anne-Marie. *L'islam des interdits*. Paris: Atélier Dominique Toutain, 2003.

Deutscher, Irwin. *Accommodating Diversity—National Policies that Prevent Ethnic Conflict*. Boston: Lexington, 2002.

Dewitte, Philippe (ed.). *Immigration et Intégration:l'état des saviors*. Paris: La Découverte, 1999.

D'Huart, Marina. *J'ai bien le temps de grandir*. Marrakesh: Traces du présence, 1998.

Diouri, Farida. *Dans tes yeux, la flamme infernale*. Paris: L'Harmattan, 2000.

Discours Royal sur Le Code de la Famille. http://www.mincom.gov.ma/french/generalites/codefamille/discours.html. (Last accessed January 21, 2005).

Djavann, Chahdortt. *Bas les voiles!* Paris: Gallimard, 2003.

Djebar, Assia. *Ces voix qui m'assiègent*. Paris: Editions Albin Michel, 1999.

Djerrari Benabdenbi, Fattouma. *Souffle de femme*. Casablanca: Eddif, 1999.

Djura. *Le vole du silence*. Paris: Editions 1 Michel Lafon, 1990.

Dore-Audibert, Andreé and Khodja, Souad. *Etre femme au Maghreb et en Mediterranée.—du mythe à la réalité*. Paris: Karthala, 1998.

During, Simon. *The Cultural Studies Reader*. London: Routledge, 1999.

Durkheim, Emile. *Les formes élémentaires de la vie religieuse*. Paris: Quadrige/PUF, 1985.

Dwyer, Kevin. *Moroccan Dialogues: Anthropology in Question*. Baltimore: John's Hopkins University Press, 1982.

Ech-Channa, Aïcha. *Miseria-Témoignages*. Casablanca: Eddif, 2004.

The Economist Magazine. *Islam in France: All over an inch of flesh*. p. 45, London, October 25, 2003.

Eddouada, Souad. *Women, Gender and the State in Morocco: Contradictions, Constraints and Prospects*. Ph.D. Dissertation, Mohammed V University, Rabat, 2003.

Eickelman, Dale F. *Knowledge and Power in Morocco*. Princeton, NJ: Princeton University Press, 1992.

———. "Islamic Liberalism Strikes Back," *Middle East Studies Association Bulletin*, vol. 27, no. 2, December 1993, p. 163–68.

El Aoufi, Noureddine (ed.). La *Société Civile au Maroc*. Rabat: Imprimerie El Maarif Al Jadida, 1992.

El Bouih, Fatna. *Une femme nommée* Rachid. Casablanca : Le Fennec, 2001.

El Guindi, Fadwa. *Veil: Modesty, Privacy and Resistance*. Oxford: Berg, 1999.

Elhany Mourad, Farida. *La fille aux pieds nus*. Casablanca: Eddar el Beïda, 1985.

El Khayat-Benani, Ghita. *Le monde arabe au féminin*. Paris: L'Harmattan, 1985.

Eloy, Marie-Helène (ed.). *Les jeunes et les relations interculturelles—Rencontres et dialogues interculturels*. Paris: L'Harmattan, 2004.

El-Sohl, C Fawzi and Marbro, Judy (eds.). *Muslim Women's Choices: Religious Belief and Social Reality*. Oxford: Berg, 1994.

Engineer, Asghai. *The Rights of Women in Islam*. New York: St. Martin's Press, 1992.

Entelis, John P. *Culture and Counterculture in Moroccan Politics*. Lanham, MD: University Press of America, 1996.

Esack, F. *Qu'ran, Liberation and Pluralism*. Oxford: Oneworld Publications, 1997.

Esposito, John L. *Women in Muslim family law*. Syracuse, NY: Syracuse University Press, 1982

Esposito, John L. *Islam, Gender and Social Change*. Oxford: Oxford University Press, 1997.

———. (ed.). *The Oxford Encyclopedia of the Modern Muslim World*. (4 volumes). Oxford: Oxford University Press, 2001.

——— and Delong-Bas, Natana J. *Women in Muslim Family Law—Contemporary Issues in the Middle East*. Syracuse, NY: Syracuse University Group, 2002.

Esprit, Janvier. Special issue: "L'islam d'Europe"., no. 239, 1998.

Etienne, Bruno. *Islam, les questions qui fâchent*. Paris: Bayard, 2003.

———. *La France et l'islam*. Paris: Hachette, 1989.

Farah, Madelain. *Marriage and Sexuality in Islam: A Translation of al-Ghazali's Book on the Etiquette of marriage from the Ihya*. Salt Lake City: University of Utah Press, 1984.

Ferjani, Mohammed-Chérif. *Islamisme, Laïcité et Droits de l'Homme*. Paris: Harmattan, 1991.

Fernea, Elizabeth and Berzigan, Basima. *Middle Eastern Women Speak*. Austin: University of Texas Press, 1977.

Fernea, Elizabeth. *In Search of Islamic Feminism*. New York: Doubleday, 1998.

Fouilloux, Etienne. *Fondamentalismes, intégrismes: Une menace pour les droits de l'homme*. Paris: Bayard-Centurion, 1997.

Fraser, John Foster. *The Land of Veiled Women: Some Wanderings in Algeria, Tunisia and Morocco*. London: Cassell and Company, 1913.

Fremeaux, Jacques. *La France et l'Islam depuis 1789*. Paris: PUF, 1991.

Friedman, Johnathan. *Cultural Identity and Global Processes*. London: Sage, 1994.

Fysh, P. and Wolfreys, J. *The Politics of Racism in France*. Basingstoke: Macmillan, 1998.

Gabrielli, Francesco (ed.). *L'Islam en Europe*. Paris: Bordas, 1985.

Galleotti, Anna Elisabetta. Citizenship and equality: the place for toleration. *Political Theory*, vol. 21, no. 4, 1993.

Gaspard, Françoise and Khosrokhavar, Farid. *Le Foulard et la République*. Paris: La Découverte, 1995.

Geertz, Clifford. *Islam Observed. Religious Development in Morocco and Indonesia*. Chicago: The University of Chicago Press, 1968.

———. *The Interpretation of Cultures*. New York: Basic Books, 1973.

Geertz, Hildred and Rosen, Lawrence. *Meaning and Order in Moroccan Society: Three Essays in Cultural Analysis*. Cambridge: Cambridge University Press, 1979.

Geisser, Vincent. *La Nouvelle Islamophobie*. Paris: La Découverte, 2003.

Gellner, Ernest. *Saints of the Atlas*. Chicago: University of Chicago Press, 1969.

Gemie, Sharif. "Stasi Republic: The School and the 'Veil,' December 2003–March 2004" *Modern and Contemporary France*, vol. 12, no. 3, pp. 387–97, 2004.

Gerholm, Tomas and Lithman, Y.G. (eds). *The New Islamic Presence in Western Europe*. Thousand Oaks, CA: Sage Publications, 1988.

Ghayet, Ahmed. *Les Beurs—Génération Mohammed VI*. Casablanca: Eddif, 2002.

Ghazi, Walid-Fala and Nagel, Caroline. *Geographies of Muslim Women: Gender, Religion and Space*. New York: Guildford Publications, 2005.

Giddens, Anthony. *Les conséquences de la modernité*. Paris: L'Harmattan, 1990.

Glaser, Barney and Strauss, Anselm. *The Discovery of Grounded Theory*. Berlin, New York: Aldine, 1967.

Goody, Jack. *Islam in Europe*. Cambridge, UK: Polity Press, 2004.

Gozlan, Martine. *L'islam de la République. Des musulmans de France contre l'intégrisme*. Paris: Ed. Belfond, 1994.

Gray, Doris. "Transnational Muslim Women: A Qualitative Study of Conceptions of Islam in Morocco and in France," *The Journal of North African Studies*. London, New York: Routledge, November, 2006.

——. "Educated, Professional Women in Morocco and Women of Moroccan Origin in France: Asserting a New Public and Private Identity," *Journal of Middle East Women's Studies*. Bloomington: Indiana University Press, Fall 2006.

——. "Le mouvement des jeunes femmes musulmanes: Une étude comparative entre les femmes au Maroc et les femmes d'origine marocaine en France," *Questions de Communication*. Nancy, France: Presses Universitaires de Nancy, December 2006.

——. "Muslim Women in France and Morocco: Applying Grounded Theory Methodology for Research in French and Francophone Studies," *Modern and Contemporary France*. Oxfordshire, UK: Routledge, October 2006.

Gray, Kenneth. "Women Entrepreneurs in Morocco: Debunking Stereotypes and Discerning Strategies," *International Entrepreneurship and Management, 2005*. Vol. 1, no. 2, June 2005. New York: Springer Science & Business Media.

Guène, Faïza. *Kiffe, Kiffe Tomorrow*. New York: Harvest Books, Harcourt Brace, 2006.

Guénif-Souilamas, Nacira. *Des beurettes*. Paris: Editions Grasset & Fasquelle, 2000.

Guénif-Souilamas, Nacira. *Les Beurettes*. Paris: Hachette, 2003.

Guénif-Souilamas, Nacira and Macé, Eric. *Les Féministes et le garçon arabe*. Paris: L'Aube, 2004.

Guessous, Soumaya Naamane and Guessous, Chakib. *Grossesses de la honte. Enquête raisonnée sur les filles mères et les enfants abandonnés au Maroc*. Casablanca: Editions Le Fennec, 2005.

Haddad, Yvonne (ed.). *Christian-Muslim Encounters*. Gainesville, FL: University Press of Florida, 1995.

Haddad, Yvonne. *Muslims in the West: From Sojourners to Citizens*. Oxford: Oxford University Press, 2002.

Haddadou, M.A., *Les Berbères célèbres*. Algiera: Berti Editions, 2003.

Hadraoui, Touria. *Une enfance marocaine*. Casablanca: La Fennec, 1998.

Hale, Sonra. *Gender Politics in Sudan: Islamism, Socialism, and the State*. Boulder, CO: Westview Press, 1997.

Hall, Edward T. *The Hidden Dimension*. New York: Anchor Doubleday, 1966.

——. *Beyond Culture*. New York: Anchor Doubleday, 1981.

Hall, Stuart. *Critical Dialogues in Cultural Studies*. London: Routledge, 1996.

Hames, Constant. "L'Islam en France et en Europe." *Archives des sciences sociales des religions*, vol. 68, no. 1, pp. 79–92, juillet–septembre 1989.

Hammoudi, Abdellah. *Master and Disciple. The Cultural Foundations of Moroccan Authoritarianism*. Chicago: University of Chicago Press, 1997.

Hargreaves, Alec G. "Testimony, Co-Authorship and Dispossession Among Women of Maghrebi Origin in France." *Research in African Literatures*, vol. 37, no. 1, Indiana University Press, Spring 2006.

———. *Immigration, 'Race' and Ethnicity in Contemporary France*. London and New York: Routledge, 1995.

———. *Immigration and Identity in Beur Fiction—Voices from the North African Community in France*. Oxford and New York: Berg, 1997.

Hargreaves, Alec G., and McKinney, Mark (eds). *Post-Colonial Cultures in France*. London: Routledge, 1997.

Hegasy, Sonya. *Staat, Öffentlichkeit und Zivilgesellschaft in Marokko. Die Potentiale der sozio-kulturellen Opposition*. Politik, Wirtschaft und Gesellschaft des Vorderen Orientes. Hamburg: Deutsches Orient. Institut, 1997.

Hennebelle, G. (ed.). L'islam est-il soluble dans la république? *Panoramiques*, no. 27, 1997.

Hervieu-Léger, Danièle. *La religion pour mémoire*. Paris: Le Cerf, 1993.

Hessini, Lelia. "Wearing the *Hijab* in Contemporary Morocco." In *Reconstructing Gender in the Middle East: Tradition, Identity, Power*. ed. Gösek, Fatma Müge, and Shiva Balaghi. New York: Columbia University Press, pp. 40–56, 1994.

Hofert, Alamut and Armando, Salvatore (eds). *Between Europe and Islam*. Bruxelles: PIE Peter Lang, 2000.

Houari, Leïla. *Zeida de nulle part*. Paris: L'Harmattan, 1985.

———. *Femmes aux mille portes—Portraits, mémoire*. Bruxelles: éditions EPO, 1996.

Hunke, Sigrid. *Allah's Sonne über dem Abendland—Unser Arabisches Erbe*. Stuttgart: Deutsche Verlagsanstalt, 1960.

Hunter, Shireen T. *Islam, Europe's Second Religion: The New Social, Cultural, and Political Landscape*. New York: Praeger Publications, 2002.

Huntington, Samuel. *The Clash of Civilizations: Remaking of World Order*. New York: Simon and Schuster, 1998.

Irigaray, Luce. *An Ethics of Sexual Difference*. Ithaca, NY: Cornell University Press, 1993.

Isaacs, Stephen and Michael, William. *Handbook in Research and Evaluation: A Collection of Principles, Methods, and Strategies Useful in the Planning, Design, and Evaluation of Studies in Education and the Behavioral Sciences*. San Diego, CA: Edits Pub, 1995.

Jacques, André, and van Boven, Théo. *Droits de l'homme et évangile. Comment vivre l'universalité des valeurs dans la pluralité des cultures*. De l'Atelier, 1998.

Joffe, George (ed.). *North Africa: Nation, State, and Region*. London: Routledge, 1993.

Joseph, Suad and Slymonovics, Susan. "Introduction." In *Women and Power in the Middle East*. Philadelphia: University of Pennsylvania Press, pp. 1–14, 2001.

Kahf, Mohja. *Western Representations of the Muslim Woman: From Termagant to Odalisque*. Austin, TX: University of Texas Press, 1999.

Kaltenbach, Jeanne-Hélène, and Patrick, Pierre. *La France, une chance pour l'Islam.* Paris: Ed. Du Félin, 1991.

Kapchan, Deborah. *Gender on the Market—Moroccan Women and the Revoicing of Tradition.* Philadelphia: University of Pennsylvania Press, 1996.

Karam, Azza. *Women, Islamists and the State: Contemporary Feminism in Egypt.* London: Macmillan, 1998.

Kepel, Gilles. *Les banlieues de l'Islam. Naissance d'une religion en France.* Paris: Editions du Seuil, 1984.

———. *Les Banlieues de l'Islam. Naissance d'une religion en France,* Paris: Le Seuil, 1987.

———. *La revanche de Dieu: Chrétiens, juifs et musulmans à la reconquête du monde.* Paris: Seuil, 2003.

———. *The War for Muslim Minds. Islam and the West.* Cambridge: Harvard University Press, 2004.

Khayat, Ghita. *Le monde arabe au féminin.* Paris: L'Harmattan, 1988.

Khayat, Rita. *La Liaison.* Casablanca: Editions Aïni Bennaï, 2006.

Khosrokhavar, Farhad. *L'islam des jeunes.* Paris: Flamarion, 1997.

Koulard, André. *L'affaire du voile islamique.* Aix-en-Provence: Editions Fenêtre sur cour, 1991.

Kozma, Liaf. "Moroccan Women's Narratives of Liberation: A Passive Revolution?" *Journal of North African Studies,* vol. 8, no. 1, 2003.

Kramer, Jane. "Letter from Europe: Taking the Veil," *New Yorker,* pp. 59–71, November 22, 2004.

Krieger-Krynicki, A. *Les musulmans en France. Religion et Culture.* Paris: Maisonneure et Larose, 1985.

Krier, Isabelle and El Hani, Jamal Eddine (eds) *Le Féminin en Miroir – Entre Orient et Occident.* Casablanca: Editions Le Fennec, 2005.

Kristeva, Julia. *Etrangers à nous-même.* Paris: Fayard, 1990.

Kritzman, Lawrence D. (ed.). "France's identity Crisis," special issue of SubStance, no. 76–77, 1995.

Laala Hafdane, Hakima. *Les femmes marocaines—une société en mouvement.* Paris: L'Harmattan, 2003.

Lacoste-Dujardin, Camille. *Des mères contre les femmes.* Paris: La Découverte, 1996.

———. *Dialogue des femmes en ethnologie.* Paris: La Découverte, 2002.

Lamchichi, Abderrahim. *Islam et musulmans de France: pluralisme, laïcité, citoyenneté.* Paris: L'Harmattan, 1999.

Lapid, Yousouf (ed.). *The Return of Culture and Identity.* Boulder: Lynne Rienner, 1996.

Lapidus, Ira M. *A History of Islamic Societies.* Cambridge University Press, 2002.

Laskier, Michael M. *North African Jewry in the Twelfth Century: The Jews of Morocco, Tunisia and Algeria.* New York: New York University Press, 1994.

Layachi, Azzedine. *State, Society and Democracy in Morocco: The Limits of Associative Life.* Washington, DC: Center for Contemporary Arab Studies, Georgetown University, 1998.

LeBor, Adam. *A Heart Turned East—Among the Muslims.* New York: Thomas Dunne Books, 1997.

Léger, Jack-Alain. *A contre Coran*. Paris: Editions Hachette, 2004.

Leila. *Mariée de force*. Paris: Oh, 2004

Leveau, Rémy, and Withol de Wenden, Catherine. *La beurgeoisie: Les trois âges de la vie associative issue de l'immigration*. Paris: CNRS Editions, 2001.

Lévi, Alma et Lila. *Des filles commes les autres: au-delà du foulard*. Entretiens avec Véronique Giraud et Yves Sintomer. Paris: La Découverte, 2004.

Levi-Strauss, Claude. *The Elementary Structures of Kinship*. Boston: Beacon Press, 1969.

Lewis, Bernard and Schnapper, Dominique (eds.). *Muslims in Europe*. London: Pinter, 1994.

Lewis, Bernard. *The Muslim Discovery of Europe*. New York: W.W. Norton & Company, 2001.

Lewis, Reina. *Gendering Orientalism: Race, Femininity and Representation*. London and New York: Routledge, 1996.

Lionnet, Françoise. *Autobiographical Voices: Race, Gender, Self-Portraiture*. Ithaca, NY: Cornell University Press, 1989.

Lionnet, Françoise and Scharfman, Ronnie (eds). "Post-Colonial Conditions: Exiles, Migrations and Nomadisms," special issue of Yale French Studies, no. 82, 1993.

Long, Elizabeth (ed.). *From Sociology to Cultural Studies*. Oxford, UK: Blackwell Publishers, 1997.

Ludden, David. *Reading Subaltern Studies: Critical History, Contested Meaning and the Globalization of South Asia*. London: Anthem, 2002.

Maalouf, Amin. *In the Name of Identity—Violence and the Need to Belong*. New York: Arcade Publishing, 2001.

Macleod, Arlene. *Accommodating Protest: Working Women, the New Veiling, and Change in Cairo*. New York: Columbia University Press, 1991.

Maghraoui, Driss. "French Identity, Islam and North Africans: Colonial Legacies Postcolonial Realities," *French Civilization and its Discontents*, ed. Tyler, Stovall, and Georges van den Abbeele. New York, Oxford: Lexington Books, 2003.

Maher, Vanessa. "Women and Social Change in Morocco," *Women in the Muslim World*, ed. Lois Beck and Nikkie Keddie. Cambridge, MA: Harvard University Press, 1978.

Majid, Anouar. *Unveiling Traditions: Postcolonial Islam in a Polycentric World*. Durham, NC: Duke University Press, 2000.

Manji, Irshad. *The Trouble with Islam: A Wake-Up Call for Honesty and Change*. East Mississauga, Ontario: Random House of Canada, 2003.

Marchand, René. *La France en danger d'Islam: Entre Jjihad et Reconquista*. Paris: L'Age d'Homme, 2002.

Marzouki, Ilhem. *Le mouvement des femmes en Tunisie au XXème siècle: Féminisme et politique*. Tunis: Cérès, 1993.

McClintock, Anne. *Imperial Leather: Race, Gender, and Sexuality in the Colonial Contest*. New York: Routledge, 1995.

Meddeb, Abdelwahab. *La Maladie de l'Islam*. Paris: Seuil, 2002.

Meddeb, Abdelwahab and Petit, Philippe. *Face à l'islam: Entretien avec Philippe Petit*. Paris: Textuel, 2004.

Méliane, Loubna. *Vivre Libre*. Paris: Pocket, 2004

Mernissi, Fatima. *Beyond the Veil*: *Male-Female Dynamics in Modern Muslim Society*. Bloomington, IN: Indiana University Press, 1987.

—— (ed.). *La femme et la loi au Maroc*. Alger: Ed. Bouchene, 1991.

——. *Women and Islam*: *A Historical and Theological Inquiry*. Oxford: Blackwell Publishers, 1991.

Mernissi, Fatima and Lakeland, Mary Jo. *The Veil and the Male Elite*: *A Feminist Interpretation of Women's Rights in Islam*. Cambridge, MA: Perseus Publishing, 1992.

——. *Dreams of Trespass* – *Tales of a Harem Girlhood*. New York: Basic Books, 1994.

Merriam, Sharan B. *Case Study Research in Education*. *A Qualitative Approach*. San Francisco: Jossey-Bass Publications, 1988.

Metcalf, Barbara Daly (ed.). *Making Muslim Space in North America and Europe*. Berkeley: University of California Press, 1996.

Metz, Jean-Baptiste. *La foi dans l'histoire et dans la société*. Paris: Le Cerf, 1979.

Miller, Susan Gibson. *Disorienting Encounters*: *Travels of a Moroccan Scholar in France in 1845–1846*. Berkeley and Los Angeles: University of California Press, 1992.

Miller, Susan Gibson and Rahma, Bourquia (eds.). "Introduction." In *In the Shadow of the Sultan*: *Culture, Power, and Politics in Morocco*. Cambridge: Harvard University Press, pp. 1–16, 1999.

Milliot, Louis. *Introduction à l'étude du droit musulman*. Paris: Recueil Sirey, 1953.

Minces, Juliette. *La génération suivante*. *Les enfants de l'immigration*. Paris: Editions de l'Aube, 2004.

——. *Le Coran et les femmes*. Paris: Hachette, 1996.

——. "Le Foulard islamique à l'école: un état des lieux." *Hommes et migrations*, no. 1201, pp. 18–24, septembre 1996.

Ministère de l'emploi et de la solidarité—Ministère de l'intérieur—Agence pour le développement des relations interculturelles. *L'Islam en France*. Paris: La Documentation Française, 2001.

Mokkedem, Malika. *L'interdite*. Paris: Grasset, 1993.

——. *La Transe des insoumis*. Paris: Grasset, 2003.

Morin, Edgar. *La Méthode*, *l'humanité de l'humanité*, tome 5: *L'identité humaine*. Paris: Seuil, 2003.

Morocco. *Code du Statut Personnel*. *Bulletin Officiel du Maroc*. Books 1 and 2, May 1958. Updated and reprinted in Mohammed Chafi, *Code du statut personnel annoté*. Marrakech: Imprimerie Walili, 1996.

Morocco. *Dahir berbère de 1930* (Berber Decree). Bulletin Officiel du Maroc. May 1930.

Mortimer, Mildred (ed.). *Maghrebian Mosaic*. *A Literature in Transition*. Boulder: Lynne Rienner Publishers, 2001.

Moruzzi, Norma Claire. "A Problem with Headscarves: Contemporary Complexities of Political and Social Identities." *Political Theory*, vol. 22, no. 4, 2004.

Motahari, Mortada. *La Question du Hijab*. Paris: Editions Al Bouraq, 2000.

Moulay Rchid, Aberrazak. *La femme et la loi au Maroc*. Casablanca: Le Fennec, 1991.

Murata, Sachiko. *The Tao of Islam. A Sourcebook on Gender Relationships in Islam*. New York: State University Press, 1992.

Nashat, Guity and Tucker, Judith E. *Women in the Middle East and North Africa: Restoring Women to History*. Bloomington: Indiana University Press, 1999.

Nasr, Seyyed Hossein. *Ideals and Realities of Islam*. Chicago: ABC International Group, 2000.

Negrouche, Nasser. "Derrière le voile," *Le Monde Diplomatique*, February 2004.

Nielsen, Jorgen. *Towards a European Islam*. London: Macmillan Press, 1992.

Noelle-Neumann, Elisabeth. *The Spiral of Silence: Public Opinion—Our Social Skin*. Chicago: University of Chicago Press, 1993.

Nökel, Siegrid (ed.). *Der neue Islam der Frauen*. Bielefeld: transcript Verlag, 2001.

Nökel, Sigrid and Werner, Karin (eds.). *Der neue Islam der Frauen*. Bielefeld: transcript, 1999. (not 2001)

Nonneman, Gerd and Niblock, Tim (eds.). *Muslim Communities in the New Europe*. Reading: Ithaca Press, 1996.

Nordham, Charlotte (ed.). *Le foulard islamique en questions*. Paris: Editions Amsterdam, 2004.

Nouri, Fatima. *Tafami*. Nantes: Opéra, 1998.

Orlando, Valérie. *Nomadic Voices of Exile, Feminine Identity in Francophone Literature of the Maghreb*. Columbus: Ohio University Press, 1999.

Ossman, Susan (ed.). *Places We Share: Migration, Subjectivity, and Global Mobility*. Lanham, MD: Lexington Books, 2007.

Oufkir, Malika, *Stolen Lives—Twenty Years in a Desert Jail*. Miramax, 2001

Oulehri, Touria. *La répudiée*. Casablanca: Editions Afrique-Orient, 2001.

Oumassine, Damia. *L'argenier des femmes égarées*. Casablanca: La Fennec, 1998.

Ousmaal-Ouatah, Saïda. "Le choix de porter le voile en France," *Migrations société*, vol. 16, no. 96, pp. 179–96, novembre–décembre 2004.

Pamuk, Orhan. *Snow*. London: Faber and Faber, 2004.

———. *Istanbul. Memoirs and the City*. New York: Random House, Vintage Books, 2006.

Peach, C. and Gleb, G. "Muslim Minorities in Western Europe." *Ethnic and Racial Studies*, vol. 18, no. 1, January 1995.

Pennell, C.R. *Morocco since 1830: A History*. New York: New York University Press, 2000.

Le Port du foulard islamique à l'école. Les documents de travail du Sénat. Série Législation comparée. No, LC 128, novembre 2003.

Rabinow, Paul. *French Modern: Norms and Forms of the Social Environment*. Chicago: University of Chicago Press, 1989.

———. *Reflections on Fieldwork in Morocco*. Berkeley: University of California Press, 1977.

Ramadan, Tariq. *Western Muslims and the Future of Islam*. New York, Oxford: Oxford University Press, 2004.

———. *Arabes et musulmans face à la mondialisation: le défi du pluralisme*. Lyon: Tawhid, 2003.

———. *Musulmans d'Occident—construire et contribuer*. Lyon: Tawhid, 2002.

Rassan, Amal. "Women and Domestic Power in Morocco." *International Journal of Middle Eastern Studies*, pp. 171–79, September 1980.

Rausch, Margaret. "Ishelhin Women Transmitters of Islamic Knowledge and Culture in Southwestern Morocco," *The Journal of North African Studies*, vol. 11, no. 2, June 2006, p. 173.

Rchid, Abderrazak Moulay. "La Mudawwana en question," *Femmes, culture et société au Maghreb*, vol. 2, ed. Rahma Bourqia, Mounira Charrad and Nancy Gallagher. Casablanca: Afrique Orient, 1996.

Rosello, Mireille. *France and the Maghreb—Performative Encounters*. Gainesville, FL: University Press of Florida, 2005.

Rosen, Lawrence. *The Culture of Islam: Changing Aspects of Contemporary Islam*. Chicago: University of Chicago Press, 2002.

———. *The Anthropology of Justice: Law as Culture in Islamic Society*. Cambridge: Cambridge University Press, 1989.

———. *Bargaining for Reality: The Construction of Social Relations in a Muslim Community*. Chicago: University of Chicago Press, 1984.

Roy, Olivier. *La laïcité face à l'islam*. Paris: Stock, 2005.

———. *Globalized Islam*. New York: Columbia University Press, 2004.

Ruedy, John. "Introduction." *Islamism and Secularism in North Africa*, ed. John Ruedy, pp. xxiii–xxi. New York: St. Martin's Press, 1994.

Saadawi, Nawal. *The Hidden Face of Eve: Women in the Arab World*. Boston: Beacon Press, 1980.

Safi, Omid. *Progressive Muslims: On Justice, Gender, and Pluralism*. Oxford: Oneworld Publications, 2003.

Said, Edward. *Orientalism*. New York: Vintage Press, 1979.

———. *Culture and Imperialism*. New York: Random House, 1993.

Said, Bobby. *A Fundamental Fear. Eurocetrism and the Emergence of Islamophobia*. London: Zed Books, 1997.

Samad, Yunas and Eade, John (eds.). *Community Perception of Forced Marriages*. Bradford: Community Liason Unit, 2002.

Samie, Amal. *Mourir pour deux idées*. Casablanca: Afrique Orient, 1998.

Saqj, Rachida. *Marocaines en mâle-vie*. Casablanca: Eddif, 1998.

Sbai, Noufissa. *L'enfant endormi*. Rabat: EDINO, 1987.

Schimmel, Annemarie. *Islam—An Introduction*. New York: State University of New York Press, 1992.

———. *My Soul is a Woman—The Feminine in Islam*. New York: Continuum International Publishing Group, 1997.

———. *Deciphering the Signs of God*. New York: State University of New York Press, 1994.

Sebbar, Leïla. *Sept filles*. Paris: Editions Thierry Magnier, 2003.

Sebti, Fadéla. *Vivre musulmane au Maroc: Guide des droits et obligation de la femme marocaine*. Casablanca: Le Fennec, 1989.

———. *Moi Mireille, lorsque j'étais Yasmina*. Casablanca: Le Fennec, 1995.

Senni, Aziz. *L'ascenseur social est en panne . . . : J'ai pris l'escalier!* Paris: L'Archipel, 2005.

Sfeir, Antoine. *Les réseaux d'Allah*. Paris: Plon, 1997.

Shadid, W.A.R. and van Konigsfeld, P.S. *Religious Freedom and the Position of Islam in Western Europe: Opportunities and Obstacles in the Acquisition of Equal Rights*. Kampen: Kok Pharos, 1955.

Sölle, Dorothee. *The Silent Cry. Mysticism and Resistance*. Minneapolis: Fortress, 2001.

Sonbol, Amira El Azhary (ed.). *Women, the Family and Divorce Laws in Islamic History*. Syracuse: Syracuse University Press, 1996.

Sorman, Guy. *Les enfants de Rifaa—musulmanes et modernes*. Paris: Fayard, 2003.

Spensky, Martine. "Identités multiples: L'affaire du 'foulard.'" In *Modern and Contemporary France*, no. 42. pp. 48–50, July 1990.

Spivak, Gayatri. "A Critique of Postcolonial Reason. Can the Subaltern Speak?" In *The Norton Anthology of Theory and Criticism*. New York: Norton & Company, 1999, pp. 21–97).

———. *In Other Worlds—Essays in Cultural Politics*. New York: Methuen, 1987.

Stora, Benjamin. *La gangrène et l'oubli*. Paris: La Découverte, 1991.

Stowasser, Barbara Freyer. *Women in the Qur'an, Traditions and Interpretations*. Oxford, OH: Oxford Press, 1996.

Strauss, Anselm and Corbin, Juliet. *Basics of Qualitative Research. Techniques and Procedures for Developing Grounded Theory*. Thousand Oaks, CA: Sage Publications, 1998.

Syed, Mohammed Ali. *The Position of Women in Islam*. Albany: State University of New York Press, 2004.

Termine, Emile. *France, terre d'immigration*. Paris: Gallimard, 1999.

Tillion, Germaine. *Le harem et les cousins*. Paris: Seuil, 1966.

Todorov, Tzvetan. *Nous et les autres, la réflexion française sur la diversité humaine*. Paris: Seuil, 1981.

Tozy, Mohammed. *Monarchie et Islam politique au Maroc*. Paris: Presses De Sciences Po, 1999.

Tozy, Mohammed and Albera, Dionigi. *Traditions anthropologiques en Méditerranée*. Paris: Maisonneuve Et Larose, 2003.

Tribalat, Michèle. *Faire France. Une enquête sur les immigrés et leurs enfants*. Paris: Éditions La Découverte, 1995.

———. *De l'immigration à l'assimilation. Enquête sur les populations d'origine étrangère en France*. Paris: Éditions La Découverte, 1996.

Trimingham, J. Spencer. *The Sufi Orders in Islam*. New York and Oxford: Oxford University Press, 1971.

Tucker, Judith (ed.). *Arab Women—Old Boundaries, New Frontiers*. Bloomington: Indiana University Press, 1993.

UNDP (United Nations Development Programme) and Arab Fund for Economic and Social Development. *Arab Human Development Report 2003—Building a Knowledge Society*. New York: United Nations Publications.

UNESCO. *Social Science Research and Women in the Arab World*. London and Dover, NH: Frances Pinter, 1984.

Venel, Nancy. *Musulmanes françaises: des pratiquantes voilées à l'université*. Paris: L'Harmattan, 1999.

Vertovec, Steven and Rogers, Alistair (eds.). *Muslim European Youth*. Aldershot, UK: Ashgate, 1998.

Vianès, Michèle. *Un voile sur la République*. Paris: Editions Stock, 2004.

Vidal, Dominiqe and Bourtel, Karim. *Le Mal-Etre Arabe. Enfants de la Colonisation*. Marseille: Agonne, 2005.

Wadud, Amina. *Inside the Gender Jihad—Women's Reform in Islam*. Oxford, UK: Oneworld Publications, 2006.

———. *Qur'an and Woman. Rereading the Sacred Text from a Woman's Perspective*. New York: Oxford University Press, 1999.

Waltz, Susan E. *Human Rights and Reform: Changing the Face of North African Politics*. Berkeley: University of California Press, 1995.

Weber, Edgar. *L'islam en France ou La paix sainte*. Paris: L'Harmattan, 1992.

Weber, Max. *Die protestantische Ethik und der Geist des Kapitalismus*. Weinheim: Beltz Athenäum (Ersterscheinung 1905), 2000.

Weibel, Nadine B. *Par-delà le voile. Femmes d'islam en Europe*. Paris: Editions Complexe, 2002.

Westermarck, Edward. *Ritual and Belief in Moroccan Society, Volume I and II*. New Hyde Park, NY: University Press, 1968.

Wieviorka, Michel. *L'avenir de l'islam en France et en Europe: Les Entretiens d'Auxerre*. Paris: Ballard, 2003.

Woodhull, Winifred. *Transfigurations of the Maghreb: Feminism, Decolonization and Literatures*. Minneapolis: University of Minnesota Press, 1993.

Yacoubi, Rachida. *Ma vie, mon cri*. Casablanca: Eddif, 1996.

———. *Je dénonce*. Paris-Mediterrané, 2002.

———. *Ma vie mon cri*. Paris: Paris-Méditerrané, 2003.

Yamani, Mai (ed.). *Feminism and Islam*. Berkshire: Ithaca Press, 1996.

Yassine, Nadia. *Full Sails Ahead*. New Britain, PA: Justice and Spirituality Publishing, 2006.

Yazbeck, Haddad (ed.). *Islam, Gender and Social Change*. Oxford: Oxford University Press, 1997.

Yegenoglu, Meyda and Alexander, Jeffrey. *Gendering Orientalism: Towards a Feminist Reading of Orientalism*. Cambridge: Cambridge University Press, 1998.

Yin, Robert K. *Case Study Research. Design and Methods*. Newbury Park, CA: Sage Publications, 1989.

Zayzafoon, Lamia Ben Youssef. *The Production of the Muslim Woman*. New York: Lexington Books. 2005.

Zeghal, Malika. *Les islamistes marocains—Le défi à la monarchie*. Paris: La Découverte, 2005.

Ziai, Fati. "Personal Status Codes and Women's Rights in the Maghreb." In *Muslim Women and the Politics of Participation: Implementing the Beijing Platform*, ed. Mahnaz Afkhami and Erika Fried. Syracuse: Syracuse University Press, 1997.

Zouari, Fawzia. *Ce voile qui cherche la France*. Paris: Editions Ramsay, 2004.

Index

About the Author

Doris H. Gray teaches in the French and Francophone Department of Florida State University in Tallahassee, Florida, from where she received her Ph.D. with distinction in 2005. Prior to becoming an academic she worked as a journalist and for a decade as a foreign correspondent for the German Press Agency in Nairobi, Kenya. She also taught for two years at Al Akhawayn University in Morocco. She is the recipient of a Fulbright Fellowship for Morocco. Her research interests are in women of the developing world and immigrant women in Europe.

Her scholarly articles have appeared in the *Journal of North African Studies*, the *Journal of Middle East Women's Studies, Modern and Contemporary France* and in the French journal *Questions de communication*. She has published a book chapter "Women entrepreneurship in Morocco — Vanguards of Change in the Muslim World" in *Perspectives of Women Entrepreneurship in the Age of Globalization*.